The Welsh at
Mametz Wood
The Somme 1916

To Wendy

my muse, researcher and inspiration who has given me so much help in preparing the manuscript, and for helping me find these forgotten men.

The Welsh at Mametz Wood

The Somme 1916

DR JONATHAN HICKS

First impression: 2016

The publishers wish to acknowledge the support of
Cyngor Llyfrau Cymru

Cover photograph: John Knott
Cover design: Y Lolfa

ISBN: 978 1 78461 238 2

Published and printed in Wales
on paper from well-maintained forests by
Y Lolfa Cyf., Talybont, Ceredigion SY24 5HE
website www.ylolfa.com
e-mail ylolfa@ylolfa.com
tel 01970 832 304
fax 832 782

Foreword

I FIRST VISITED Mametz Wood in August 2004 on a tour of the battlefields of the Great War with my wife and three young sons.

Driving along a rutted track towards the site of the memorial to the 38th (Welsh) Division on a sunny day, the wood stood verdant and lush on the hillside to our left. We arrived beneath the Welsh dragon and marvelled at the symbolism of the piece of German barbed wire clasped in its claw.

In the distance, some 200 yards away, lines of gleaming white headstones stood proudly erect within a low brick boundary wall. We entered the cemetery and began to walk along the rows, noting the names and ages of these men who would never again return to Wales.

The sky now began to turn grey; dark clouds blew in and cast a spectral gloom over this silent village. I instructed my sons to stand still, close their eyes and imagine they were soldiers climbing the rise to attack the German positions in Mametz Wood in July 1916.

A flash of lightning suddenly lit up the sky. 'Imagine it's a flash of gunfire,' I told them, now deeply caught up in my imaginary re-creation of events all those years ago.

We started our climb up the flint-strewn slope towards the edge of the wood, which, with the light fading, had taken on a quite different aspect. What had been the lush trees of summer now became a sinister line of blackness.

Then it happened.

A crack of thunder – a wall of sound that cast aside the trappings of a family holiday and became the deafening explosion of shells some ninety years before. We needed no further bidding and headed for the sanctuary of the car.

Having returned to the present, to happier times, we left Mametz Wood to its awful memories.

Dr Jonathan Hicks
April 2016

Contents

Preface

THIS WORK IS a new interpretation of the battle for Mametz Wood in July 1916, telling the story of those terrible days from the viewpoint of soldiers on both sides, using their own words. I have used primary sources, including personal accounts and photographs which are published for the first time, as well as material translated from the original Welsh; in addition, the memories left behind by German survivors are presented (many unpublished in English before) to give hitherto unseen balance to the conflict.

The attack of the 38th (Welsh) Division on the German positions in Mametz Wood in July 1916 – the second week of the Battle of the Somme – would cost it some 4,000 casualties. It led to a slur on the honour of the division that has endured for a century.

In his introduction to a history of the 38th Welsh Division, Field Marshal Earl Haig wrote 'I do not think that there is any Division which fought under my command in France which cannot point to at least one occasion when its actions reached the highest level of soldierly achievement.' He then cited two occasions for this Division which immediately came to his mind, neither of which was during the battle for Mametz Wood.

Instead he cited the attack north of Ypres on the first day of the Battle of Passchendaele (Third Ypres), 31 July 1917 when it 'met and broke to pieces a German Guard Division', and 'a most brilliant operation' at Pozières, 21–24 August 1918.

Haig did not consider the performance of the 38th (Welsh) Division at Mametz Wood to be a success, but the fact remains that this citizen force, composed of miners from the Rhondda, farmers from Caernarvon and Anglesey, coal trimmers from the docks at Barry and Cardiff, bank workers from Swansea and men from a whole host of other backgrounds and occupations from the counties of Wales, came together and fought in savage hand-to-hand fighting with an enemy from the most effective army in Europe at that time and drove them out of Mametz Wood, leaving behind them the broken bodies of their comrades, many of whom still lie in that wood, far from home.

This book is dedicated to the men who fought there in the second week of July 1916, those who died and who were buried in France, and those who are still missing. It is a salutary fact that more than half the casualties of the Great War have no known grave.

CHAPTER 1

Raising The 38th (Welsh) Division

THE 38TH (WELSH) Division was established following a speech made by Lloyd George, the then Chancellor of the Exchequer, at the Queen's Hall in London on 19 September 1914. In it he said:

> I should like to see a Welsh Army in the field. I should like to see the race that faced the Normans for hundreds of years in a struggle for freedom, the race that helped to win Crecy, the race that fought for a generation under Glyndŵr against the greatest captain in Europe – I should like to see that race give a good taste of their quality in this struggle in Europe; and they are going to do it.[1]

Two days later, at a conference of prominent Welshmen at 11 Downing Street, which Lloyd George chaired, it began to take shape. A committee was formed out of this meeting and it was decided to launch the scheme for a Welsh Army Corps at a national conference to be held at Park Hall in Cardiff at 4 p.m. on Tuesday, 29 September.

Already thousands of Welshmen had signed up in response to the recruiting drive encapsulated in Kitchener's famous poster so, if a Welsh Army was to be formed, a change in recruiting methods would be needed to fill its ranks. From now on, men joining the Army who resided in Wales, or who were of Welsh descent, should join a unit which would bear the name of Wales. At this time Wales had three infantry regiments: The

Royal Welsh Fusiliers, The South Wales Borderers and The Welsh Regiment. (The Welsh Guards were not to be formed until the following year.) In addition, a resurgent recruiting drive was required which had to reach out to all parts of the Principality.

In 1908, the various Volunteer Forces had merged as part of the Haldane Army Reforms into the Territorial Force. In September 1914, the Welsh Territorial Division consisted of 18,000 men. If a Welsh Army was to be raised in addition to this, a further 40,000 to 50,000 Welshmen were required.

The Park Hall Conference of 29 September was held under the chairmanship of the Earl of Plymouth. The Report of the Executive Committee later stated: 'The enthusiasm and scenes of patriotic fervour which characterised the proceedings will be an abiding memory with all who were privileged to attend.'[2] Lloyd George spoke and his speech was well received. 'Realising the righteousness of the cause for which the British Empire was fighting, the delegates at the conference expressed their readiness to work whole-heatedly in raising this great Cymric Army to supplement the large contribution which Wales had already made to the British Forces since mobilisation began.'[3] (To say nothing of the contribution made by Merchant Navy up to this point.)

An impression had been created that the thousands of men who had already enlisted were to form part of the new Welsh Army Corps, but as they had already joined other

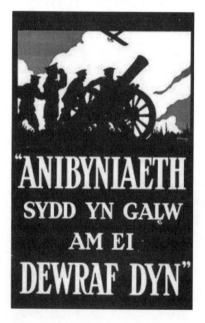

Welsh recruiting poster

regiments this notion had to be dispelled at the meeting. In fact, sufficient men had already enlisted from Wales to form an Army Corps but they had been distributed amongst other regiments. What was required now was a drive to raise another one. This was hugely optimistic and Lloyd George's speech was redundant as soon as he made it, for where was such additional manpower to come from? The month had already seen the peak in the number of men volunteering to serve and the following months saw less than a third of this figure enlist. One also needs to consider that recruitment in Wales was not necessarily that of Welshmen. According to the 1911 census, just over 17 per cent of the population of the county of Glamorgan had been born in England; in Monmouthshire this rose to over 22 per cent. It has also been pointed out that of those soldiers of the 1st Rhondda Battalion who died between August 1914 and December 1916, over 18 per cent were born in England; for its sister battalion, the 2nd Rhonddas, the figure is over 21 per cent.[4] The difficulty though is that after its losses at Mametz Wood the ranks were filled from the next available draft, regardless of where they enlisted – as was the case with other battalions who lost significant numbers in action.

Nevertheless, the enthusiasm for this proposal was certainly evident from the reaction of the audience. Lloyd George reminded listeners of Wales' martial past, affirming that just because Welshmen had suppressed their military activities on a national scale, it did not mean that they had lost their virile and patriotic qualities. He called on Welshmen to 'stand manfully by the flag of freedom, fair play, honest-dealing, progress of Europe.'[5]

A National Executive Committee was formed with the purpose of setting up the new Welsh Army Corps and it first met at the Law Courts in Cardiff on 2 October 1914. The initial difficulty they faced was that the Regular Army and the Territorial Force would continue to require an influx of men from Wales. It was estimated that, by 30 September 1914, 50,000 men had enlisted in Wales for service in the Royal Navy,

Army and Territorial Force.[6] A further meeting took place three days later which submitted a memorandum that the minimum height requirement for the Welsh Army Corps be reduced to 5ft. 3ins. (The 14th Welsh had, for example, set a minimum height requirement of 5ft. 6ins.) Permission was also requested that the three battalions about to be allotted to the Fourth New Army be included in the Welsh Army Corps, these being the Swansea, North Wales and Rhondda Battalions. Permission was further requested to include the battalions of Welshmen being raised in London, Liverpool and Manchester.

Permission was granted on 10 October by the War Office for the raising of the Welsh Army Corps, to comprise two Divisions, but at their next meeting on 16 October the Committee discussed a worrying aspect of this permission: that being that 'every effort must be made to complete existing Welsh units to establishment before recruits are encouraged to enlist in the new units of the Welsh Army Corps.'[7] The committee at this stage had no control over recruitment and therefore determined to appoint a Superintendent of Recruiting in Wales.

Recruits parade outside the City Hall, Cardiff in 1914

Recruiting issues occupied the work of the committee until the end of November. By now the height requirement had been further lowered with the introduction of 'Bantam' Battalions, with a minimum height of 5ft. The idea was also conceived that the men of the new Welsh Army Corps should wear a distinctive uniform of homespun cloth, *Brethyn Llwyd* – a grey wool produced in Wales. Manufacturers were instructed and large amounts of the cloth were sourced. The cloth was hardwearing but ultimately was only used in training, being discarded for the khaki uniform of the rest of the British Army as soon as the unit went overseas. The similarity of the Welsh cloth to that of the German *feldgrau* was undoubtedly noted.

Four Service Battalions were recruited by 31 October, totalling 3,000 men. These were:

13th (Service) Battalion Royal Welsh Fusiliers (1st North Wales)
10th (Service) Battalion Welsh Regiment (1st Rhondda)
13th (Service) Battalion Welsh Regiment (2nd Rhondda)
14th (Service) Battalion Welsh Regiment (Swansea)

At a meeting that was to have widespread consequences, on 2 November the committee met at Shrewsbury and decided that the Lords Lieutenant and County Committees should select the officers for the Welsh Army Corps.

Nine days later the committee met and resolved to invite the St David's Centre of the St John Ambulance Association to form one of the three Field Ambulance units to be attached to the new Corps. Three regional training centres were also to be established: The Royal Welsh Fusiliers were to train at Llandudno; The South Wales Borderers at Colwyn Bay and The Welsh Regiment at Rhyl.

On 18 November the committee decided, on the suggestion of the General Officer Commanding-in-Chief, Western Command, Sir Henry Mackinnon, that three Infantry Brigades should be formed as follows:

The 16th Welsh in training on a north Wales beach

1st Brigade – Llandudno – Brigadier-General Sir Owen
    Thomas
2nd Brigade – Rhyl – Colonel Robert Henry William Dunn
3rd Brigade – Colwyn Bay – Major-General Sir Ivor
    Philipps

Sir Owen Thomas was a landowner and alderman on
Anglesey who had served during the Boer War. He was to lose
three sons during the Great War and received a knighthood in
1917 for his work in recruiting men for the division. Dunn was
a career soldier, JP and Deputy Lieutenant for Flintshire who
was to die of natural causes aged 60 in 1917. He quelled the
anti-German riot in Rhyl in May 1915.

Sir Ivor Philipps was the only one of the three to serve
overseas during the Great War. Born in 1861, he had served
in the Indian Army for ten years from 1893, seeing action in
Burma, and in the Miranzai and Isazai Expeditions. He was in
China as Quartermaster-General from 1900–1, before retiring

with the rank of major in 1903, and was awarded the Distinguished Service Order in 1900 for his work during the Boxer Rebellion. Philipps later joined the Pembrokeshire Yeomanry, which he commanded from 1908 to 1912. He became a Liberal MP in 1906. When the war began he served in the War Office and in November 1914 was promoted to Brigadier-General in charge of 115th Infantry Brigade. In January 1916 he was given command of the 38th (Welsh) Division. It was to be his old brigade that was given the task of making the first attack on Mametz Wood on 7 July.

Sir Ivor Philipps

During November 1914 further units were formed:

14th (Service) Battalion Royal Welsh Fusiliers
15th (Service) Battalion Royal Welsh Fusiliers (1st London Welsh)
10th (Service) Battalion South Wales Borderers (1st Gwent)
15th (Service) Battalion Welsh Regiment (Carmarthenshire)
16th (Service) Battalion Welsh Regiment (Cardiff City)

In addition, elements of the following arms were added: Royal Field Artillery, Royal Engineers, Army Service Corps and the Royal Army Medical Corps. This brought the total strength of the Corps up to approximately 7,000 men.

During December the following new units were formed:

16th (Service) Battalion Royal Welsh Fusiliers
17th (Service) Battalion Welsh Regiment (Glamorgan)
123rd Field Company Royal Engineers
124th Field Company Royal Engineers
43rd (later 38th) Signal Company Royal Engineers
1st (later 129th) Field Ambulance
2nd (later 130th) Field Ambulance

In the first two months recruitment had been slow, but by December the numbers had increased and by the end of that month the estimated strength was some 10,000 men.

The following year saw the recruitment of a Pioneer Battalion and the appointment of Major-General Sir Ivor Philipps to command the three brigades. January 1915 also saw the recruitment of four new units:

11th (Service) Battalion South Wales Borderers (2nd Gwent)
151st Field Company Royal Engineers
3rd (later 131st) Field Ambulance
1 Brigade Field Artillery

This brought the strength of the Corps up to 16,000 men.

On 17 February it was reported to the committee that 20 Welsh Canadians had been sent by the Canadian Pacific Railway to join the Welsh Army Corps. The men were allocated to the 10th South Wales Borderers. During the month the following new units were raised:

19th (Service) Battalion Royal Welsh Fusiliers
12th (Service) Battalion South Wales Borderers
18th (Service) Battalion Welsh Regiment
38th Sanitary Section Royal Army Medical Corps
18th (Service) Battalion Royal Welsh Fusiliers (2nd London Welsh)

This brought the strength of the new Corps up to Divisional size – approximately 20,000 men – but it was clear by March 1915 that a change to recruiting methods was necessary if a second Division was to be formed. A stronger recruiting authority was required in each county and at the end of May the overall strength stood at 29,660 officers and men, and by June this had risen to over 35,000. It was noted at a meeting of 14 July that General Sir Henry Mackinnon had on more than one occasion since the turn of the year informed the committee that the Army Council considered it more important to provide men for the battalions already at the Front and Reserve companies for the New Armies than to raise a second Division of the Welsh Army Corps.

Before the storm of steel – St David's Day 1915, Colwyn Bay

Departing from Cardiff Station in 1915

At a meeting of the committee on 27 October this view was reinforced by Lord Derby and the members decided that recruitment for the Welsh Army Corps should be brought to a close.

The 38th (Welsh) Division thus comprised of three infantry brigades, each containing battalions from Welsh regiments.

113rd Brigade was under the command of Brigadier-General L.A.E. Price-Davies V.C. and comprised:

13th Royal Welsh Fusiliers (1st North Wales)
14th Royal Welsh Fusiliers (Caernarvon and Anglesey)
15th Royal Welsh Fusiliers (London Welsh)
16th Royal Welsh Fusiliers

114th Brigade was led by Brigadier-General T.O. Marden and was formed from:

10th Welsh (1st Rhondda),
13th Welsh (2nd Rhondda)
14th Welsh (Swansea)
15th Welsh (Carmarthenshire)

Brigadier-General H.J. Evans was in command of 115th Brigade, which consisted of:

17th Royal Welsh Fusiliers (2nd North Wales)
10th South Wales Borderers (1st Gwent)
11th South Wales Borderers (2nd Gwent)
16th Welsh (Cardiff City)
19th Welsh (Glamorgan Pioneers)

These battalions were concentrated at Winchester during August 1915 and eventually departed for France during the first week of December 1915. It was the start of active service that was to see the division involved in some of the fiercest fighting on the Western Front.

CHAPTER 2

Mametz Wood –
The Overture

AFTER LEAVING WINCHESTER the division marched to Southampton and embarked on a troopship for France. They landed at Le Havre then entrained for Rocquetoire, a commune in the Pas-de-Calais department, south-east of St Omer, the General Headquarters of the British Expeditionary Force. This move was completed by 5 December. By the end of the month the Divisional artillery had arrived and the Division moved south-east to Saint-Venant, where it was held in reserve.

In January 1916 the Division entered the line in the Neuve Chapelle sector, relieving the 19th Division. It held a section of the line from Le Picantin in the north to Givenchy in the south and remained here until June 1916, taking part in several trench raids, until on 11 June it set off for the Somme battlefield to take part in the great offensive.

An unknown officer of the division wrote of 'The sturdy column that swung its way down the hedge-bound lanes in the early mornings of the end of June, singing and laughing in the happiness of relief from the fetter of the trenches in Flanders.'[1]

They were headed for the area around Mametz Wood, a place that has a special resonance for the people of Wales, current Welsh soldiers and the relatives of those who fought there. What was to take place there during those days of July was to stay with the Division for the remainder of the war and beyond.

The Divisional Ammunition Column Football Team

On the night of 3/4 July, a patrol from the 2nd Battalion of the Royal Irish Regiment entered Mametz Wood and subsequently reported that the wood was very dense with thick undergrowth and movement for infantry was not easy. They spotted a tripwire at the edge of the wood but thought this would only be a serious obstacle at night. About 100 yards inside the southern edge of the wood was a small, shallow trench or dip but they came across no fortified defences within the area they explored. The patrol reported that Strip Trench, which ran north-south at the southern edge of the wood, was strongly wired and well traversed. Trees had fallen across the trench and made movement along it difficult. Wood Trench, which ran east-west, was strongly wired. They also noted several machine gun positions.

The soldiers interviewed an unnamed Frenchman who gave them information on the types of trees to be found in the wood: oak, nine feet in girth; birch, two feet in girth; beech, six feet in girth and some ash trees. The average height of the trees was 30 to 45 feet. On the north-eastern border there was some strong undergrowth of hawthorn and briar. A thicket of tall hornbeam, 90 to 120 feet in width, was reported at the south-western end.

During the patrol they also captured a prisoner who told them that the Germans had withdrawn from the wood to their second line to the north, outside Bazentin-le-Petit Wood. They had penetrated deeper into the wood to check on this and found a party of Germans asleep. They dispatched them and took the breech blocks from two field guns, rendering them useless. One of the patrol found that the Germans were still occupying Quadrangle Trench to the east but not in great strength.

In his Special Order of the Day for 5 July, Major-General Ivor Philipps ordered the following to be read out to every Platoon and Section on parade:

To the Officers, N.C.O.s and Men of the 38th (Welsh) Division,
You have worked hard for many months with an energy and zeal beyond praise to fit yourselves for the task you have voluntarily undertaken. You have undergone the hardships of a winter campaign with fortitude. You have earned the praise of your Corps Commanders for your courage, discipline and devotion to duty. You have now held for six months a section of the British line in France, during which time you have not allowed one of the enemy to enter your trenches except as a prisoner, and on several occasions you have entered the enemy's lines. 11 Officers and 44 N.C.O.s and men have already received rewards from the King for gallant and distinguished conduct in the field. Your fellow countrymen at home are following your career with interest and admiration. I always believed that a really Welsh Division would be second to none. You have more than justified that belief. I feel that whatever the future may have in store for us I can rely upon you, because you have already given ample proof of your worth. During the short period in the Training Area you worked hard to qualify yourselves for still further efforts. I thank you most sincerely for the loyal and wholehearted way in which you have all supported me and for the way in which each one of you has done his utmost to carry out the task allotted to

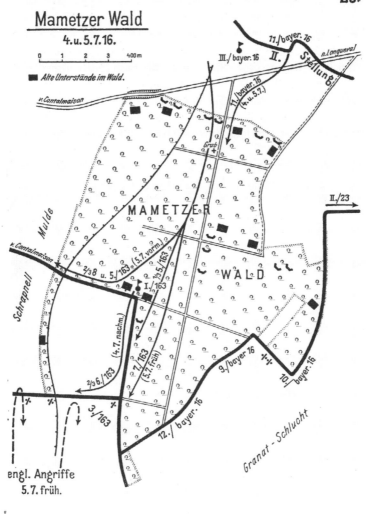

20.

Mametzer Wald
4. u. 5. 7. 16.

0   1   2   3   400 m

■ Alte Unterstände im Wald.

The German positions on 5 July 1915

him. With such a spirit animating all ranks we can one and all look forward with confidence to the future, whatever it may have in store for us.

You are today relieving the 7th Division, which has attacked and captured German trenches on a front of a little less than one mile and for a depth of about one and a half miles. In this attack the village of Mametz was captured, the enemy have suffered very heavy casualties. 1,500 German officers and men were taken prisoners and six field guns were captured.

The 1st Battalion, Royal Welsh Fusiliers and the 1st Battalion, Welsh Regiment of the 7th Division have both distinguished themselves in this attack, and I am confident that the young battalions of the famous Welsh regiments serving in the 38th (Welsh) Division will maintain the high standard for valour for which all three Welsh Regiments have been renowned throughout the war.[2]

The scene was now set for the epic action that was to follow.

CHAPTER 3

7 July –
The First Movement

WHILE THE BATTLE of the Somme has become synonymous with failure, and the appalling British Army casualty figure of 57,470, of whom 19,240 were killed on 1 July, the first day of the offensive, is often seen as an example of the futility of the Great War, it is frequently overlooked that the battle was only just beginning and the fighting was to continue until 18 November 1916, resulting in many more deaths on both sides.

After the disaster of the first day, the German Army was driven back in several sectors, including beyond the villages of Mametz and Fricourt, and by 5 July the British were facing them across the valley near Mametz Wood.

The official history of the 38th Division, in itself a disappointingly slim volume, gives scant attention to the assault on Mametz Wood. While a chapter is entitled 'Capture of Mametz Wood', the detail is very thin. But it does claim that the task was of some magnitude, so much so that the capture of Mametz Wood had been left out of the orders for 1 July by General Headquarters. It was to have been bypassed when the attacking lines of infantry reached the area, as was anticipated.

Taking the woods in the area, including Trônes Wood, Bazentin-le-Petit Wood and Bazentin-le-Grand Wood, was now seen as vital if the advance was to continue. The 38th (Welsh) Division was allocated the task of capturing Mametz Wood and on 5 July they moved into trenches in the area from which they could view the ground.

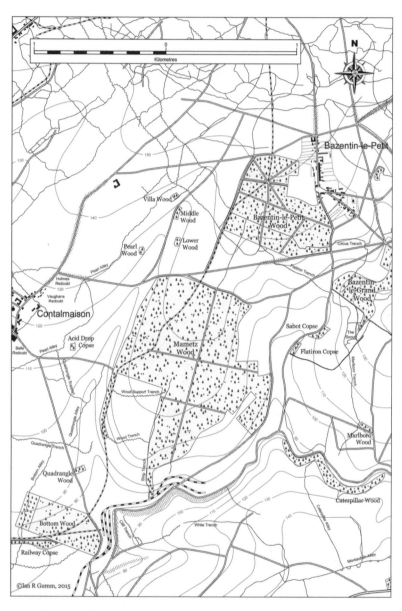

Map of Mametz Wood and its environs

Mametz Wood was, and still is, the largest wood on the Somme. It covers an area of over 200 acres, being close to a mile in length, and is situated south of Bazentin-le-Petit Wood, overlooking a valley. An attack from this direction would have to be made across open ground, first downhill from the British trenches, then up rising ground to the edge of the wood itself.

Two copses were situated to the north – Flatiron and Sabot copses. Both were held by the Germans who could bring enfilading machine gun fire on any attackers who crossed the exposed ground to attack the wood. If any attempt was made to take these two positions first, then similar supporting fire could be brought into play from inside Mametz Wood and the two Bazentin woods. The German second line ran across the northern edge of Mametz Wood, some 300 yards away, and was ideal for moving in reinforcements, if required.

This, then, was the situation to the east of Mametz Wood. To the west the British area was held by soldiers of the 17th Division, who would provide support. In opposition were elements of the Prussian Guard, and a citizen army was being charged with evicting them; soldiers who had received little or no training in wood fighting were expected to drive out an experienced, battle-hardened enemy. It was anticipated that this would be a straightforward task, but as the official history of the Royal Welsh Fusiliers comments: 'The wood seems to have been a puzzle. There was still, for some reason, a belief that the enemy would relinquish it, though why he should do so with such easy access to it is not clear.'[1]

XV Corps Headquarters failed to capitalise on the intelligence gathered by the patrols of 3 and 4 July, and the official history of the Great War states: 'It would appear that if XV Corps had encouraged more vigorous action on the afternoon of the 3rd a hold on Mametz Wood could have been secured and Wood Trench and Quadrangle Trench occupied. The last-named objective was taken on the morning of the 5th, but the others were to cost many lives and much precious time.'[2]

The opportunity for a quick victory had been lost.

The attack on Mametz Wood was to begin on 7 July. The 17th Division would attack a small copse to the west, known as Acid Drop Copse. They would also attack the western edge of the wood to draw enemy fire away from the advance by elements of the 38th Division, who would be attacking the area of Mametz Wood known as The Hammerhead. Once these attacks had achieved their objectives, both divisions would advance north along the central track inside the wood, known as a 'ride', and clear the Germans out of the wood.

115th Brigade

The 115th Brigade, comprising the 17th Royal Welsh Fusiliers, the 10th and 11th South Wales Borderers, the 16th Welsh and the 19th Welsh (Pioneers), was given the responsibility for the attack on The Hammerhead. This brigade was under the command of Brigadier-General Horatio John Evans who was, at 56, the oldest of the brigade commanders during the Battle of the Somme. Evans was a career soldier who was to be replaced some six weeks after the battle. His analysis of the fighting can be found in a later chapter. Evans was described by Llewelyn Wyn Griffith of the Royal Welsh Fusiliers as 'physically strong, with a hard and clear face, and the bearing of a man who has lived wisely.'[3]

In the Operation Order for the attack planned for 7 July, two main objectives were specified – Acid Drop Copse and Mametz Wood. The first attack was to begin at 2 a.m. when the 17th Division was to seize Quadrangle Support Trench and Pearl Alley Trench to the west of Mametz Wood. At 8 a.m. 17th Division was to take part in a combined attack with the 38th (Welsh) Division. This was to be delayed by thirty minutes if the 2 a.m. attack proved unsuccessful.

The 115th Infantry Brigade was to attack the centre of Mametz Wood, working westwards and then northwards, while at the same time the 17th Division would attack Mametz Wood from the south-west to capture the remainder of the wood. An intense preliminary bombardment was ordered from 7.20 a.m. to 8 a.m., after which a series of barrages would be fired. If the 2 a.m. attack was unsuccessful, the bombardment would commence at 8 a.m., with a reduction in duration of ten minutes. To shield the advancing troops a smoke barrage would be formed on the eastern portion of Mametz Wood and around Flatiron Copse and Sabot Copse.

The role of 113th Brigade was to provide heavy rifle and machine gun fire on the southern end of Mametz Wood from their positions in White Trench and Cliff Trench from 8 a.m. to 8.30 a.m., regardless of the starting time of the assault; light trench mortar fire would also strike the southern portion of Mametz Wood.

Evans was unimpressed by the orders he had been given. According to Griffith:

> The General was cursing last night at his orders. He said that only a madman could have issued them. He called the Divisional Staff a lot of plumbers, herring-gutted at that. He argued at the time, and asked for some control over the artillery that is going to cover us, but he got nothing out of them. We are not allowed to attack at dawn; we must wait for the show at Contalmaison, well away on our left.[4]

Evans' reconnaissance of the ground made it clear to him that an attack on a narrow front was all that was possible and he decided that this could be no more than one battalion wide. He chose the 16th Battalion of the Welsh Regiment.

The commanding officer of the 16th Welsh, Lieutenant-Colonel Frank W. Smith, realised immediately that his right flank would be exposed to fire from the area of Flatiron Copse and he suggested that the plan be altered to allow him to attack at first light. This was not possible because the attack had to be co-ordinated with that of the 17th Division.

But Evans was overruled and when the attack took place two battalions were used. The 11th South Wales Borderers would attack with its left flank as close to Caterpillar Wood

Lieutenant-Colonel Frank W. Smith (seated) with officers of the 16th Welsh

as possible and the 16th Welsh would be tight against their right flank. Each battalion would have no more than a 250-yard frontage for the attack. It was planned that the problem of flanking fire was to be eased by the use of a smoke screen.

In the early hours of 7 July a reconnoitring patrol was to be sent out to the south-eastern corner of Mametz Wood if assurances were received that the artillery would not be shelling that portion of the wood. By 8 a.m. the following morning, half an hour before the assault was to begin, all communication wires had been cut by the German shelling. Nevertheless, the British artillery stuck to its schedule but no smoke barrage was formed, as the wind was not favourable. This was to have catastrophic

Shells bursting in Mametz Wood

consequences for the attacking battalions, as it meant that the German defenders inside Mametz Wood and Flatiron and Sabot copses would have unhindered views of the advancing lines of British infantry.

At 8.30 a.m. the officer commanding the 115th Machine Gun Company was ordered to push forward two additional machine guns to the west of Caterpillar Wood to enfilade the German trenches at the eastern edge of the wood.

At the same time, the 11th South Wales Borderers and 16th Welsh rose to their task as soon as the artillery stopped and immediately came under fire from the German machine guns in Flatiron and Sabot copses.

The communication wires had still not been repaired, so having no idea as to the success of the attack, at 8.45 a.m. the staff officer, Captain H.V. Hinton, was ordered to go forward as quickly as possible to Caterpillar Wood to find out how the attack was progressing. At 9.19 a.m. Headquarters were informed that the attack by the 11th South Wales Borderers and the 16th Welsh had been launched at the appointed time of 8.30 a.m. At 10 a.m. messages were received by the officers commanding these battalions that they were being temporarily held up by heavy machine gun fire coming from the southern edge of Mametz Wood and from the direction of Bazentin Wood and Flatiron Copse.

A report from Captain Hinton timed at 9.25 a.m. was received at 10.10 a.m. In it he stated that the attack was being held up by fairly heavy enemy rifle and machine gun fire about 200 yards from the northern side of the wood, and about 400 yards from the southern side of the wood. Casualties did not appear to be heavy. The soldiers of the 11th South Wales Borderers and 16th Welsh were returning fire and throwing bombs. He suggested a further artillery bombardment to assist the attack; this was immediately granted. In addition, the 115th Machine Gun Company was ordered to send forward more machine guns towards Caterpillar Wood to deal with the enfilade fire apparently coming from Bazentin-le-Grand Wood.

Confirmation of the additional artillery bombardment came at 10.25 a.m.; it would commence at 10.45 a.m. and last for thirty minutes. This information was immediately sent forward to the attacking battalions with instructions to dig themselves in and then to attack once more at the cessation of the bombardment. The officer commanding the 10th South Wales Borderers was sent for to be given instructions to move up his battalion to support this renewed attack when it came.

Another report now came in from Captain Hinton, timed at 9.50 a.m., which stated that the situation was getting worse. The machine gun fire and artillery fire was becoming heavier and the enemy held a trench on the edge of Mametz Wood from which they were pouring fire on to the remnants of the two battalions, which were still in the open.

The officer commanding the 10th South Wales Borderers had still not arrived so another message was sent to him. Captain Hinton, meanwhile, sent another report, timed at 10.25 a.m., wherein he stated that the attacking lines were now 300 yards from the wood and the casualties were as follows: 16th Welsh – 1 officer and 60 other ranks; 11th S.W.B. – 5 officers and 30 other ranks. He requested immediate artillery support.

Hinton returned to Headquarters at 11.30 a.m. and reported that at around 10.45 a.m. the German machine gun fire was heavy so that the next assault would be slow, but casualties were not heavy and the situation was not serious. The four companies of the 10th South Wales Borderers were now ordered forward in support.

At 11.10 a.m. telephone communication between the front line and brigade headquarters was re-established. The officer commanding the 16th Welsh reported that the British shells were falling short into his position and causing casualties. Still the 16th Welsh pushed forward and, by 1.30 p.m., the officer commanding reported that his casualties were increasing. At the same time Captain Hinton reported that the 10th South Wales Borderers had arrived. Forty-five minutes later they went into action in support of the two attacking battalions.

The wires were now cut again, so information from the front line dried up. Brigadier Evans went forward himself to Caterpillar Wood to ascertain the situation. He arrived there at 4.40 p.m. and found the two attacking battalions and the supporting battalion holding a line about 250 yards from the eastern edge of Mametz Wood, partially dug in and somewhat disorganised. The soldiers were exhausted, having been in continuous action for over eight hours. They had few officers left and had taken around 400 casualties.

Evans took control of the situation, preparing the remaining soldiers for another attack to begin at 5 p.m. But it proved impossible to reorganise the units by that time, plus there was insufficient time to correctly site the trench mortars and machine guns to provide support. Evans, therefore, postponed the attack and asked for a further artillery bombardment to clear the enemy from the front of the wood and to give him time to bring up the machine guns and reorganise the battalions. Before this could happen, orders were received to withdraw and this was accomplished without any further casualties, leaving two companies of the 17th Royal Welsh Fusiliers behind to hold Caterpillar Wood and Marlborough Wood.

The attack had failed and blame had to be apportioned. The Brigade War Diary stated that the artillery bombardment was ineffective owing to the difficulty of observation as it was impossible to accurately register the guns, and that the volume of fire directed at the Bazentin woods and Flatiron Copse was insufficient to quell the enfilade fire that poured into the attacking ranks. Evans claimed that he had not been consulted with regard to the details of the artillery preparation. Neither did he agree with the final dispositions of the units as laid down in the Divisional Orders. He felt they were not in accordance with his reconnaissance of the ground over which they had attacked. He also stated that no close reconnaissance of the ground had been possible owing to the British artillery fire preventing patrols being sent out. Nor had it been possible to accurately locate the position of the machine guns on the northern flank which caused such heavy casualties.

However, there had been some successes. The Stokes Trench Mortar Battery at Caterpillar Wood under Lieutenant K.H. Noel silenced at least two guns situated in the southern part of Mametz Wood, and the machine guns under Captain Job of the 115th Machine Gun Company successfully reduced the fire coming from the Bazentin woods, Flatiron Copse and Sabot Copse.

The Brigade War Diary firmly lays the blame on the failure to provide the smoke barrage, and the delay in obtaining artillery support, as this had to be referred to 'higher authority'. Unlike the 113th Brigade later, no blame was attached here to the soldiers of 115th Brigade. It was an operational issue alone which had prevented them from being successful.

But there were other factors that had affected the chances of the attack being successful. The weather had changed and rain fell, which meant that movement became very difficult in the resulting mud. The attack by the 16th Welsh and the 11th South Wales Borderers had been made too close to the German second line positions to the north of Mametz Wood, which allowed the Germans to take a heavy toll of the attackers through enfilading fire. The artillery fire, as Evans had feared, was not properly co-ordinated and not only left the men exposed to uninterrupted German fire but also meant that shells fell short, causing casualties to their own side.

In addition to all these problems, there was the added matter that the attack by the 17th Division to the west also failed, so the anticipated co-ordinated effect came to nothing. The attack had cost 400 casualties in the three battalions engaged and nothing had been achieved. These battle weary units were withdrawn and, at the end of the day, Lieutenant-General Horne (XV Corps) informed Haig that he was not happy with the conduct of General Philipps who was removed from command on 9 July 1916.

16th Welsh (Cardiff City)

The National Executive Committee, responding to Lloyd George's 19 September speech calling for a 'Welsh Army', asked Alderman J.T. Richards, the Lord Mayor of Cardiff, to raise a complete battalion from the city. In November the recruiting campaign began and command of the battalion was given to Captain Frank Gaskell, who was at home in Llanishen, a suburb of Cardiff, recovering from wounds.

Eight weeks later the battalion's ranks had been filled. The men were attested and enrolled at The Custom House in Cardiff, then were given a short leave to sort out their affairs before travelling to Porthcawl for training. At the turn of

Frank Gaskell with some of the Glamorgan Constabulary recruits to the 16th Welsh

the year the battalion moved to Colwyn Bay, stopping off at Cardiff to parade through the home city, with some of the recruits wearing the 'Welsh Grey' cloth uniform. In August 1915 the men moved to Winchester with the other units of the 38th (Welsh) Division. At the end of November the battalion paraded at the Arms Park in Cardiff, before embarking on 4 December for France.

The next few months were spent at positions in the Givenchy-Festubert-Laventie area, where approximately 50 casualties were sustained. The 16th Welsh had lost Frank Gaskell on the night of 15 May 1916 while visiting a forward position. A German sniper's bullet hit his ammunition pouch, causing it to explode, and he died of his wounds two days later.

He was succeeded as Commanding Officer by Major Frank W. Smith. Smith had served in the Matabele War in South Africa and the Boer War, where he had been awarded the Distinguished Conduct Medal. An Inspector with the Glamorgan Constabulary in Bridgend before the war, he was mobilised with the Glamorgan Yeomanry in August 1914. He had been a notable rugby player and had been vice-captain of Cardiff Rugby Football Club, playing against New Zealand and South Africa.

Smith had become one of the first company commanders of the 16th Welsh and the *South Wales Echo* of 11 December 1914 reported that 'The men were delighted to see at their head such a genial, able and diligent officer.'[5] He landed in France with the battalion in December 1915 and was promoted to the rank of major. During his early duty at the Front he was wounded by the accidental discharge of a bomb and was repatriated to London for treatment, re-joining the battalion on his recovery. He was later awarded the Distinguished Service Order and Mentioned in Dispatches.

The 16th Welsh War Diary records that on 5 July the battalion was in bivouacs at Carnoy. A party of eight officers, divided into three groups, was sent out to carry out a reconnaissance of the approaches to the new position at Queen's Nullah. The party was heavily shelled; two officers were killed and two were wounded.

The dead officers were Second Lieutenant James Hubert Waddington, aged 20, a native of Swansea, who is buried in Morlancourt British Cemetery Number 1, and Second Lieutenant Wilfred Brynmor Williams, whose parents lived in Llantwit Vardre, Pontypridd. He was buried in Dantzig Alley British Cemetery.

On 6 July there was an inspection of the men's arms and equipment and Major-General Sir Ivor Philipps' letter was read to the battalion. In the evening they proceeded to the valley north of Caterpillar Wood. It was noted that between there and Mametz Wood there was a slope which hid the soldiers from the enemy's view.

The War Diary for the 16th Welsh states:

> 8.30am Battalion under orders, drawn up on their own side of the slope facing Mametz Wood in lines of Platoons with a two platoon frontage. 11 S.W.B. in support, 10 S.W.B. in reserve. Our Artillery ceased firing at the wood at 8.30am and the first lines of the battalion proceeded over the crest of the slope but instantly came under heavy machine gun frontal fire from Mametz Wood and enfilade fire from Flatiron Copse and Sabot Copse and the German second system which ran between Mametz Wood and Bazentin Petit Wood. Battalion suffered heavily and had to withdraw to their own side of the crest. Battalion made two more attacks, but position was too exposed for any hope of success and orders were received to cease operations. 11 S.W.B. attempted to approach the wood through a gulley running between Caterpillar Wood and the slope mentioned above but machine gun fire drove them back. Weather very wet, this adding greatly to exhaustion of troops. Battalion received orders to return to their bivouacs. Moved off 10.30am. Arrived 4.00am on the 8th.[6]

They made two more attacks that day but the War Diary comments 'the position was much too exposed for any hope of success and orders were received to cease operations.'[7]

Five 16th Welsh officers were killed, six wounded and 268

other ranks killed, wounded or missing. The officers killed were: two brothers who were serving as second lieutenants: Leonard and Arthur Tregaskis, Second Lieutenant John Edwin Howell, a farmer's son from Llanelli, who died aged 23 and whose body was never identified, Captain J.L. Williams and Second Lieutenant W.B. Williams.

The continuing wet weather added greatly to the exhaustion of the soldiers. At 10.30 p.m. they moved off to return to their bivouacs, arriving there at 4 a.m.

As the days passed following the capture of the wood, the scale of the casualties and the names of those killed, wounded and missing began to filter back to Wales. The newspapers printed photograph after photograph and gave the scant details of the casualties' lives. Storekeepers, coal trimmers, tramway men, colliers – a whole cross-section of the Welsh working class were listed as the full horror of the extensive casualty list became public knowledge.

One of the first sets of names to be reported was those of two former members of the Glamorgan Constabulary – Company Sergeant-Major Richard Thomas of Bridgend and Sergeant Robert John Harris of Aberkenfig. Their deaths were reported thus:

Three unknown soldiers of the 16th Welsh

Both were in the same battalion of the Welsh Regiment (the 16th), joining with Inspector Smith, now the C.O. The first announcement of the death of Company Sergeant-Major Richard Thomas came from Regimental Sergeant-Major John Thomas, who was his fellow police sergeant at Bridgend. In a letter to his wife, written on 10 July and received on Saturday afternoon, Thomas wrote: 'Just a line to let you know I am all right. Wish I could say the same about all the other boys. Poor Dick Thomas was killed yesterday morning where the big fighting that you read about in the newspapers is going on. Captain Herdman and he were leading the company into action, and Dick was about the first to be knocked over. The captain was wounded. Bob Harris was also killed near the same spot. Trinder was wounded and is now is hospital. No doubt it will be a terrible shock to Mrs Thomas. Colonel Smith is all right, but we are very much upset over the loss of Dick. He used to keep the lot of us alive with his jokes.' Only a few weeks ago he spent a brief furlough with his family at Bridgend. He was of a genial disposition, and was extremely popular not only as a (rugby) football player, but as a police officer in every place where he had been stationed. He was 36 years of age, and leaves a widow and two children to mourn the loss of one who was well beloved by all his comrades, and by all the people who knew him in the sphere on which he moved.[8]

Dick Thomas was a well-known rugby player for Mountain Ash, Bridgend and Cardiff. He played for Wales against South Africa in 1906, against Ireland and France in 1908, against Scotland in 1909, as well as against England and Scotland three seasons later. A former miner from Ferndale, he had later joined the Glamorgan Constabulary. He played for the Glamorgan Police team in their final match before the Great War, against his hometown team of Ferndale. He was also a boxer, winning the competition open to the Police of Glamorgan and Monmouthshire at a Nazareth House 'assault-at-arms' just a few years before the outbreak of the war. In addition, he was the Glamorgan Police heavyweight champion on three occasions.

Sergeant Robert Harris, the son of Mr and Mrs John Harris,

of Llechwen Farm, Ynys-y-bŵl, Pontypridd, had joined the Glamorgan Constabulary in 1908, and in 1911 was serving at Nantymoel; he subsequently served at Aberkenfig. A newspaper report of his death described him as being 'exceedingly popular among the officers and men of the Glamorgan Constabulary.'[9] His body was never found and he is commemorated on the Thiepval Memorial.

The confusion that ensued over the casualties is evident in the fact that Lance Corporal William Edward Trinder of the same battalion was not wounded, as stated above, but was killed during the attack on 7 July, and his body was never recovered. Before the war he had also been a member of the Glamorgan Constabulary, being stationed at Caerau, Maesteg. He too is remembered on the Thiepval Memorial.

Another Company Sergeant-Major of the 16th Welsh killed during the attack on 7 July was Albert Willshire, a 38-year-old veteran. He had served with the 2nd Battalion of the Welsh Regiment in India and at the outbreak of the war he rejoined his regiment, being posted to the fledgling battalion as an

Dick Thomas

Robert Harris

experienced N.C.O. who would be invaluable in training the new recruits. He was a married man with three children, who, in civilian life, was employed by Messrs. Walkey, Thomas and Co., paper merchants. He had also been an enthusiastic football player.

In a letter to Willshire's wife conveying the sad news, Captain M. Boyd stated:

> I hear on all hands of his great courage. All the officers with the company being killed or wounded, your husband led the company in the last attack, just before being killed. He went out and brought in a machine gun that was in danger of capture. He was a brave man amongst a splendid lot, the whole regiment being thanked by the General for their great bravery. To me in particular he is a serious loss for his never-failing cheerfulness and devotion to duty, while the men have lost a friend as well as a sergeant-major.[10]

The attack on The Hammerhead claimed the lives of several men from my hometown of Barry.

Corporal Edgar James Gilbert was 24 years of age and before joining the Army he was a cutter at W.J. Windsor's 'outfitting establishment' in Holton Road in Barry. His friend Lance Corporal G. Jenkins of the same battalion wrote a letter to his parents on 17 July:

> It is with bitterest regret that I have to inform you of the death in action of your son Edgar. As you are aware by the papers, active operations have taken place this month, and our battalion took its share in the brilliant and successful assault on July 7, resulting in the capture of a now notorious position. It was during this action that Edgar fell, whilst a determined rush was being made. Believe me, I hardly know how to express my feelings of sorrow and sympathy, but I can at least say that mere words fall short of just expression. We both were in school together and met again at Porthcawl in December 1914 when the Battalion was formed under the control of our late Lieut.-Colonel Frank Gaskell. Edgar and I shared alike during our period of training and actual warfare, and he showed qualities that greatly helped to minimise the many

hardships of war. His noble death I feel very acutely, and I cannot help feeling that his splendid sacrifice, crowned by death, for God, for King and Country, has been a national gain. The loss to you may be hard to understand and hard to bear, but let us comfort ourselves by the noble thought that no sacrifice could be higher.[11]

Private Charles Breckenridge was also killed during the attack on the first day. He had been a postman who lived with his wife Florence at 8 Woodlands Road, Barry, and was killed when the battalion was swept with machine gun fire from The Hammerhead, plus from Flatiron Copse and Sabot Copse on their right.

Major J.H. Hicks, for the Colonel in charge of Records, No. 4 District, wrote to Breckenridge's widow:

Madam, I beg to inform you that I have this day received notification from the War Officer to the effect that your husband, the late 24472 Private C. Breckenridge, The Welsh Regiment, has had a reverent and proper burial according to the rites of his religion. He was buried south east of the Bois de Mametz, 1 mile west-north-west of Montauban, 5 miles east of Albert.[12]

Sadly, Charles Breckenridge's grave was lost during the remaining years of the war and he is commemorated on the Thiepval Memorial as one of the missing.

Another Barry postman was also killed on that day – Corporal Sydney Charles Hambleton. Before enlisting he had been employed at the General Post Office, Barry Dock, and had been a local postman for 16 years. He was the second son of Mr and Mrs Sydney Hambleton of 68 Morel Street, who had lost another son, Corporal Philip Hambleton, who had died in Malta on 7 December 1915. Another son, Corporal Frederick Hambleton, served in France with the Welsh Guards and survived the war. Sydney Hambleton left a wife and a daughter to mourn his loss. The commanding officer of his Company wrote to Sydney's wife that he had been in the front line of the attack on Mametz Wood and the platoon was practically wiped out. The officer wrote: 'But the men followed me gallantly and it was cruel to see them fall before a hail of bullets. He was a fine soldier and of great assistance.'[13] He and Breckenridge are also commemorated on the Barry Post Office Memorial.

Mrs Hoare of 4 Arthur Street in Barry received news on Sunday 17 July of her husband's death. Lance Sergeant Charles Hoare was 29 years of age and had two brothers in the Army. He was also killed during the 16th Battalion's attack on Mametz Wood.

Sergeant David Thomas was also killed on 7 July. He was 26 years of age and before enlisting had been employed at the offices of the Barry Railway Company. He lived in Miskin Street, Barry, and was a well-known local footballer, playing as a forward for Penarth, Aberavon and Liverpool. He left a widow and one child.

Lance Corporal Arthur Thomas from Forrwst Street Cardiff was killed during the advance and lies close to Mametz Wood as his body could not be identified later. He is commemorated on the Thiepval Memorial.

One soldier who should not have even been on the battlefield

Private Charles Breckenridge   Arthur Thomas

that day was Private George Henry Wright who died of his wounds on 10 July, aged just 17. A native of Dinas Powys, he had lied about his real age in order to enlist. His father was a sapper in the Royal Engineers. George is buried at Heilly Station Cemetery.

The death of Private C.J. Irwin of the 16th Battalion of the Welsh Regiment was conveyed to his wife at 42 Russell Street, Cardiff, by his officer with the words, 'The men followed me gallantly, and it was cruel to see them fall before the hail of bullets. They gave their lives cheerfully for the dear homeland and the folks at home.'[14] Irwin's body, like to so many others who fell that day, was never identified and he is commemorated on the Thiepval Memorial to the missing.

A Welshman killed while endeavouring to save the life of another was Private Herbert Brisen of the 16th Battalion of the Welsh Regiment. Originally from 15 Alpha Street, Coedpenmaen, Pontypridd, he died on 7 July. One of the officers of the battalion, in a letter to Mr J.E. Teasdel, engineer and manager of the Pontypridd Tramways, wrote: 'Brisen died in trying to save others, and I had recommended him for honours. He fought well and died nobly.'[15] Before enlisting Herbert Brisen was employed at the Great Western Collieries, Pontypridd. His body was never identified and he is also remembered on the Thiepval Memorial.

Sportsman Robert Charles Blackmore was killed during the first day of the attack, aged 26. A Lance Corporal with the 16th Battalion (Welsh) Regiment, he was a well-known 'pedestrian' or walker who was often a winner at the Cardiff Stadium and other local race

Jack Irwin

meetings. He had been a member of the publishing staff of the *South Wales Echo* and had once won a £50 prize at a pedestrian event. He was also a sprinter and, at the Naval and Military Carnival at Stamford Bridge in August 1915, he came second in the 300 yards race, later being presented with a silver cup.

There were several pairs of brothers killed during the fighting at Mametz Wood. Private Henry John Morgan and Private Charles Morgan, the sons of Mr W.J. and Mrs E. Morgan of 1 Eyre Street, Splott, Cardiff, left their employment with the Blaenavon Steel and Iron Company to join the Cardiff City Battalion. Both men served in 'A' Company.

Lieutenant W.J. Richards, in a letter to their distraught parents, wrote that they were killed by German snipers, adding 'Your sons were very good soldiers and they did their duty to the last.'[16] Neither of the brothers has a known grave and they are recalled on the Thiepval Memorial; Charles died aged 22, and Henry aged 26.

Perhaps the most famous pair of brothers to be killed were Lieutenants Leonard and Arthur Tregaskis of the Welsh Regiment. News of the fate of one of his sons was received at their father's home, the message from the War Office reading: 'Deeply regret to inform you that Lieutenant Leonard Tregaskis of the Welsh Regiment, was killed in action on July 8. Army Council express their sympathy.'[17]

The Tregaskis brothers lie side by side in Flatiron Copse Cemetery

At the outbreak of war the two brothers returned home from Canada, travelling 5,000 miles to enlist. Leonard was employed by Spillers and Bakers for 13 years, before emigrating to Canada in 1913. He was a keen motorist as well as a member of the Whitchurch Hockey Club. In his last letter, which was received at their family home just a few days before the brothers were to be killed, Leonard stated that 'things are becoming interesting'.[18]

Albert and Ernest Oliver enlisted in the 16th Welsh on the same day, 4 December 1915, and had consecutive service numbers – 24115 and 24116. Albert Thomas Oliver was killed on 7 July 1916 and is buried at Flatiron Copse Cemetery, close to Mametz Wood. His brother, Ernest George Oliver, died just three days later and is buried in Dantzig Alley British Cemetery, Mametz. Both brothers were members of the Salvation Army, playing in its band. They were originally from Pontypridd. Albert was 23 and had been a coal miner. Ernest was a year older and was also a miner. Their older brother John served with the 1st Welsh; he survived the war.

Originally a butcher by trade, William Thomas Evans was working as a ranch hand in Canada at the outbreak of the war. He paid his own way back to Britain in order to enlist, arriving

The three Oliver brothers and their family

at Liverpool after a voyage on the SS *Hesperian* (which was sunk in September 1915 by the same German U-boat that had sunk the *Lusitania* four months previously). Believing that the war would be over by the time he arrived in France, he joined the police force in Cardiff, finally joining the 16th Welsh after Christmas in 1914.

He may have given an interview to a reporter from *The Porthcawl News*, as an article ran as follows:

> Among the Cardiff City Battalion while stationed at Porthcawl was a Canadian, who was a rancher in a large way at Alberta. He paid his own fare to this country, and when asked why he came over here to enlist, quietly replied: 'I thought that my Mother Country wanted men, so I came over here to respond to her call.' Surely this is what we can truly term 'True patriotism'.[19]

Evans was promoted to sergeant and then transferred to the Machine Gun Corps, eventually being discharged early in 1919 with the rank of warrant officer class 2. He had been gassed and this affected his health for the remainder of his life.

Captain John Lewis Williams of 'C' Company of the Cardiff City Battalion died of his wounds on 12 July 1916, aged 34.

He had been struck by a piece of shell, which necessitated the immediate removal of his left leg. Sadly, he did not recover and was buried in Corbie Communal Extension Cemetery. One of the principals in the firm of Greenslade and

William Thomas Evans, third from the left

Williams, coal exporters of Cardiff, he had joined the Welsh Regiment shortly after the outbreak of war and received several rapid promotions.

A famous rugby player who played for both Cardiff and Wales, he was described thus:

> To use the commonplace expression that Captain J.L. Williams was one of the most popular players who ever wore the blue and black jersey of the Cardiff Rugby Club is but to tell the simple truth. He was loved as much for his manliness as for his skill. It was about a dozen years ago that he won his way into the Cardiff team from Whitchurch by sheer merit, and for a number of years he and R.T. Gabe formed a wonderful left wing. They were the very acme of polished cleverness in all they did. In 1905–6 J.L. Williams scored the phenomenal number of 35 tries.
>
> By Cardiff Ruggerites Johnny Williams will always be remembered for his glorious runs on the left wing, which, in addition to their effectiveness, were the very poetry of motion. Perhaps the most sensational try he ever scored on the Cardiff Arms Park was against the first South African team on New Year's Day, 1906. This was the occasion on which he beat the famous full-back A.F. Marsburg on the goal-line and scored his try by plunging into a pool of mud and water. Ringing cheers from the throats of 40,000 spectators greeted J.L. Williams as he returned to his place in the field after his brilliant performance. He played in seventeen games for Wales.[20]

Private Edward James Bennett from Cardiff died on 7 July alongside his pals in 'C' Company. A builder before the war, he had enlisted in December 1914. His commanding officer wrote to the parents: 'He was in the front line of action, and went through very severe fighting, and both officers and men felt the loss of a true and faithful soldier and comrade.'[21] A keen sportsman, he was killed aged 21. His body was unable to be identified and he is recalled on the Thiepval Memorial.

Private William Davies, aged 37, was also killed during the attack on 7 July. He was laid to rest in Flatiron Copse Cemetery. His commanding officer, Eddie Williams, sent a decorated scroll to the family that read:

It is with feelings of deepest regret I have to inform you of the Death of Private W. Davies. My Platoon, which formed the front line of the attack on Mametz Wood, was practically wiped out. The men followed me gallantly, and it was cruel to see them before the hail of bullets. They gave their lives cheerfully for the dear Homeland and the folks at home.[22]

Private Charles Harris was killed on 7 July whilst advancing with the 16th Welsh. His widow received the following letter from Eddie Williams:

It is with feelings of deepest regret I have to inform you of the death of your husband. My platoon, which formed the front line of the attack on Mametz Wood, was practically wiped out. The men followed me gallantly and it was cruel to see them fall before the hail of bullets. They gave their lives cheerfully for their dear homeland and the folks at home.[23]

Charles Harris is remembered on the Thiepval Memorial. He was 33 years of age and left a wife and three children.

Eddie Williams had to write many such letters and the similarities between these are evident. He resigned his commission in August of 1917 owing to ill-health contracted while on active service. On 7 July he had to feign death for 14 hours as he was lying so close to the German positions. When night fell he made his way back to his own lines and took part in the subsequent fighting in the wood. His brother Oswald, a

Captain John Williams   Private Edward Bennett   Private William Davies

51

first-class graduate from Oxford, was also an officer with the 16th Welsh but he went missing, aged 21, during a bombing raid on the German trenches on 9 April and his name is on the Loos Memorial. The family were from Risca, Monmouthshire.

Private Walter Pinkard served with the Machine Gun Section of the 16th Welsh. He was killed on the first day of the attack, aged 27. He was buried between Caterpillar Wood and Mametz Wood but his grave was lost. Lieutenant Richards wrote home to Pinkard's wife in Splott, Cardiff, to say:

> He was in action on 7 July, and as we had no news of him afterwards, he was posted as missing. News has now reached me that his body was found and buried by another regiment. As you are aware, he was a Machine Gunner, and I am sorry to say that all the men on his gun were either killed or wounded by the explosion of an enemy's shell.[24]

He had married on 19 July 1914 and enlisted in November of the same year. He had one son.

Lance Corporal Osman James Poole was also killed on 7 July during the attack of the 16th Welsh. He left a wife and

five children, the youngest only five weeks old. Before the war he was the assistant storekeeper at the Junction Dry Dock, Cardiff. A native of Heath Troon, Staffordshire, he was buried in Flatiron Copse Cemetery.

Sergeant Frederick Rowlands also died that day, aged 27. He had lived at 15 Wood Street, Pontycymmer,

Osman Poole with his wife and son

Bridgend, with his wife. Born in Welshpool, he had enlisted in Porthcawl and is also buried in Flatiron Copse Cemetery.

Oscar Harmer of Cardiff served with the 16th Welsh, and then with the King's Shropshire Light Infantry. While with the Cardiff City Battalion, he was the personal runner for the commanding officer, Lt-Col. Frank Gaskell, and he was by Gaskell's side when he was fatally wounded by an enemy sniper. He survived the battle for Mametz Wood and was awarded the Distinguished Conduct Medal while serving with the K.S.L.I. in 1918. The citation read:

> For most conspicuous gallantry and devotion to duty. In the attack
> on Fresnoy-le-Petite, 19th September, 1918, when all the officers of
> his company had become casualties, he reorganised the company
> and took command. Later, with half a platoon and one Lewis
> gun, he captured an enemy post, from which he silenced a hostile
> machine gun with Lewis gun fire, and succeeded in keeping down
> the fire of enemy snipers. The post was repeatedly attacked by the
> enemy with bombs and rifle grenades, but chiefly due to his fine
> example and energy all attacks were repulsed, though nearly all his

Sergeant Frederick Rowlands, standing extreme left, and the other men of his company

53

men were wounded. Eventually he successfully withdrew his men under cover of darkness.[25]

Four of the McConnell brothers from Roath in Cardiff enlisted in the 16th Welsh. Thomas McConnell died of his wounds on 19 May 1916, and the three other brothers all took part in the attack of 7 July. Samuel was killed in action that

Private Oscar Harmer sitting extreme right

John and James McConnell with other soldiers of the 16th Welsh

54

day and his body was unable to be identified later. Before the war he had worked as a labourer on the railway. John and James survived the war – James rising to the rank of Corporal. Another brother, William, served with the 9th Welsh and was demobilised in April 1919.

Major James Robert Angus rendered valuable leadership with the 16th Welsh on the 7 July and was Mentioned in Dispatches for 'showing a fine example of leadership and disregard of danger by constantly exposing himself to fire.' He was a police officer in Barry before war broke out and had served in the Boer War with the Grenadier Guards. A former member of the Glamorgan Police rugby team, Angus was accidentally drowned aged 45 while bathing in a river in September 1917.

Second Lieutenant J.P. Lloyd was wounded on 7 July and evacuated home to a London hospital to recover. He was hit by two machine gun bullets, in the right thigh and left hand, then rolled back to the top of the ridge he had just come over and crawled 400 yards on one hand and one leg. He was found by a man of the Royal Army Medical Corps who dressed his wounds, but who was soon killed by a German bullet. Lloyd was later picked up by stretcher-bearers.

An anonymous soldier made his feelings clear as to the success of 'The Great Push' when he wrote to *The Cardiff Times*:

'We are out to win this time, and win quickly, but the people at home must not expect civilisation to prevail without loss. Frank Gaskell's old lot performed nobly. They had a hot time a few days ago, but Cardiff will feel proud of its boys when the facts can be made known.'[26]

Major James Angus

10th South Wales Borderers (1st Gwent)

The 10th Battalion of the South Wales Borderers was the first of the three new S.W.B. battalions to be formed in Wales. Recruiting for it was commenced at Ebbw Vale and Cwm, men being drawn mainly from Abercarn, Abertillery, Crumlin, Newport, Pontnewydd and Tredegar. By the end of October 1914, nearly 300 men had enlisted, and by the end of the year the figure had reached 600. The battalion proceeded to Colwyn Bay to begin its training before being sent to France.

They marched to bivouac between Mametz and Carnoy on 5 July and the following day they proceeded to trenches as the reserve to the 16th (Welsh) Regiment and the 11th South Wales Borderers. This was the case the following day as well. On this day Lieutenant-Colonel Sidney John Wilkinson D.S.O. was killed, and 20 other ranks were wounded, with two being killed.

Wilkinson was 38 and had served in the Second Boer War. He was the Commanding Officer of the battalion and was killed in Caterpillar Wood bringing his men forward.

11th South Wales Borderers (2nd Gwent)

Recruitment for the 11th South Wales Borderers did not proceed as quickly as that of its sister battalion. Breconshire and the Pengam area were assigned as its recruiting areas but, by the time of its move to Colwyn Bay in the first week of January 1915, it had only collected about 160 men. Another 180 men arrived on 19 January and by April it was complete.

The 11th South Wales Borderers marched to bivouac at Carnoy on 5 July. The following evening at 8 p.m. they marched to Caterpillar Wood, arriving in position at 2.30 a.m.

They began their attack on Mametz Wood at 8.24 a.m. The attack failed so they reformed and launched a second attack at 11 a.m., which also failed. Lieutenant Hamer, the acting Adjutant, was killed. Eight officers were wounded and 120 other ranks were killed, wounded or missing.

In a letter to Hamer's father regarding the death of his son, his Colonel wrote:

He being my adjutant, I knew him well, and was very fond of him. Besides being a thoroughly reliable and painstaking officer, he was also a charming companion, and popular with all ranks. I have lost a friend and the regiment has lost a splendid officer; but if we feel this, it is nothing to your loss. A real brave man, he died a gallant death, and I am so thankful to say a painless and instantaneous one.[27]

Hamer's orderly wrote to the family as well:

Our battalion were ordered to attack Mametz Wood but Mr Hamer need not have gone beyond Battalion Headquarters. News came back that several of the officers had been wounded, so he bravely ran up to see whether he could render any assistance. The last time he was seen alive, he was crawling out under heavy machine gun fire trying to find Captain Browning, who was badly wounded. He must have exposed himself, as he was shot in the head and killed instantaneously. I had been his servant since he had been in France and feel his death very keenly. Had he been spared, he had a bright future before him as he had been appointed Adjutant and was about to be made captain.[28]

An unnamed fellow officer wrote:

We were together in the Valley before attacking Mametz Wood. In that attack he was a perfect adjutant, rushing everywhere, always thinking of the exposed position of the men and never paying heed to his own personal safety. A great gloom fell on the whole battalion when the news filtered back to the reserve that he had been killed. Four days afterwards we managed to get the body and he was buried in the little valley south east of Mametz Wood within 200 yards of the spot where he was shot. We put up a little cross with his name on to mark his grave.[29]

Sadly, this grave could not be located after the war and he is now commemorated on the Thiepval Memorial.

Lieutenant Thomas Pryce Hamer

Thomas Pryce Hamer was 33 and from Llanidloes, Montgomeryshire. Before the war he had been the proprietor of a local leather manufacturing business, which he left in his father's charge when he enlisted in the North Wales Pals Battalion of the Royal Welsh Fusiliers as a private before gaining his commission in the South Wales Borderers. He was a well-known footballer, having been the captain of Llanidloes Football Club for several seasons and had represented Wales at centre-back in an amateur international in 1910 against England, a 6–0 defeat at Huddersfield on 19 February.

The officer he had attempted to rescue, Captain Charles Eric Browning from Dulwich in London, survived the war, rising to the rank of major. He was awarded the Distinguished Service Order and Croix de Guerre in October 1918 for leading a raid on Bulgarian positions. During the Second World War he served in the RAF as a pilot officer.

William John Harries was born in Llanelli in 1886 and was later a quarryman. He served with the 11th South Wales Borderers and was killed on 7 July. He is buried in Flatiron Copse Cemetery.

Second Lieutenant Ewart Gladstone Salathiel died of wounds received at Mametz Wood on 17 July, aged 27. He was buried in Rogerstone Baptist Chapel yard in Monmouthshire. He had studied at University College of Wales, Aberystwyth, and played for the college's tennis team. Salathiel was a teacher at the Cwmffrwdoer Council School, Pontypool, before the war.

The survivors were relieved at 3 a.m. on 8 July by 113th Brigade and they returned to their bivouacs.

17th Royal Welsh Fusiliers (2nd North Wales)

The 17th R.W.F. had replaced the 17th Welsh early in 1915 and was recruited mainly from north Wales.

On 6 July, the 17th Royal Welsh Fusiliers were occupying the line at Montauban Alley, north-east of Mametz village. The following day they moved up to prepare for the attack on Mametz Wood, the battalion being in reserve so their casualties were slight.

19th Welsh (Glamorgan Pioneers)

The final battalion assigned to 115th Brigade was the 19th Welsh, a Pioneer Battalion. Their role was primarily that of construction, repair and general engineering duties, but these could be combined with bombing and general fighting. The War Diary notes their arrival in the area on 6 July when three companies marched to Minden Post before commencing work on road repairs. They were joined later in the day by their final company and the Headquarters staff.

On 7 July the battalion moved to Loop Trench and waited all day for orders. The following day they moved back to Minden Post. 'B' Company dug a trench and sap at Queen's Nullah, and 'C' Company was engaged in road repairs.

113th Brigade

On 5 July at just after midnight the 15th Royal Welsh Fusiliers reported that their front was being heavily shelled. In response, the British batteries opened up on the German batteries and increased their rate of fire onto Mametz Wood, at the request of the brigade's commanding officer, Brigadier-General Price-Davies VC.

Llewelyn Alberic Emilius Price-Davies was a career soldier who had served in the second Boer War, winning the Victoria

Brigadier-General Price-Davies

Cross there, aged 23. He saw the limitations of a volunteer army and had expressed these concerns to his brother-in-law, the Chief of the Imperial General Staff, Field Marshal Henry Wilson.

The 16th Royal Welsh Fusiliers reported that they too had been heavily shelled during their relief and for most of the night. By 5.30 a.m. the situation was much quieter as the German shelling reduced. There was also some shelling of the 13th Royal Welsh Fusiliers in White Trench.

By 11 p.m. on the 5 July the position of the battalions of 113th Brigade was reported to be as follows: the 13th Royal Welsh Fusiliers were holding Caterpillar Wood and White Trench, with the remainder of the battalion in Dantzig and Fritz trenches. The 14th Royal Welsh Fusiliers had two companies in Dantzig Trench. The 15th Royal Welsh Fusiliers were holding Cliff Trench, with the final battalion, the 16th Royal Welsh Fusiliers in Caftet Wood. This alteration in their Front was due to the brigade sidestepping, the 14th Royal Welsh Fusiliers handing over their Front to two battalions – the 6th Dorsets and the 9th Northumberland Fusiliers, and the 13th Royal Welsh Fusiliers moving up on the right of the 15th Royal Welsh Fusiliers and taking over White Trench and Caterpillar Wood from troops from other brigades. A platoon of cyclists from 15 Corps attached to the brigade, plus a machine gun section took over Marlborough Wood. Orders for the attack were received at 11 p.m.

The brigade was already taking a large number of casualties by this time. On 6 July alone, as the result of the German artillery fire, the total was: three officers wounded and 32 other ranks killed with 84 other ranks wounded. The vast majority of these are remembered on the Thiepval Memorial, perhaps giving some evidence as to the destructive power of the German shellfire.

Two brothers were killed on this day while serving with the 14th Battalion of the Royal Welsh Fusiliers. Alfred Edward Colyer is buried in Delville Wood Cemetery but his brother George Colyer has no known grave and is remembered on the Thiepval Memorial. Alfred was 23 while George was 18. Both brothers were born in London.

On the morning of 7 July the soldiers of the four battalions held their positions and watched as the attack of 115th Brigade began. When this attack failed, the brigade then lent its support to the attack by 17th Division. Firstly, they received orders to reconnoitre Strip Trench and then to demonstrate to the south of Strip Trench to keep the German defenders' attention from the attack by battalions of 17th Division in the direction of Wood Trench, the 16th Royal Welsh Fusiliers moving northwards in support.

The two patrols sent forward reported that Strip Trench was strongly held. How close they managed to get to the German trench system in broad daylight can only be conjectured, as it was certainly a hazardous exercise. They had advanced along a communication trench and this method was subsequently used by a party of 30 bombers under Lieutenant Cundle, followed by two companies from the 15th Royal Welsh Fusiliers. They were exposed to German views as they came down the hill and the leading bombing party sustained several casualties. The attack, which had relied on surprise, was soon abandoned.

Three officers were wounded this day and four other ranks were killed, with 63 wounded. One of the men of the 15th Battalion killed during the abortive bombing attack was Private Thomas Alfred Mullings from Shoreditch in London. He is buried in Dantzig Alley British Cemetery, Mametz.

13th Royal Welsh Fusiliers (1st North Wales)

This battalion was recruited mainly from Rhyl in north Wales and its surrounding area.

The War Diary of the 13th R.W.F. states that by 7.30 p.m. of the evening of the 5 July they were in Fritz Trench and Dantzig Alley. These were occasionally shelled during the evening to give the Fusiliers a taste of what was to come. The Germans also shelled the village of Mametz.

The following day a heavy bombardment was reported with shrapnel and high explosive shells falling on Quadrangle Alley, Quadrangle Support Trench, Wood Support Trench, Mametz Wood, Acid Drop Copse and the second lines. This shelling of the wood and copse had an almost unforgettable impact on the soldiers of the Welsh Division.

At 8.30 p.m. on the evening of the 6 July 'A' and 'C' companies of the 13th R.W.F. moved forward to the front line, 'A' Company occupying White Trench from a gap on the left to Beetle Alley. 'C' Company was moved into Caterpillar Wood. The British artillery bombardment continued during the night.

At 2 a.m. 17th Division made an attack on Acid Drop Copse as part of their contribution to the assault.

The War Diary reported later:

> At 8.00am a joint attack was made by a part of 17th Division on the west side and a part of the 38th Welsh Division on the east side of Mametz Wood. The attack was preceded by a heavy bombardment by our Artillery and during the attack a barrage was put over the German 2nd system and also a screen of smoke shells to cover the attacking troops.[30]

It continued: 'During the morning the enemy retaliated with Artillery fire, HE and shrapnel on Dantzig Alley, and the batteries behind Bottom Wood and Shelter Wood. The attack duly failed. Second Lieutenant R.E. Swain killed in action.'[31]

Robert Ernest Swain died of his wounds on 8 July, aged 23, but his body was never identified after the war so, like so many others, he has no known grave. He had returned from Australia in June 1914, enlisted in the 2nd King Edward's Horse, and fought at Festubert and Messines. He was transferred as an officer to the Royal Welsh Fusiliers and had two brothers at the Front.

'6.00pm: a bombing attack was made by the 15th R.W.F. from Cliff Trench; the attackers were repelled by superior numbers. Rained heavily during the day and night, the result being that the trenches were in a very bad condition.'[32]

'7 July: night passed fairly quietly. Artillery fire being greatly subdued.'[33]

14th Royal Welsh Fusiliers (Caernarvon and Anglesey)

Formed mainly from men who lived in the Llandudno and surrounding area, the 14th Battalion of the Royal Welsh Fusiliers had arrived in the area on the 5 July, relieving elements of 91st Brigade in the front line in Quadrangle Trench. The following day 'A' and 'B' companies came to Dantzig Alley, with the others bivouacking near Carnoy. On 7 July the other companies moved up to Dantzig Alley, with the Battalion Headquarters coming up to an old German dugout in Pommiers Trench.

15th Royal Welsh Fusiliers (London Welsh)

The 15th Battalion of the R.W.F., formed from Welshmen who lived in London, arrived to relieve the 1st Warwicks in Queen's Nullah, Bottom Wood, Bunny Alley, Bunny Trench, White and Cliff trenches at 8 p.m. on the evening of 5 July. During 6 and 7 July, the War Diary records that these trenches were systematically bombarded by a German battery of 5.9-inch guns.

At 6.30 p.m. on 7 July a small operation was organised under Lieutenant R.V. Jones, the officer commanding 'A' Company, against the southern portion of Mametz Wood. This operation was not pushed onwards as German machine gun fire opened up as they approached the wood. Lieutenant

F.W. Harris was wounded, along with 11 other ranks killed or wounded.

At 2.30 a.m. that night they were relieved by 16th R.W.F. and they went into Brigade Reserve at Minden Post. During these three days the battalion lost three officers wounded and 67 other ranks killed or wounded.

16th Royal Welsh Fusiliers

The final battalion of 113th Brigade was the 16th Royal Welsh Fusiliers, which was comprised of the overspill of men from the 13th R.W.F. On 5 July, 15 officers and 600 other ranks left Ribemont and relieved the 2nd South Staffordshires in the trenches between Mametz and Mametz Wood. The remainder of the battalion went to Morlancourt; the relief was completed by 10 p.m.

The following day they were withdrawn from the trenches owing to overcrowding and went into bivouacs near Carnoy. On 7 July they relieved the 15th R.W.F. as above, in the front line trenches.

114th Brigade

10th Welsh (1st Rhondda)

Comprised of men recruited from the Rhondda Valleys, the 10th Welsh had been formed through the initiative of the miners' trade union leader David Watts Morgan, who commenced recruitment on 5 September 1914. (Morgan himself enlisted as a private in the battalion and was later transferred to the Labour Corps. He was awarded the D.S.O. for his bravery at Cambrai in 1917.) The battalion was commanded by Lieutenant-Colonel P.E. Ricketts, previously an officer in the Indian Cavalry.

The battalion arrived at the Citadel, some three miles from Mametz Wood, on 5 July and bivouacked. It was used on 7 July and the following two days in supplying working and carrying parties for the troops in front.

Officers of the 10th Welsh

13th Welsh (2nd Rhondda)

The 13th Welsh was formed in the same manner as its sister battalion (above) and the War Diary records that the battalion left Heilly at 2.30 p.m. on 5 July and marched the ten miles to the Citadel, arriving at 8.30 p.m., then went into bivouacs for the night. The following day was spent in reconnoitring roads and preparing the men for action.

At 4 a.m. on 7 July they moved to Minden Post in reserve to the 115th Infantry Brigade. At 5 p.m. they were moved to Pommiers Redoubt, the trenches here reported as being in a very bad state.

Officers of the 13th Welsh

14th Welsh (Swansea)

On 9 September 1914 the War Office approved a request that this battalion be raised and it was formed around the Training Corps of Swansea Football and Cricket Club, who had made a miniature firing range under the grandstand of their ground and turned the playing field into a training ground.

The 14th Welsh left Heilly on 5 July and went to support at the Citadel. On 7 July four officers were accidentally wounded by the explosion of a percussion bomb – Lieutenant (Temporary Captain) H. Jones, Second Lieutenant F. Roderick, Second Lieutenant D.E. Evans and Second Lieutenant A.F.H. Kelk. None of them were seriously wounded but a Court of Enquiry heard from Second Lieutenant J.A. Wilson who said that, on the evening of 7 July, the four officers who were subsequently wounded, along with Captain A.H. Dagge, Lieutenant John Strange and himself, were practising the throwing of Number 19 bombs. The four injured officers comprised one group and they were throwing the bombs to each other, about 30 yards apart. The bombs had been used for the same purpose earlier but this time one went off and injured each one of them.

15th Welsh (Carmarthenshire)

The battalion was raised by the Carmarthenshire County Committee and was the only battalion to be formed in this manner.

The 15th Welsh marched into the divisional reserve on the afternoon of 5 July, with officers reconnoitring the ground the following day. On 9 July they were bivouacked to the rear of Pommiers Redoubt, with the assault on the wood commencing the following day.

Royal Engineers

151st Field Company

Attached to the Welsh Division was the 151st Field Company of the Royal Engineers. They arrived at Minden Post after dark on the evening of 5 July. On 6 July two sections were ordered to go with the 11th South Wales Borderers to be ready to go forward to consolidate the position and make a reconnaissance. They marched off at 8.30 a.m. and were in position in Caterpillar Wood by 2 a.m. the following morning. When the attack failed they withdrew to the Loop at dusk.

123rd Field Company

The 123rd Field Company of the Royal Engineers saw little involvement on 7 July.

124th Field Company

The third Field Company of the Royal Engineers who served with the 38th Division at Mametz Wood was the 124th Company who waited all day on 7 July for orders to move from Queen's Nullah into Mametz Wood to consolidate it as soon as it was taken. When it became clear that the attack had been unsuccessful, they were ordered back to their bivouacs at Halt Dump.

Signal Company

The job of the Signal Company attached to the division on 6 July was to lay two cables from the Divisional Headquarters to 115th Brigade, a distance of five miles. On 7 July the brigade moved to new positions, so the telephone lines were extended, with cable being laid to Caterpillar Wood. However, this was shot away by German artillery as soon as it had been laid. Several attempts were made to repair it but each time the line was cut as soon as it had been repaired.

Bad weather then set in, causing trouble with the buried lines. New lines were again laid to 115th Brigade so that communication by telegraph and telephone was now possible. On 8 July a direct line was laid from Divisional Headquarters to 113th Brigade and on 9 July a line was laid to 122nd Brigade of the Royal Field Artillery on the Mametz-Fricourt Road.

Royal Field Artillery

The artillery of the 38th Division had not yet arrived, so the front was covered by the artillery of the 7th and 21st Divisions, who were well acquainted with the ground but were unfamiliar with the infantry they were now to support, a defect which had unfortunate results during the fighting that was to come. The attacking battalions later felt that, had they had their own divisional artillery, it would have been easier to emphasise to them the necessity of putting an intense bombardment on Flatiron and Sabot copses before the attack of 7 July began.

In fact, 121st Brigade had taken part in the bombardment, the 122nd (Howitzer Brigade) were in action the following day, 119th Brigade arrived on 8 July and 120th Brigade arrived on 9 July.

119th Brigade

The 119th Brigade of the Royal Field Artillery was not involved in the attack on 7 July, arriving on 8 July.

120th Brigade

The 120th Brigade of the R.F.A. went into action at 7 p.m. on 9 July between Mametz and Carnoy. On 10 July they moved their fire to the enemy trenches in front of Bazentin-le-Grand Wood and the enemy forces counter-attacking Contalmaison.

121st Brigade

The third brigade of artillery attached to the Welsh Division was the 121st. On 6 July they laid out their lines of fire on Mametz Wood but their fire on 7 July was directed at points to the west of the wood. The many defective fuses in use were blamed for the inaccuracy of the artillery barrage, as was the height of the trees, which caused the shells to burst short.

The Field Ambulance Brigades

130th (St John) Field Ambulance

The 130th was one of three mobile Field Ambulances raised to support the new Welsh Division, but was the only one entitled to use the title 'St John' in its name and to wear the St John insignia. It was raised predominantly from trained St John men from across the South Wales coalfield – the Amman, Garw, Ogmore Vale and Rhondda valleys, plus Gwent. They trained at Criccieth and Prestatyn in early 1915 before moving to Winchester in August 1915 for their final training.[34]

They received orders on 5 July to proceed to Morlancourt that evening and to take over the Advanced Dressing Station at Citadel from the 23rd Field Ambulance and the Main Dressing Station in the old church at Morlancourt.

The ADS consisted of dugouts built to form a dressing room, and with bunks to accommodate 20 casualties. The Main Dressing Station at Morlancourt was a derelict church, dating from 1741. The 130th was instructed to only admit sitting cases; all stretcher cases were to go to the 131st Field Ambulance and the sick to the 129th Field Ambulance.

The Chancel was screened off and prepared for its use as an operating room. The Vestry was used as a dispensary and dispensary stores. On being assessed, the patient was passed on to the South Aisle, supplied with a blanket, food and cigarettes, before being evacuated through the exit door or placed to lie on a stretcher in the lower room. Thirty-six casualties were seen that day, mostly gunshot wounds to limbs and a few shellshock cases.

At 6.30 a.m. on 7 July, four officers and 108 other ranks of the stretcher subdivision left Headquarters at the Citadel and reported to Minden Post, bringing forward rations, wheeled stretchers and cooking utensils. Six motorcars accompanied them, while three horse ambulances reported to the Divisional Collecting Station.

Captain Ffoulkes, Captain Jones, along with Lieutenants Elliott and Burke, plus their stretcher-bearers, were ordered to occupy Triangle Post and to liaise with the regimental medical officers of the 16th Welsh and the 11th South Wales Borderers who had their aid posts in Caterpillar Trench.

At 9 a.m. four abandoned German dugouts were found on the slope of Caterpillar Wood in a protected position. These were cleaned out and the wounded were placed into them. Others were sheltered in bivouacs constructed from waterproof sheets. Walking cases were directed along Caterpillar Trench which was the only communication trench leading back to the Loop and it was too narrow to convey stretcher cases.

Captain Ffoulkes reported: 'All walking cases evacuated along Caterpillar Trench, Loop Trench and Triangle, lying cases over the open to right of Caterpillar Trench eventually joining Loop Trench.'[35]

On account of the now sodden condition of the ground and the heavy shell and machine gun fire of the enemy, it was found impossible to convey all the cases from Caterpillar Wood. As the casualties grew, Captain Ffoulkes asked for a way to be found to expedite the number of casualty evacuations from the battlefield. Sergeants Hopkins and King decided on a route and five teams of stretcher-bearers then began to carry the casualties across open ground, parallel to the trench. They came under sniper fire and had to seek the protection of the trench for its length before chancing the open ground again, carrying the five wounded men three miles to Triangle Post.

The rain continued to fall and Hopkins made a second attempt to retrieve the wounded over open ground. It was during this attempt that Lance Corporal William James West from Cwmcarn was killed by a shell burst. Two other men, Private W.E. Jones and Sergeant Hill, were wounded.

The constant shelling, machine gun fire and the deteriorating conditions underfoot meant that further attempts to evacuate the casualties were abandoned for the day. More stretcher-bearers were called forward to the Regimental Aid Post and

Men of the 130th (St John)
Field Ambulance

treatment of the wounded men continued there throughout the night.

Sergeant Hopkins reported: 'At daylight we buried Lance Corporal West in a hollow at the bottom of Caterpillar Trench. We put a cross above his body, and wrote his number, rank, name and unit on the same, with copying pencil. The position is roughly 40 yards to the right on the west of the trench.'[36] West's grave was lost and he is now remembered on the Thiepval Memorial.

Sergeant Thomas George Hopkins was awarded the Military Medal on 17 September for his gallantry at Mametz Wood; in 1918 he was awarded the Distinguished Conduct Medal. Military Medals were also awarded to Lance Corporal Trevor John Nicholas, Private William Henry Jones and Private William John Ridgeway of the 130th Field Ambulance.

Between 6 a.m. and noon the unit assessed 29 casualties. Between noon and 9 p.m. the figure rose to 67. The number of casualties treated at Morlancourt from 9 p.m. on 7 July to 9 p.m. on 8 July was 119.

131st Field Ambulance

The 131st Field Ambulance was at Morlancourt by 6 July. At 8 a.m. on 7 July, two N.C.O.s and 40 other ranks went to the Triangle and opened an aid post under Captain David of the Royal Army Medical Corps. The Sanitary Section of the

38th Division, plus a Medical Officer, formed a new Divisional Collecting Station at Minden Post. Six Medical Officers were at work at Minden Post – each in his own tent or dugout. Two were in the main dugouts; two were in the smaller dugouts and one in each of the operating tents. There were thus six streams of patients being dealt with at any given time at six dressing rooms.

The Reverend Peter Jones Roberts, a Wesleyan Methodist Minister, is described by Llewelyn Wyn Griffith as 'going to bury other people's boys'[37] on 7 July. Roberts had just heard of the death of one of his sons, killed at Fricourt, just a few miles from Mametz Wood where he was stationed with the 38th Division. Roberts braved German artillery fire to ensure other sons were buried properly, though he was unable to locate his own son's grave. He was 51 when war broke out and was assigned to Home Service only, but he was not content with this and lobbied to be allowed to serve abroad, which was granted at the end of 1915. His son was killed while running to the aid of one of his fellow officers on 3 July and is commemorated on the memorial at Ovillers Military Cemetery.

CHAPTER 4

8 and 9 July –
The Interlude

GENERAL HENRY HORNE, commanding officer of XV Corps, wrote home to his wife on 7 July: 'We are stuck in the Wood. It is very difficult to find out what is going on, but I expect we shall make some progress by evening. The Germans are fighting hard, but reports and examinations of prisoners show that they are hard put to it to hold on.'[1]

A day later he wrote: 'I am creeping slowly along around Mametz Wood but I have not got it yet. A wood is a very difficult thing to manage; it offers full scope for the German machine guns.'[2]

Horne telephoned and then visited Philipps on 8 July and told him his next plan of attack was inappropriate. When this revised plan was not put into action, Horne summoned Philipps on 9 July and dismissed him from his post. Horne had planned to replace him with Major-General Charles Guinand Blackader, who had commanded an Indian brigade at Neuve Chapelle and Loos in 1915, and a Territorial brigade during the Easter Rising in Dublin in 1916, before he was proposed as Philipps' successor. He was eight years younger than Philipps and had seen service on the West African Frontier and the Boer War, where he had taken part in the defence of Ladysmith. He had then been promoted to command the 2nd Battalion of the Leicestershire Regiment.

However, Haig overruled Horne and gave temporary command of the division to Major-General Herbert Edward Watts, commanding 7th Division. Watts was 58 and the son of a vicar. Commissioned in 1880 he had served in the Boer War and was Mentioned in Dispatches eight times during the Great War.

A plan for an attack on 9 July had been worked out by the 38th Divisional staff. The brigades which had not taken part in the attack on 7 July, the 113th and 114th, were now to be used. The 114th was to provide the main attack on the central ride, while the 113th was to capture Strip Trench. This plan was cancelled when Philipps was replaced and nothing of significance happened on 9 July except for the command of the Division passing to Major-General Watts. An unsupported attack by the 17th Division on the day was completely unsuccessful.

113th Brigade

On 8 July, despite no attacks taking place, 113th Brigade lost two officers and 33 other ranks wounded, with eight other ranks being killed and four reported missing. Three other ranks who perished lie in the same row at Morlancourt British Cemetery. They are Private Arthur Edward Evans, from Neath, who had lied about his age to enlist and died of his wounds aged just 18, as did Private William Griffiths from Ruabon, Denbighshire, and Private John Hatton from St Helens in Lancashire.

At 3.30 p.m. that day, an enemy deserter reported that the Germans were evacuating Contalmaison. It was decided to send patrols into Mametz Wood to see if an evacuation was also taking place there. An artillery barrage was used as cover and the patrols were sent out. They soon ran into machine gun fire from the edge of the wood which halted their progress.

Preparations were now being made for an attack by the brigade on Mametz Wood to take place that night. Wood fighting is difficult at the best of times but this was an extremely ambitious plan and problems with communication and identification of units, friend or foe, were bound to occur. Two further patrols from the 16th Royal Welsh Fusiliers were sent forward under the cover of darkness to reconnoitre the wood.

At 2 a.m. on 9 July, a telephone report stated that there was no sign of the 14th Royal Welsh Fusiliers. An hour later, it was established that owing to the congestion in the trenches they had been unable to move into their starting positions. By now it was too late to start the attack and the 14th R.W.F. were withdrawn.

The Brigade's position was now as follows: 13th R.W.F. in Fritz Trench and Dantzig Alley; 14th R.W.F. and 13th R.W.F. at Minden Post; 16th R.W.F. at Cliff Trench-Valley and Trench-Bunny Alley.

At 5.30 a.m. orders were received to prepare for an attack that afternoon. This was later postponed until 10 July.

13th Royal Welsh Fusiliers (1st North Wales)

Wiring and trench strengthening parties were now organised and the soldiers of the 13th R.W.F. spent 8 July engaged in making their defences more secure. German shelling recommenced.

During the night that followed 'A' Company in White Trench was relieved by the 14th Welsh Regiment and moved to the west end of Dantzig Alley. One company of the 13th R.W.F. was sent to Pommiers Redoubt and the strongpoint. 'C' Company in Caterpillar Wood was also relieved by elements of the 14th Welsh and proceeded to Dantzig Alley.

At 2.30 p.m. on 9 July the two companies in Dantzig Alley were withdrawn and bivouacked on ground south of Mametz Cemetery, which must have provided comforting surroundings. The German artillery now began to shell Mametz village and subsequently Second Lieutenant H.T. Edwards was taken to hospital suffering from shellshock.

14th Royal Welsh Fusiliers (Caernarvon and Anglesey)

On 8 July the battalion moved to bivouac at Minden Post and the following morning moved off at 1 a.m. to Mametz to take part in an attack, but received orders later to return to their bivouac.

One officer and five other ranks were killed on 9 July, with 22 other ranks wounded and three missing. Only one of those killed has a known grave: Private David Morley of the 14th Battalion who was buried in Dantzig Alley British Cemetery. He was a cabman from Regent's Park, London.

A letter from his sister to the war office stated: 'Having received official intimation that my brother was wounded in action on the 12th of July [*sic*], I am writing to ask if you could give me any information as to his whereabouts. You did not state any particulars on the form you sent and I have not heard from him personally.'[3] David Morley forfeited three days' pay while he was in training at Kinmel Park for going absent without leave for three days. He left a widow and a daughter, born in 1915.

15th Royal Welsh Fusiliers (London Welsh)
At noon on 9 July the battalion moved through the shattered remnants of Mametz village and occupied Fritz and Dantzig trenches in preparation for a general attack in the wood; this operation was cancelled at 2.30 p.m. and they were ordered back to Minden Post. They were ordered forward again when orders were received at 11.55 p.m. that they were to be ready to attack the wood at 3.15 a.m.

16th Royal Welsh Fusiliers
July 8 was described as a quiet day and 9 July saw some shelling while they prepared for the attack to take place on 10 July.

114th Brigade
10th Welsh (1st Rhondda)
On 9 July the battalion moved to Pommiers Redoubt and prepared to attack the following day.

13th Welsh (2nd Rhondda)

At 10 p.m. on 8 July, preparations were made for the 13th Welsh to dig an assembly trench from which an attack could be made on the wood. This idea was subsequently abandoned. Work continued repairing the existing trenches on 9 July, as well as improving the pathway to Minden Post. The Officer Commanding attended a conference with the Brigadier-General and the men were readied for the following day's attack.

14th Welsh (Swansea)

On 8 July the battalion moved into the front line in White Trench and spent the following day there.

15th Welsh (Carmarthenshire)

This battalion moved to Pommiers Redoubt on 9 July and prepared for the following day's assault on Mametz Wood.

115th Brigade

17th Royal Welsh Fusiliers (2nd North Wales)

On 8 July the 17th R.W.F. spent the day cleaning their equipment. Despite this they still suffered ten other ranks wounded. The following day the battalion suffered ten more other ranks killed and two wounded. One of those killed was Private John Henry Hughes, aged 26. A native of Llanystumdwy, Criccieth, Caernarvonshire, he is remembered on the Thiepval Memorial.

Private John Hughes

10th South Wales Borderers (1st Gwent)

The 10th S.W.B. spent 8 and 9 July in bivouac between Mametz and Carnoy.

11th South Wales Borderers (2nd Gwent)

The 11th S.W.B. were in their bivouac until 8 a.m. on 9 July when two companies were ordered to Caterpillar Wood and Marlborough Wood to relieve the 10th Welsh.

16th Welsh (Cardiff City)

July 8 saw a roll-call at noon and Brigadier-General Evans expressed his appreciation of the conduct of his men during the attack on the first day.

19th Welsh (Glamorgan Pioneers)

On 8 July one company was engaged in road repairs and on 9 July the 19th Welsh were consolidating certain points against enemy counter-attacks.

151st Field Company Royal Engineers

The weather by now was very wet and the communication trenches were reported to be mainly impassable with wet mud. On 8 July the only work carried out during the day was the improvement of a trench across Caterpillar Wood ravine and the preparation of the northern banks of the ravine for use as a firing line.

Once night fell it was a different story. Two sections under Second Lieutenant Jones were detailed to carry out wiring in front of Marlborough Wood. One section put in a trench stop and a Lewis Gun emplacement in a trench running north-east from Marlborough Wood, while a fourth section, under Sergeant Edwards, prepared machine gun emplacements in Caterpillar Wood and communication trenches between them and the old German dugouts.

July 9 saw the company withdrawn from Marlborough and

Caterpillar woods to the Loop, and thence to Minden Post where orders were received detailing how they would support the attack to take place the next day. Liaison Officers were ordered to be found by the 19th (Pioneer) Welsh to keep in touch with the first battalions attacking, so as to send back information that when the attack was sufficiently progressed the consolidating parties could enter the wood. It was reported that the left Liaison Officer was in touch, but the one on the right could not be contacted.

One officer, Lieutenant T.C. Freeth, was sent to hospital suffering from shellshock on 8 July.

124th Field Company Royal Engineers
At 10 a.m. on 9 July their bivouac was shelled by the German artillery and Driver W. Jones, aged 34 from Cymer, Port Talbot, was killed. He was later buried in Dantzig Alley British Cemetery, Mametz. The company was consequently ordered to Minden Post.

119th Brigade Royal Field Artillery
On 8 July they received orders of a probable action the following day, so the batteries were moved forward and came into action south-west of Fricourt. The following day they were in action all day, registering on a portion of Mametz Wood.

121st Brigade Royal Field Artillery
On 8 July their 18-pounder batteries fired on Mametz Wood. The Forward Observation Officer reported German infantry were advancing from Pearl Alley down a communication trench towards the wood. The brigade was ordered to turn its fire onto the north-west corner for 20 minutes. The following day, night firing was again carried out on the wood.

CHAPTER 5

10 July – The Second Movement

THE CARDIFF TIMES reported on the preparations being made for the next attack:

> Mametz Wood this evening still harbours a strong enemy force, said to be composed of units of the Prussian Guard – tucked away in dugouts and well supplied with machine guns. But slowly and surely our net is being drawn round this strong tactical position, and the final issue here is only a question of time.
>
> That the Germans are fighting with such tenacity in this region is conclusive proof as to the value they attach to every yard of ground in front of their second line. As I have before said, it is recognised by our Army that progress up to a certain point is bound to be slow, indeed desperately slow, and horribly costly to both sides, and then, when, as we are all confident it ultimately must, the weak link snaps, events may march with dramatic intensity. Therefore 'patience and trustfulness in the indomitable spirit of our troops' forms the most fitting message at the moment.

The writer went on to comment on the casualties incurred:

> I learn that a very large proportion of the casualties consist of slightly wounded men – a reassuring fact it is well to keep in mind when referring to the total of our losses. Also that the percentage of head wounds is surprisingly small compared with previous battles, a condition due in a large measure to the effective protection given

by our shrapnel helmets and also to the fact that machine gun fire is responsible for the bulk of the injuries received.[1]

The casualties, despite this optimism, had been heavy.

Major-General Watts' plan of attack for 10 July was essentially the same as that which had been worked out by Philipps before his dismissal, but Watts placed importance on the parity of status of the two brigades to be engaged – the 113th and 114th.

The artillery plan was altered and this time proper support was to be given to the attacking infantry. In order to fool the Germans, the barrage was to lift from their front line positions as usual, as if in readiness for a British attack, and then, as the defenders emerged from their dugouts, the barrage would once more pound the original positions. This way the Germans would be caught in the open by the returning shellfire. This approach had been used successfully by the French on previous occasions.

This time a creeping barrage was to be used as well. The shellfire would advance slowly north, behind which the waves of British infantry would follow.

The odds appeared to be in favour of the attackers. A superiority of three to one was calculated but this, of course, did not include the advantage the Germans had of firing from behind cover, and of using machine guns sited in emplacements.

The plan for the attack was: 114th Brigade, 14th Welsh and 13th Welsh on the right, and 113th Brigade, with 16th R.W.F. leading and the 14th R.W.F. close behind on the left.

The official history of the Welsh Regiment describes what happened next.

At 3.50am the smoke barrage commenced at Strip Trench and drifted northeast effectively. At 4.05am the 13th and 14th Welsh advanced in waves of platoons at 100 yards interval in accordance with tactical instructions issued by the Fourth Army. It is very doubtful if this was a suitable formation considering the strength of the enemy's machine guns, and it had already been abandoned by the French, who advanced as we did later in the war, by 'packets'.[2]

113th Brigade

This time the attack would start from the south-east, given the withering machine gun fire from the north that so severely curtailed the attack of 115th Brigade on 7 July. The 16th Battalion Royal Welsh Fusiliers was to attack the southern-western edge of the wood, the attacking waves being in eight lines, four paces between each man, and the lines being 100 yards apart. Special bombing parties were arranged on the left of each line. Their job was to deal with Strip Trench and Wood Trench to the battalion's left.

They were ordered to form up in lines behind White Trench by 3 a.m., and at 4 a.m. to crawl out in front of that trench and lie down. Vickers machine guns and Lewis Guns would pour fire into the south of the wood and into Strip Trench. While this was going on an artillery bombardment was taking place. The 14th Royal Welsh Fusiliers would support the attack, followed by the 15th Royal Welsh Fusiliers. The 124th Field Company Royal Engineers and the Pioneer companies would be in support in Queen's Nullah.

The artillery bombardment was to start at 3.30 a.m. and last until 4.15 a.m. Their target area was the area up to the first cross-ride and The Hammerhead. From 3.55 a.m. to 4.25 a.m. a smoke barrage was to be formed if the weather was favourable, but if conditions were not then the attack was go ahead as scheduled anyway. When 4.15 a.m. came the artillery barrage would gradually lift to the north and west of the cross-ride before continuing on Wood Support Trench. The objective for the 16th and 14th Battalions was the first cross-ride. The 15th Battalion was to send a patrol up the valley and along the railway line to ascertain if an approach to the wood was feasible from that direction. At 6.15 a.m. the artillery barrage was to lift to the second cross-ride. An hour later it was to lift to pour fire onto the extreme northern edge of the wood. At 8.15 a.m. the barrage would move onto the German second line which sat in front of Bazentin-le-Petit Wood to prevent reinforcements being rushed into Mametz Wood.

The problem with the planning of artillery fire at this stage of the war was that of communication. It had already proved an issue over the open topography during the first week of the Battle of the Somme. In a wood where visual contact from outside was virtually nil, the artillery had only timed barrages to rely on. The plan relied on the infantry reaching their objectives within a limited time span and progressing no further, which meant not being able to take into account local conditions on the ground. On this occasion it was ordered that every effort should be made to relay information as to the progress of the advance. The Brigade Signal Officer was ordered to arrange for a visual receiving station to be set up at Cliff Trench and for personnel to man the telephone station in Queen's Nullah. Given the confused nature of wood fighting, there was little chance of this being a success and the burden would fall on company runners to bring information from the wood back to these positions, but with information that was only as good as the moment the runner had left the advanced position. The Signal Company's War Diary states the frequency with which the telephone lines were cut, despite numerous repairs.

The scant instructions given to the officers and men concerning wood fighting were highlighted in the Operation Order No. 57 issued on 9 July to 113th Infantry Brigade: 'Men should be warned that roads, and especially cross roads, should be avoided. All lines of defence should be made behind a road or railway and not in front. When in the wood the advance should be made in small columns.'[3]

Brigadier-General Price-Davies met with the officers of the

14th and 16th Royal Welsh Fusiliers and they changed the time of the attack to 4.12 a.m. so that they should reach the edge of the wood just as the barrage lifted to its second target. Colonel Carden of the 16th R.W.F. was told that he should not start the attack until the 114th Infantry Brigade began theirs, as their starting position was further away than that of his battalion. Later Major McLellan of the 16th stated that when he advanced the 114th were already down the slope and were observed to be retiring, which caused his battalion to waver. At this point Carden restored the discipline of the men and the attack was pressed forward:

> Lieutenant-Colonel Carden was a gifted leader with a touch of fanaticism. He addressed his battalion before going into action; 'Make your peace with God. You are going to take that position, and some of us won't come back – but we are going to take it.' And tying a coloured handkerchief to his walking-stick he said, 'This will show you where I am.'[4]

But Carden's words seem to have had little effect. Even before the 16th Royal Welsh Fusiliers reached the wood, on seeing the left flank of the 114th Brigade retiring, there was a hesitation in the advance. Carden, accompanied by Captain G.C.W. Westbrooke and Lieutenant A.V. Venables, restored the situation and led the men forward once more. Carden was a conspicuous figure with his stick and his handkerchief held high and he was soon hit. He got up to lead his men to the edge of the wood where he was struck once more and killed. It was suicidal bravery and meant that the 16th

Lieutenant-Colonel Ronald Carden

Battalion had lost its commanding officer when they needed him most, to organise their advance amidst the undergrowth and trees of Mametz Wood.

Ronald James Walter Carden was born in London or France in 1876. He was the son of a baronet and was serving with the 17th Lancers (Duke of Cambridge's Own). There was such a shortage of experienced officers for the New Armies that the appointment of volunteers from cavalry units which were not immediately required for action, Indian Army officers on leave or retired officers (known as 'dug-outs') was extremely common. Carden gained his Majority in 1907 and, at 38 when the war started, he may well have been on retired pay. He was buried in Carnoy Cemetery.

George Cecil Westbrooke, twice Mentioned in Dispatches, later won the Military Cross and was promoted to Major by the end of the war and later became a Colonel. He was a master at Ruthin School in north Wales and lived in the School House. Venables, who lived in Sheffield, was also later Mentioned in Dispatches.

At 5.15 a.m. the 15th Royal Welsh Fusiliers were ordered to advance to carry on the preceding lines of the 16th R.W.F., which, it had been reported from Divisional Headquarters, were wavering. In fact the 15th had moved forward before this time in response to appeals from the 16th for support.

By now the 16th were at the edge of the wood and the 14th R.W.F. had gone too far to their right, which meant that when the 15th R.W.F. advanced they could see no sign of the 14th Battalion. The 16th and 15th battalions entered the wood and bombed up Strip Trench, meeting the Dorset Regiment in Wood Trench. At 5.55 a.m. the 15th R.W.F. sent for reinforcements but these were refused for some reason.

There was understandably considerable confusion when the battalions entered the wood. The thick undergrowth and mangled trees meant danger at short distances. The line gradually made its way forward though, driving the Germans back and reached the first cross-ride around 6.30 a.m. At this time a message was received at Brigade Headquarters from Divisional Headquarters that the barrage had been lifted as the 13th Welsh of 114th Brigade were through the wood. This was intended to prevent casualties from the British artillery on its own troops. Colonel J.C. Bell, of the 15th Royal Welsh Fusiliers, had also sent back a message saying that the second objective had been captured. This was not true; only the first objective had been captured and this further added to the confusion.

Lieutenant-Colonel Flower was now sent forward with the remaining two companies of his battalion to find out the real situation and to reorganise the brigade.

The subsequent report gives some indication as to the state of things at Headquarters: 'Meanwhile reports from the Front had been most confusing and conflicting, but all demanded reinforcements either to save the situation or confirm success. Several officers had been despatched for new, but very little resulted.'[5]

At 7 a.m. Brigadier Price-Davies ordered the Royal Engineers and the Pioneers forward before going forward himself with Lieutenant-Colonel Gosseth. Price-Davies walked up Strip Trench and was between Wood Trench and Wood Support Trench when he saw a party of men running back in panic. He ordered the last two companies of the 15th Royal Welsh Fusiliers into the southern end of the wood.

The situation at 9 a.m. was that the 113th Brigade was in touch with units of 114th Brigade at the first cross-ride but the units though were intermingled – hardly surprising given the ground they were fighting over – and had few officers. The Royal Engineers and Pioneers were labouring to consolidate this position, harassed as they were by German machine gun fire and their own artillery fire. The artillery barrage should by now have been firing on the German second line, not on the wood at all.

The Germans still held Wood Support Trench at this stage but the units in the wood were in no condition to advance further. The 17th Royal Welsh Fusiliers of 115th Brigade arrived piecemeal and were ordered to advance on both sides of the main north-south ride. This was to have commenced at 12.30 p.m. but the Officer Commanding, Lieutenant-Colonel J.A. Ballard, became a casualty and the attack was delayed as his replacement was not immediately available. When he did arrive, an advance of around 200 yards was made in the centre, but the Germans still in Wood Support Trench were holding up any progress.

It was now established that there was a serious problem with overcrowding amongst the troops on the front line and the 15th and 16th Royal Welsh Fusiliers were withdrawn to ease this congestion and to keep them fresh for the next assault. The 13th Battalion which had been bombing the enemy in Wood Support Trench finally forced the stubborn defenders to surrender. This buoyed the spirits of the men in the wood and a further advance was made to within 200 yards of the northern edge of the wood by 113th Brigade at 6.30 p.m., mainly due to the work of the 17th Royal Welsh Fusiliers.

An advance was planned at 8.45 a.m. outwards from the wood in three directions but a single well-sited enemy machine gun put a stop to this and no advance was made. During the early hours of the night that followed a 'good deal of panic and wild firing'[6] ensued, but given the especially thick vegetation in this sector of the wood, and that the Germans still held the final 200 yards at least, it is unsurprising.

At 2 a.m. on the morning of 11 July the remnants of the 16th Welsh (Cardiff City) Battalion arrived and were ordered to occupy the central portion of the railway. Soon after daylight Brigadier-General H.J. Evans arrived and took command. The attack to clear the remaining Germans out of the wood could now begin.

A report in the War Diary of 113th Brigade, written by Price-Davies, evaluated the work of the Brigade thus:

The impression gained of the fight is that the initial advance from the Cliff to the Wood was carried out with great gallantry in the face of a heavy fire from the enemy's artillery and small arms. Subsequently there appeared to be no sting in the attack, and moral gradually became reduced until the smallest incident caused a panic. Providentially the enemy were in a more sorry plight, and had not sufficient numbers to counter-attack with effect. The 14th Battalion R.W.F. appear to have made no effort to re-enter the fight or to get in touch with other troops.

The success of the Brigade was very largely due to the efforts of the regular commanding officers. Colonel Carden caused the wavering lines to advance in the first instance, Lieutenant-Colonel Bell behaved most gallantly throughout, several bullets piercing his clothing, and Lieutenant-Colonel Flower was indefatigable in continuing the fight on the left flank where much energy was required. Even when so exhausted that he fell down, continually he persisted in exercising his command. Major Gwyther was unfortunately wounded early and his battalion does not appear to have taken any further part in the action after his becoming a casualty.[7]

Major Graham Howard Gwyther had joined the Royal Welsh Fusiliers in 1900, serving in the China Expedition of 1901. He was awarded the Distinguished Service Order in 1917.

Bell may have behaved 'most gallantly' but his misreporting of his actual position within the wood could have had terrible consequences.

13th Royal Welsh Fusiliers (1st North Wales)

Captain E.W. Lawrence R.A.M.C., Lieutenant H. Vivian Jones and Second Lieutenant A.H.S. Barrett were all killed in action on 10 July.

Edward William Lawrence, the Brigade's Senior Medical Officer, was killed by a shell burst, aged 28. A native of Pontycymmer in Glamorgan, he was educated at Christ College, Brecon, and University College Cardiff before taking the medical course at Edinburgh where he graduated in 1910.

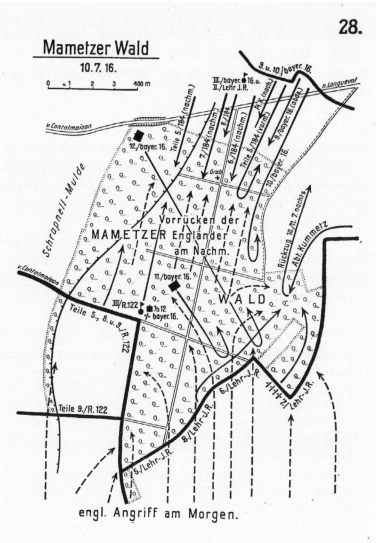

German map of the action on 10 July

He worked at the Royal Gwent Hospital in Newport before going into general practice. He had volunteered at the start of the war and is remembered on the Thiepval Memorial.

His school magazine carried the following tribute to him: 'Hotel, 1900–1903: son of Mr. A. J. Laurence [*sic*] of

Pontycymmer. Killed on active service, while serving as Capt. in the R.A.M.C., attached to the Royal Welsh Fusiliers. He was 28 years of age, and before the war had been in practice as a doctor in Bridgend.'[8]

Harold Vivian Jones was 23 years of age and was born in Builth Wells, Breconshire. He was buried in Flatiron Copse Cemetery. Major R.O. Campbell of the Royal Welsh Fusiliers, writing to Jones' father, stated: 'Vivian had a sweet smile on his face when we buried him that evening outside Mametz Wood, and he looked just like his old self, sleeping peacefully.'[9] He had been shot in the head.

Jones was captain of the University College of North Wales (Bangor) Football Team in the 1913–14 season and a member of the Officer Training Corps.

A poem was written to commemorate Harold Vivian Jones, attributed to 'Eradreba' (i.e. 'Aberdare' backwards). In fact, it was written by G.R. Thomas B.Sc., the science master at the County School, Builth Wells, where Harold had been educated before moving on to university in Bangor.

Lad of the bright, and fearless eye,
And spirits like a feather.
With buoyant mind, like upland wind,
That swept his native heather;
No futile paean can unfold,
The glory of that heart of gold.
For him no organ down the nave
Shall swell its solemn dirges;
The guns athwart his soldier-grave
Shall boom their last asperges.
At boyhood's threshold yet he donned—,
The Manhood of the Great Beyond.
And setting sun doth not excel
In majesty and splendour,
That life's eclipse with smiling lips,
Who made the Great Surrender.
The shell-scarred wood shall be the shrine,
Of noble, valiant souls like thine.

The game and not the guerdon bright,
On playing-fields inspired him;
The contest was his sole delight,
The trophy scarcely fired him,
And on that larger field of fame,
In death he won the nobler game.[10]

Like Edward Lawrence, Adrian Hamilton Silverton Barrett's body could not be identified later and he is remembered on the Thiepval Memorial. He had enlisted as a private in the Black Watch in January 1915 but by June was transferred as a second lieutenant to the 13th Royal Welsh Fusiliers. He was 21 years of age and the son of the magazine publishers Alfred and Ruby Wilson Barrett who lived in Stratford-upon-Avon.

Lance Corporal W.G. Jones of the same battalion, while recovering from his wounds at Lochee Red Cross Hospital, reported that 'At Mametz, Lieutenant Barrett was shot through the heart about 8 o'clock in the morning. He was there the next day when I passed wounded at 3 o'clock.'[11] Sadly, his body could not later be identified.

His mother visited Mametz Wood in 1920 and wrote:

I have seen it in my dreams. I have thought of the spot and pictured it myself – the spot where my son fell and where my son

Captain Ned Lawrence   Lieutenant Harold   Second Lieutenant
                        Vivian Jones   Adrian Barrett

is buried. I wanted to see the French wood, the scenery last looked upon by the blue eyes of an English boy – and that boy, my son. Nature has done her best to soften the hard marks the war has made. The undergrowth has grown up in some parts quite high: there still remain the stumps and burnt trees all bare and ghostly, that shell-fire had spoilt. But this lovely, fresh, green undergrowth is what pleased me most. I found four crosses put up in memory of the brave Royal Welsh Fusiliers. The fourth one – to the memory of the officers and men of the 13th Battalion, July 10 1916 when my boy fell – seemed to rise up as an emblem of peace and rest.[12]

Private William John Fox was also killed in action on 10 July. His platoon commander wrote: 'He had been in my platoon since the commencement of his military career, therefore I can speak of him as a soldier and a friend. He was a true soldier and a brave lad. Never before had he shown such coolness and bravery as in his last action.'[13] He had lived with his parents at 9 Digby Street, Barry, before enlisting.

Private George Briggs from Mile End, Middlesex, was killed on 10 July while serving with 'A' Company. He left a widow, Elizabeth, who was living in Walthamstow. She wrote a poignant letter to the Army: 'Would you kindly give me any information of my husband as I have not heard of him for a

Private George Briggs (extreme left)

month.'[14] His body was never identified. The day he was killed was also his birthday.

Edward Francis Leah was serving as a lance corporal when he was killed on 10 July. Born in Mordiford, near Hereford, he was the son of a gamekeeper and was educated at Mordiford and Llanarth schools. He enlisted in November 1914 and was 28 when he was killed. The Chaplain wrote:

> His platoon was advancing on a machine gun to try to capture it. In this advance he was shot in the body and died almost immediately. This happened in Mametz Wood, the capture of which will be known in the future as having been accomplished by the Welsh Division. The news has come through now that he has been buried in Mametz Wood, and there is a cross to mark his grave. I could not approach the wood, so the burial was conducted by those who followed. All the boys speak nicely of him, and they feel his loss very much. There is the great consolation that he gave his life for the cause of right and for God and country. Still, we feel the loss of our dear ones keenly. You have my deep sympathy, in which the battalion joins.

An unnamed comrade added: 'He was a fine soldier, and died a brave soldier's death.' Another added: 'He was the best friend I ever had, and when we few who are left meet, we have

a chat of those who have gone before, and Frank's name is the first on every lip. These dear old friends have now given their own young lives as well in the noble cause.'[15]

Edward Leah still lies in Mametz Wood but his grave was lost and his name is amongst those carved on the Thiepval Memorial to the missing.

Private Edward Leah

Private Mervyn Jones

Private Mervyn Jones survived the fighting at Mametz Wood but was killed in action in April 1918, aged 22. Originally from Kidwelly, he enlisted in the 13th Royal Welsh Fusiliers. He is remembered on the Pozières Memorial.

14th Royal Welsh Fusiliers (Caernarvon and Anglesey)

The 16th Royal Welsh Fusiliers moved off to the attack at 4.12 a.m. and at that time 'A' and 'C' companies of the 14th R.W.F. had formed up in four lines behind them and followed them into the attack.

The War Diary of the 14th R.W.F. notes:

At that time the 114th Brigade on our right could not be seen but as the Battalion was moving into the Hollow by the Railway some Battalions of the 114th Brigade crossed our front from the left. This caused some confusion but did not stop the advance. As soon as our line got within 200 yards of the front of the wood they were subjected to heavy rifle and machine gun fire and suffered many casualties, particularly in Officers and Senior N.C.O.s. When within 150 yards of the wood with the main ride running north and south, opposite our right a number of men from the preceding lines retired back on us shouting 'Retire'. At this stage Major Gwyther commanding the 14th R.W.F. was wounded and Major R.H. Mills was killed.

The pressure backwards was great and Captain J. Glynn Jones gave the order to reform in a hollow 150 yards from the front edge of the wood and dig in. This was done and a report sent to Brigade. About an hour later some of our men were seen advancing on the left along the narrow strip of wood in which runs Strip Trench. These were our 'B' and 'D' companies and the 15th R.W.F. At this time prisoners in some numbers were coming from the left and a white flag was shown up near the entrance to the main ride. Those were investigated and it was found that the front of the wood was fairly clear and it was decided to move in. This was done and the first objective was reached.[16]

Major Robert Henry Mills was 35 years old; he left a widow and two children at their home in Dolgellau, Merionethshire. In business with his father pre-war, he had previously served in the Boer War. He also served for 17 years in the Volunteers and Territorials. Mills was buried in Dantzig Alley British Cemetery.

The attack of the 14th Royal Welsh Fusiliers was described by Captain John Glynn Jones.

Before dawn we had our men lined out in the orthodox waves behind the rising ground overlooking the wood. In front of us lay a small valley, in the centre of which was a cutting, something like a railway cutting (the Cliff). To that cutting the ground fell steeply, and from it to the wood was a more gradual slope... Presently the silent waves of men started moving forward, and I, with my third wave, joined in. Machine guns and rifles began to rattle, and there was a general state of pandemonium, little of which I can remember except that I myself was moving down the slope at a rapid rate, with bullet-holes in my pocket and yelling a certain amount. I noticed also that there was no appearance whatsoever of waves about the movement at this time, and that the men in advance of us were thoroughly demoralised. Out of the most terrible 'mix-up' I have ever seen I collected all the men I could see and ordered them into the cutting. There appeared to be no one ahead of us, no one following us, and by this time it was broad daylight and the ridge behind us was being subjected to a terrible artillery and machine gun fire.[17]

Major Gwyther the Commanding Officer of the 14th R.W.F.

had been severely wounded at the start. The attack was now in the balance and desperate action was required to get the waves moving again.

Jones continued: 'I well remember thinking, "Here comes the last stand of the old Carnarvon and Angleseys" as I ordered the men to get ready, and posted a Lewis Gun on each of my flanks. At this stage, too, I remember seeing wounded Major Gwyther, our commanding officer, and giving him certain attention.'[18] If Jones was in the cutting at this time, it appears that Gwyther had been wounded later than is often assumed, as the battalion crossed the ground at the foot of the valley.

Meanwhile, men were crawling in from shell-holes to our front, with reports of nothing less than a terrible massacre, and the names of most of our officers and N.C.O.s lying dead in front were mentioned. Shortly after there was a lull, and from the wood in front a number of Germans – about forty – came out, with hands up. Suspecting a trick, I ordered my men to cover them, but allowed them to approach us. When they got about half-way I went out to meet them, accompanied by a sergeant, and sent them back to our headquarters.

As this appeared to point to the wood being unoccupied, I sent a small patrol to examine it; and then we all moved forward. Crossing the trench on the fringe of it, we entered the wood at the entrance of the main ride, and with two patrols in front advanced up the ride in file, as the undergrowth was very thick. Presently on our left we met men of another battalion (the 16th R.W.F.), who reported the wood taken as far as the first objective. Later I found this to be the case.[19]

The War Diary picks up the next steps:

2 Lt Stork, C.S.M. F. Thompson and Cpl. Pudner were sent out as a patrol to search the wood. They reported it clear for 200 yards except in the direction of Wood Support. This was reported to the C.O. 15th R.W.F. and we received orders to dig in where we were. The line was very thick at this time and Battalion much mixed up. When enemy threatened a small counter-attack from Wood Trench

much of our machine gun and rifle fire was masked and a great deal of effective fire was lost.

The counter-attack was however easily repulsed. The Battalion was then reorganised but owing to casualties among officers and N.C.O.s this work was difficult. Some men were therefore moved back into the line into which we had dug in around 5.00am. We remained in this position during the night of the 10/11 July during which time stragglers were found and attempts to retire by men of other units were frustrated.[20]

Corporal Frederick Daniel Moyer was killed on 10 July while serving with the 14th Royal Welsh Fusiliers. Originally from Peterborough, his body was unable to be identified later so he is recalled on the Thiepval Memorial. He had lied about his real age in order to enlist, as he was just 17 when he died.

William Anthony Jones served with the 14th Battalion of the Royal Welsh Fusiliers. He survived the fighting at Mametz Wood but was later killed that year on 1 October and is buried in Essex Farm Cemetery near Ypres. He was 22 and before the war was working as a journalist on *The Carmarthen Journal*. His parents ran The Black Lion public house in Cwmffrwd, Carmarthenshire.

Second Lieutenant Brian Harrison 14th Royal Welsh Fusiliers was killed on 10 July, aged 23, and was buried in Dantzig Alley Cemetery. Originally from Salop, he attended Arnold House School. A memorial window in Chester Cathedral was dedicated in 1921 to the school's old boys killed during the war and Harrison is one of 38 names listed on it, as is Alan Sheriff Roberts who was also killed at Mametz Wood.

Second Lieutenant A.C. Stagg of the Gloucestershire Regiment was attached to the 14th R.W.F. He died of his

Private William Jones

wounds on 10 July and was buried in Morlancourt British Cemetery Number 1. Originally from Chatham, he had enlisted in the Royal Engineers as a Sapper before being commissioned in January 1916.

15th Royal Welsh Fusiliers (London Welsh)

At 4.15 a.m. they were ordered forward in attack formation between Queen's Nullah and White Trench, formed into four lines in companies: 'A' Company leading, behind the 14th R.W.F., with 'B', 'C' and 'D' companies following.

During this attack one officer was killed, one died later of his wounds, one was reported missing and six were wounded. Twenty-two other ranks were killed, eight were missing and 140 were wounded.

The 15th Royal Welsh Fusiliers and two companies of the 13th R.W.F. were ordered into the wood as reinforcements. When they entered the thick undergrowth, control would have been difficult anyway, but with the losses of officers and N.C.O.s during the attack, the shell holes and fallen trees contributed to the confusion.

Soon there were no fewer than eleven battalions in the wood. At 2 p.m. Lieutenant-Colonel Pryce arrived from Divisional Headquarters and found the troops 'in a somewhat confused state, except for three companies of the 17th Royal Welsh Fusiliers.'[21] Ironically, the 17th Battalion had lost their commanding officer, Lieutenant-Colonel John Arthur Ballard.

John Edwards, the officer commanding 'C' Company of the 15th Royal Welsh Fusiliers wrote:

> There was a good deal of confusion in the wood, particularly during the night time. Groups fired on one another, mistaking one another for the enemy. It was impossible to see on account of the darkness, and most difficult to hear or give orders on account of the weird din. A machine gun gave the impression it was a few yards in front on account of the strange reverberation through the wood. Many of our shells fell short – or perhaps it was that they struck the tops of the tress and burst prematurely.[22]

The 22nd Brigade which was resting behind Mametz village was turned out at around 10 p.m. to make ready to go into the wood to support, but this order was cancelled shortly afterwards and they returned to their bivouacs.

Captain Glyn Jones again:

That evening there developed a terrible enemy shelling of the wood, and this resulted in perfect pandemonium. Out of the wood emerged scores of men, from every battalion in the division, all making headlong for the rear. Being more collected ourselves, and supported with a sheltered home and a steep hill behind, Sergeant Thompson and I, sometimes with the aid of revolver threats, very soon increased our force in the cutting to about 250 men.[23]

And further:

Our own guns were firing short, and in spite of our attempts to communicate with the rear this continued. The numerous casualties we sustained because of this had the effect of making the men very panicky. Further, the difficulty of seeing more than a few yards in front caused ignorance amongst the men as to where the Front lay and whether any of our fellows were there: any noise in the bush in front meant a hail of bullets into it. I, myself, saw an officer of the 15th Royal Welsh Fusiliers killed in this way.[24]

An explanation for the shelling of the northern part of the wood on 10 July is offered:

About 9.00pm... a small counter-attack supported by enemy shelling was made from the north, and a few men panicked down the central drive carrying with them at the southern outskirts of the wood several score of others who, officerless, had lost their way. The sight of these men falling back had the unfortunate effect of making our own artillery shell the northern portion of the wood, inflicting many casualties on the men digging the front trenches 300 yards within the border.[25]

Lieutenant Robert Griffith Rees was 25 when he was killed on 10 July whilst serving with the 15th Royal Welsh Fusiliers.

It was reported that:

> He was an exceedingly popular officer. Among his fellow-officers
> he was an especial favourite. He was a man of a bright, sunny
> disposition, beloved wherever he went. At Llandudno, where he
> was billeted for about nine months, his musical gifts and his skill
> as a rag-time dancer made him a welcome guest in the houses of
> his friends. He devoted himself whole-heartedly to his military
> duties, and those who heard him speak of his desire to be at the
> Front have heard of the death of such a brilliant young officer with
> mingled admiration and regret.[26]

He was re-buried in Serre Road Cemetery No. 2 after the
war.

16th Royal Welsh Fusiliers

At 3.30 a.m. on the 10 July the battalion formed up in eight
lines 500 yards from the southern edge of Mametz Wood, with
the 114th Brigade on their right flank. The attack was launched
at 4.20 a.m. and a foothold was gained in the wood. By 2 p.m.
a considerable portion of the wood was in British hands. They
were then relieved by the 13th R.W.F.

Lieutenant-Colonel Carden was killed, as was Sergeant-
Major Rees and 43 other ranks; 201 men were reported as
wounded and 64 men were missing.

A reminder of the harshness of life in the valleys of
south Wales is encapsulated in the death of Private George
Humphreys, 16th Battalion of the Royal Welsh Fusiliers, who
fell on 10 July, aged 23. His father and elder brother had both
been killed in the Senghenydd Pit disaster of 14 October 1913.
He, too, had been employed at the colliery but had survived.
Two of his other brothers were also in the Army. He was a
member of the local Wesleyan Sunday school and a member of
the Silver Band. His last words as he rushed into action were
'For my God, my King and for my dear old home.' His body
was never identified and he is commemorated on the Thiepval
Memorial.

Corporal Frederick Hugh Roberts had also been a miner at Senghenydd Pit. He had been out drinking the night before the disaster and, providentially, was too ill to get up for work that morning. He thus survived the disaster that left 439 miners and one member of the rescue team dead. Badly wounded on the 10 July, he died of his wounds on 12 July and is buried in Heilly Station Cemetery. He left his widow and children £2 5s 9d.[27]

John Hughes from Llanrwst served with the 16th Royal Welsh Fusiliers and was awarded the Distinguished Conduct Medal for his action on 31 May 1916 at Neuve Chapelle. He was on a night patrol when they came under fire which resulted in two men being killed and five wounded. Under heavy machine gun fire he carried a wounded comrade back to the safety of his own lines. He later took part in the attack on Mametz Wood. During this action he received a machine gun bullet wound to his arm that effectively ended his military service.

John Jones of Pen-y-ffordd, Chester enlisted in May 1915, aged 22. He was a collier by trade and joined the 16th Royal Welsh Fusiliers. By December 1915 he was in France and in February he was wounded. He took part in the attack on

Mametz Wood on 10 July and was reported missing, but this was not confirmed to his parents until June 1918 – an agonising wait of nearly two years.

In a letter home he wrote:

Private John Hughes

101

Well Dear Mother I am glad to tell you that I am in the best of health. Hoping that you are all same and glad for my part. We are having fine weather in France. Hoping you are having fine weather in Pen-y-ffordd. Well I was glad to see that Tom spent his holiday at home. Hoping that he enjoyed himself allright. My heart is with you tonight no matter where you may be. All the time I think of home and wonder if you think of me and fancy once more I live all those bygone happy days. My heart is with you tonight mother. My heart is with you always. Well Dear Mother, I only wish I was home with you all and would have been home enjoying myself all right now and I hope that you enjoyed your holiday alright. Well Dear I have no more news this time. I will close and kind regards to all but don't forget yourself.

This from your ever loving son,

Jack[28]

Robert Jones Evans of Llanymys, Denbigh, had landed in France on 2 December 1915. He was killed by machine gun fire on 10 July and was later buried in Dantzig Alley British Cemetery. He was just 17.

The Welsh Regiment official history speaks in mitigation  of the 16th Royal Welsh Fusiliers who were '... very strongly opposed and suffered a great deal from fire from Quadrangle Alley and Wood Trench and Wood Support in spite of the barrage directed on these positions.'[29]

Private John 'Jack' Jones

114th Brigade

The War Diary of 114th Brigade tells of its battalions coming into action on 10 July. At this point the 10th and 15th Welsh took up a position behind Pommiers Redoubt on 9 July, with the 13th Welsh in the line Marlborough Wood-Caterpillar Wood-Montauban Alley-Pommiers Redoubt, and the 14th Welsh in Beetle Alley and White Trench.

The plan for the attack by 114th Brigade stated that an artillery barrage would fall on the southern portion of the wood from the first cross-ride. A smoke barrage would commence at 3.55 a.m. and last for 30 minutes, falling near Strip Trench. At 4.15 a.m. the barrage would lift to north of the first cross-ride and continue until 6.15 a.m. At that time it would lift to the second objective for a further hour until at 7.15 a.m. it would fall on the northern edge of the wood for an hour. Finally, at 8.15 a.m. it would concentrate fire on the German Second Line. The barrage would lift gradually backwards at the rate of 50 yards every three minutes.

In addition to this a Heavy Mortar would bombard The Hammerhead, supported by four Stokes Mortars. Throughout the attack the 114th Machine Gun Company would fire from Marlborough and Caterpillar Woods on the open ground between the German Second Line and Mametz Wood, in order to prevent any reinforcements reaching the wood and hitting any Germans who attempted to flee from the wood. The artillery would also be bombarding this area. Six more machine guns would cover the advance of the infantry from Montauban Alley.

At 4 a.m. on the morning of the 10 July the 13th and 14th Welsh advanced to attack. The 14th on the left would take the southern triangle of wood, and the 13th Welsh on the right were to capture The Hammerhead. The 14th Welsh attack was made on a two-platoon frontage in eight lines, each about 100 yards apart, while the 13th Welsh assault was made on a four-platoon frontage in four lines, again with around 100 yards between each line. Both were to advance at 4.05 a.m. while the smoke barrage was still falling.

The 10th Welsh were to be in immediate support at White Trench, while the 15th Welsh were held in reserve in Pommiers Redoubt.

The attacking battalions were to progress north through the wood until they reached its northern edge, which was the third and final objective, keeping the central ride to their left. They were also briefed that artillery fire would sound much louder in the wood than it did outside. The Royal Engineers and Pioneers were instructed where to make the strongpoints.

Reports were to be sent when each objective had been captured, and failing this, hourly reports from 4.15 a.m. were ordered, including negative reports. No specific instructions were given to the ratio of guards to prisoners, merely that these escorts should be as small as possible.

The Brigadier-General of 114th Brigade wrote his report on 16 July. Patrols were sent out on the nights of 8/9 and 9/10 and reported that the ground was passable everywhere on the line of advance and that the wood was not wired at its edge. The artillery bombardment commenced on time at 3.30 a.m. and the 114th Trench Mortar Battery fired 275 bombs with good effect on The Hammerhead. The smoke barrage commenced on time and the smoke drifted north-east to good effect. At 4.05 a.m. the infantry began their advance.

The 13th Welsh suffered heavy casualties and reinforcements from the 10th Welsh were ordered forward from 4.38 a.m. to 5.10 a.m. The battalion from 113th Brigade on 114th's left gave way at this point. Colonel Ricketts, the officer commanding 10th Welsh, was hit twice before the battalion had completely advanced.

Progress in the wood seems to have been swift with a message timed at 4.50 a.m., from Colonel Hayes commanding the 14th Welsh, stating that they had reached the second objective, the northerly cross-ride, and asking for the guns to lift their barrage from this area. This was well ahead of schedule as the barrage was not timed to even reach the second cross-ride until 6.15 a.m. Major Bond of the 13th Welsh sent a similar message, timed 5.10 a.m., that they were through the wood. All the units were ordered to fall back and consolidate with the assistance of the Royal Engineers and Pioneers.

At 5.55 a.m. a message from the 13th Welsh arrived calling for reinforcements. Men could be seen coming out of the wood, and then stopping before going back in. At this point the Germans, still in the north of The Hammerhead, counter-attacked. Major Anthony and all his bombing party were killed, except for one officer, by fire from the sunken road to the north. Once more men were seen retiring from the wood so Major Phillips and two companies of the 15th Welsh were sent forward to clear the north of The Hammerhead and to push on to the second cross-ride. By 8.15 a.m. they had reached the cross-ride where the soldiers began to consolidate their position. However, they had failed to clear the northern end of The Hammerhead and from here the Germans got in behind them, shooting down two platoons. The remaining soldiers then fell back and were ordered to dig in.

It was now that Colonel Hayes had to lend one company of the 10th Welsh to 113th Brigade's 15th Royal Welsh Fusiliers to assist them in consolidating their position. Perhaps this was at the heart of Price-Davies' later reported disappointment in the performance of his brigade. Wood Support was still in German hands and this meant that the whole of the advance on the left was held up. The Germans were also reinforcing their position at the north of The Hammerhead by using the sunken road which was screened from the British machine guns located in Caterpillar and Marlborough woods, and they launched several counter-attacks on the junction of The Hammerhead with Mametz Wood.

At 10.30 a.m. Colonel Hayes was placed in command of all the 114th Brigade's troops in the wood and was ordered to advance once again to the second cross-ride. At 11 a.m. the 19th Pioneers reported being unable to carry out their work on the communication trench to the south-east corner of the wood owing to casualties being caused by German rifle fire. The 15th Welsh also reported yet another enemy counter-attack on the eastern edge of the wood. Hayes attacked but was unable to dislodge the Germans in The Hammerhead. The bulk of the 15th Welsh fell back, leaving Lieutenant Evans and some men of the 15th Welsh holding a precarious position at the edge of The Hammerhead.

Marden now could see numerous men on the outskirts of the wood and contemplated going over to the wood himself to reorganise them. Orders came through from Divisional Headquarters that at 2.30 p.m. two battalions of the 115th Infantry Brigade would sweep through the wood after 30 minutes' artillery bombardment 100 yards north of the second cross-ride.

The 10th South Wales Borderers of 115th Brigade, who had been held in reserve at Pommiers Redoubt, made this attack and they almost reached the north edge of the wood but the attack was held up by German machine guns.

Marden eventually obtained permission to enter the wood at 3 p.m. and heard that Price-Davies and Colonel Pryce of 38th Division had agreed a plan to sweep through the rest of the wood. At 4.30 p.m. the advance began, meeting with no opposition until it was again within 100 yards of the northern edge of the wood when the German machine guns opened fire. The site of these troublesome machine guns appears to have been a trench outside the wood and to the north. The 14th Welsh and 17th Royal Welsh Fusiliers attempted an attack on it but were held up by the thick undergrowth. A bombing party did manage to get into the trench but it was decided that all troops should withdraw some 300 yards from the northern edge and dig in to await an artillery bombardment.

From 8 p.m. to 8.30 p.m. the artillery opened up on the north edge of Mametz Wood and when it ceased the soldiers again attacked but were driven back. They then took up positions for the hours of darkness. German dead lay in great

numbers, especially in the eastern part of the wood, while the
114th Infantry Brigade had lost 48 officers and 1,240 other
ranks killed, wounded or missing but had taken 190 German
prisoners.

On the right the 13th Welsh came under fire from the
machine guns placed in The Hammerhead. They suffered
heavy casualties and were beaten back on two occasions. A
third attempt was made and they managed to get a foothold
in the wood. The 14th Welsh were attacking in the centre and
were to some extent covered from enfilade fire by the flanking
battalions and managed to reach the wood more or less as
the artillery barrage was lifting from the edge. On the left the
14th R.W.F. had suffered heavily as it attacked close behind
the 16th R.W.F. and Brigadier Price-Davies committed the 15th
and 13th R.W.F. to the attack almost immediately so that they
were then in close support to the battalions already engaged.
On the right the 10th Welsh were added to the attack making
a total of seven out of eight battalions of the two brigades
engaged in action. The attack was a reasonable success with all
the objectives being taken ahead of schedule. It had not been
without cost. Casualties had mounted throughout the first
hour of the attack such that in the seven battalions that went
into battle, five of the commanding officers had been killed or
seriously wounded. Added to this was the loss of many of the
junior officers, which resulted in the control of the thousands
of men in the wood becoming increasingly difficult.

To the right the Germans reinforced The Hammerhead and
this created havoc for a while amongst the attacking Welshmen.
To ease this situation the 15th Welsh, the eighth battalion to
be committed, were sent in to the attack. Lieutenant-Colonel
Hayes (14th Welsh) succeeded in capturing the central ride,
though his right was held up since there was little by way of
support. Marden committed the reserves at his disposal to the
attack. These were the 17th R.W.F. who went to support 113th
Brigade on the left, and the 10th S.W.B. who went to support
114th Brigade on the right of the attack. They arrived in the

fighting by about 2.40 p.m. and added fresh impetus to the attack such that the 10th S.W.B. reached a point to the north of the second cross-ride and were able to get patrols out to the northern edge of the wood.

By 6.30 p.m. that day the 17th R.W.F. had reached to within 20 to 30 yards of the northern edge of the wood and The Hammerhead had been taken by the 10th S.W.B. as the German troops were forced to withdraw. The bulk of the wood east of the central ride was in the Welshmen's hands, though to the west it was necessary to turn a flank along the railway line facing the north-western corner of the wood. The rest of the division came under heavy fire from the German second line and withdrew to the cover of the wood for some 200 to 300 yards. The day's fighting ended there but it left the men tired and jumpy, and throughout the night there was much wild firing.

10th Welsh (1st Rhondda)

Second Lieutenant A.P. Figgins left a detailed account of the part they played:

> The 10th Welsh Regiment was in support to the 13th and 14th Welsh who launched the attack at 4.15am on the 10 July. The 13th Welsh on the right lost direction and went left so that the right portion of the wood was unattacked.
>
> At 4.30am approximately 'A' Company of the 10th was sent to support the 13th. In quick succession all four companies of the 10th went up in support. The Battalion lost heavily going down the slope from White Trench to the railway on account of the enfilade fire from machine guns in the unattacked portion of the wood. (Lt.-Col. Ricketts wounded on the slope 4.45am.)
>
> One platoon of 'A' Company led by Mr Cowie gallantly advanced to the flank and in face of the machine gun fire captured the particular portion of wood, including the machine gun and several prisoners (Mr Cowie killed).[30]

Second Lieutenant Henry Benedict Cowie, known as 'Harry',

Second Lieutenant Henry Cowie

had joined the Glamorgan Yeomanry in October 1914 and served as a Private before being commissioned into the Welsh Regiment. His Lieutenant wrote to his parents:

I deeply regret to have to convey to you the sad news of Harry's death; he was killed on the 10th while bravely leading his platoon in a charge. It will be some slight consolation to you to know that his death was instantaneous, the bullet piercing his heart. We are glad to know that he died as he lived, gallantly and cheerfully.[31]

He was buried in Dantzig Alley Cemetery. Harry Cowie was 22 years of age and had lived in Merthyr Tydfil.

Figgins continued:

Arriving on the edge of the wood the whole Battalion was taken on with mixture of 13th and 14th Battalions, up through the wood to first objective, which was reached by 6.15am. The 10th commenced digging in, and later as soon as the other battalions reorganised they followed suit – the 14th on our left reaching to the middle drive [sic] and the 13th on our right. Two lines were dug here – one on the drive forming the 1st objective and the other thirty yards in the rear.

At 9pm the 10th had orders to advance to the second objective, which was done in two files of two companies each. One file was strongly opposed by machine gun fire and sniping and returned to the trench to reorganise. This file again advanced after about twenty minutes and went through to the second objective. Thence the Battalion proceeded out on the middle drive and up the drive to within 300 yards of the north edge of the wood, where in accordance with orders, we again dug in. Our left rested almost on the railway.

The night was spent in this position and except for enemy machine gun fire from our left front across the clearing the hours of dark were uneventful. Our own shrapnel was causing numerous casualties throughout the night.

On the morning of the 11th the Battalion was relieved and returned again to the trenches along the first objective. The 13th and 14th Welsh were relieved also and went right out of the line immediately.

At 4pm the Battalion again advanced to take up a position lining the railway, just left of our previous night's position. Thence we advanced and dug in 50 yards from the western edge of the wood, with out right almost on the north western corner of the wood. The 15th Welsh were on our left.

At Dusk the enemy commenced a heavy bombardment with H.H.E. and torpedoes – the latter apparently coming from an enemy trench on the ridge north east of the wood. Heavy losses were incurred here and our men were withdrawn to the railway. Here we found the 16th Welsh who had not been able to advance owing to the South Wales Borderers being held up on their right.

The enemy commenced searching the railway with H.E.s and losing more men here we manned our previous night's trench, which was unoccupied owing to the withdrawal of a battalion of R.W.F. who should have been on our right.

The 10th Welsh were relieved about 6am on the morning of the 12 July and returned to the Citadel.[32]

Second Lieutenant Herbert Francis Jones was killed on 10 July while serving with the 10th Welsh. He is remembered on the Thiepval Memorial, as he has no known grave.

Frederick Samuel King served with the 10th Battalion of the Welsh Regiment and took part in the attack. He was later twice Mentioned in Dispatches for his conduct.

Sergeant William Henry Loud was originally from Worle in Somerset, but by 1911 he was living in Cwmparc, Rhondda, and was employed as a collier/hewer. He joined the Glamorgan Constabulary in 1914 and served in Maesteg. When war broke

Frederick King survived the war and is pictured here later in life as a Yeoman of the Guard

Private William Loud. 13th Welsh (2nd Rhondda)

out he had enlisted in the 10th Welsh. He was killed on 10 July and still lies in Mametz Wood, as he is commemorated on the Thiepval Memorial as one of the missing.

At 4.05 a.m. the order was given to advance, moving left 150 yards to connect with the 14th Welsh, and the lines of men proceeded steadily down the slope towards Mametz Wood. The advance was made in lines of sections in simple file. On reaching a line 100 yards beyond the road at the bottom of the cliff, the line extended and went forward at a steady pace, gradually becoming faster until the wood was reached.

German machine gun fire from the right of Mametz Wood caused heavy losses on the extreme right, but it was reported that few casualties were incurred elsewhere. The defenders in the wood fired rapidly until the 13th Welsh reached close quarters when the Germans surrendered.

The men of the 13th then formed themselves into small

parties and began to clear the wood, advancing rapidly until the British barrage was reached which resulted in many casualties. Major Bond was one of those killed at this point. When it was realised that it was a British and not an enemy barrage that was causing the causalities the battalion was ordered to withdraw. During this withdrawal they fell in with the 10th Welsh who were moving up in support, and got in touch with the 14th Welsh.

G. D'Arcy Edwardes served with the 1st (Royal) Dragoons. He was killed while organising an attack on an enemy machine gun in The Hammerhead and was buried in Dantzig Alley British Cemetery. Edwardes was an only son and had been educated at Eton and Sandhurst. Gazetted to the 1st Royal Dragoons in 1907, he served with his regiment in India and South Africa, returned home in 1914, and went straight to the Western Front.

Colonel Hayes, commanding the 14th Welsh, ordered the men to dig in along the ride. It was then ascertained that Major Edwards had been hit and Captain Johnson took charge of the Battalion. Second Lieutenant R.S. Rees had been killed and three other officers wounded.

While they were digging in, it was discovered that the right of the line was 100 yards in advance so it was withdrawn to the line of consolidation. At this point Second Lieutenant Purdie and Second Lieutenant Crossman went into the wood to scout. Later Crossman returned to say that Purdie had been killed. Thomas Paterson Purdie's body was never identified and he is commemorated on the Thiepval Memorial. He was the son of a ship-owner from Bothwell in Lanark and was 19 years old. He was killed leading his platoon against two concealed German machine guns. These were afterwards captured and put out of action.

At about 9.30 a.m. Colonel Hayes ordered the battalion forward and they moved to the second objective. This order was then countermanded and they were moved back. At 4.30 p.m. the battalion advanced in single file through the wood

Second Lieutenant Thomas Purdie

and commenced to dig in along the ride.

A while later about 100 men and three officers moved forward to a line that was being consolidated some 300 yards from the north edge of the wood. Second Lieutenant Crossman was then discovered to be missing.

Second Lieutenant Guy Danvers Mainwaring Crossman was an M.A. graduate of Worcester College, Oxford, and was a master at Lawrence House School, St Anne's-on-Sea, before joining the Universities and Public Schools Corps as a Private in October 1914. He was gazetted Second Lieutenant, The Welsh Regiment, in August 1915 and had been on the Western Front since February 1916.

Colonel Park, Commanding Officer, Welsh Regiment wrote home to Crossman's parents: 'He was doing exceptionally well, and carried out two or three enterprises in No Man's Land with the greatest coolness, which in my opinion requires the very greatest form of courage.' A Captain Dunkley wrote: 'A fine and gallant officer: our success on the day in question was largely due to his excellent work.' Lieutenant L.W. Arkell added: 'He did the best work of anyone in the wood. Before that I had heard him spoken of as the coolest man in the battalion' and Lieutenant H. Davies: 'He showed exceptional bravery in the attack; his coolness was quite a revelation.'[33]

Lawrence House School's magazine carried the following tribute to him:

During his years here as master, Mr Crossman won the regard
of all by his transparently upright life, and, when war broke out,
enlisted as a Private, feeling that it was his duty to do so, although

as an older man he might well have excused himself, nor did the life in the least appeal to him. He eventually was offered a commission in The Welsh Regiment, where he gained the highest praise of his superior officers as an absolutely reliable and painstaking officer. To those who knew his thoroughness in all that he undertook, this was exactly what one would expect.[34]

Guy Crossman's body was recovered from the wood and he now lies buried in Flatiron Copse Cemetery, next to Mametz Wood. He was 31.

On 19 July the newspapers announced the death of Major Charles Edward Bond, aged 48, of the 13th Battalion of the Welsh Regiment, who had been killed on 9 July:

The Welsh Regt. which has taken such a prominent part in the recent fighting has lost another officer well-known in South Wales, in the person of Major C.E. Bond, whose death in action was announced in Swansea on Tuesday. The deceased officer leaves a widow and 3 children. In civil life he was a cashier at the Swansea Branch of the Capital & Counties Bank. A volunteer officer of many years standing, he retired at the inception of the Territorial Force with the honorary rank of major. For a time he was commandant for Swansea district of the Glamorgan National Reserves, an organisation which furnished the Army with a large number of well-trained officers and men at the outbreak of the present war. Major Bond, in his capacity as recruiting officer at Swansea passed 1,200 men into the Army before himself re-enlisting. At the invitation of General Pearson he was the first officer to enrol in one of the new local service battalions. An extremely popular officer, he held the full confidence of all ranks.[35]

Private George Rees Protheroe of the 2nd Rhondda, 13th Battalion Welsh Regiment died of his wounds while being conveyed to the dressing station from the battlefield. He had joined the Army 18 months previously and arrived in France in December 1915. Corporal W.J. Evans of the Royal Army Medical Corps wrote home to Protheroe's wife stating that

Major Charles Bond, seated left, and other officers of the battalion

Private Protheroe, who was suffering from wounds to his face and side, had died in his arms as he approached the dressing station. Private Protheroe had written home the night before he went bomb throwing saying: 'If I get wounded, tell them I died doing my duty for King and country.'[36] George Protheroe is commemorated on the Thiepval Memorial.

Sergeant Joseph Scott of the 13th Battalion was killed in action on 10 July. His body was never identified. He was to have married earlier in the month but his leave was cancelled. His fiancée received a letter from a fellow sergeant:

Dear Miss Jones or Em, if I may call you so,

It gives me great pain to write and tell you of the death of your fiancé and my great friend and fellow sergeant in the same platoon, as I daresay you remember. But I must tell you I am proud of him for he died like a hero with his face to the foe in Mametz Wood. Often he would speak to me of you and his wish was always that if anything happened to him one or the other would write to his mother and you and let them know whatever his fate was to be.

I may say he is sorely missed by the few of us who are left and we all extend our deepest sympathy to his widowed mother and yourself. The name of Sergeant Joseph Scott along with others we are proud to honour and we speak of them in the mess with reverence. Yes, often by the few of us who are left. They will remain in our memory when we take off our hats to remember those gallant men.

Yours sincerely,
Sergeant Peter Williams
No. 8 Platoon[37]

Of the officers of the 13th Welsh, Lieutenant W.S. Jeffreys was killed, as were Second Lieutenants W.M. Harvey and L.S. Rees.

William Stanley Goldsmith Jeffreys was a native of Newport and was killed on 10 July. He has no known grave. He attended the Newport International School, then Sherborne School from 1911–14. He briefly attended University College Wales, Cardiff, before enlisting.

William Mitchell Harvey was 22 when he was killed on 10 July. Originally from Shropshire, he has no known grave.

Lieutenant William Jeffreys

Private Daniel Davies

Laurence Sinclair Rees from Slough was killed on the same day, aged 26, and is also commemorated on the Thiepval Memorial.

Private Daniel Davies was born in Cwmavon. Aged 30, he was killed on 10 July but his body was unable to be identified. He left a widow, Mary, who was living in Pontrhydyfen, Port Talbot.

Private George Richards also served with the 2nd Rhondda Battalion. He survived the fighting at Mametz Wood and served with the battalion until October 1918. George was present in July 1987 when the memorial to the 38th Welsh Division was unveiled at Mametz Wood.

Private Edward Price, 13th Battalion Welsh Regiment, was wounded during the fighting. Originally from Aberbargoed, he had a wife and a baby daughter. Whilst attacking Mametz Wood, he was shot by a young German officer. The bullet went through the trigger of his rifle, through his hand and came out at the back of his wrist, and he was unable to fire it, so he bayoneted the German and, as he did so, the German was calling for his mother.

George Richards at Mametz Wood in 1987

Private Edward Price

He took the officer's pickelhaube, short sword and belt. They are the objects he is poking fun at on the hospital bench. His hand was permanently disfigured. Despite his bravado in the photograph, Price still had nightmares about killing the German until he died in 1952. He was transferred to the Labour Corps as the result of his injury and was eventually discharged in December 1917 as no longer being fit for war service.

14th Welsh (Swansea)

On 10 July the ground they had to cross to the wood was estimated at 1,000 yards. 'B' Company under Captain Godfrey was on the right, 'C' Company under Captain Dagge on the left. The battalion attacked on a two-platoon frontage in eight waves. 'A' Company under Captain Milbourne Williams was in support and 'D' Company under Second Lieutenant Wilson was in reserve.

Some 676 N.C.O.s and men took part in the attack. The ground was level for about 300 yards, then went down the steep cliff, about a thirty-foot drop, with paths in various places, then up a gradual rise to the edge of the wood. The advance was made in quick time, with some 80 to 100 yards between the waves. The casualties were very slight until the edge of the wood was reached, and the enemy was unprepared owing to the waves going in so close to the bombardment. The German barrage had commenced only after the last wave had left the cliff and caused little effect.

When the wood was entered it was found that, owing to the intense bombardment, the fallen trees and thick undergrowth made it very difficult to penetrate. The rides were almost indistinguishable from their surroundings, and it was difficult to establish the correct direction. A mixing of the units was now inevitable and the battalion was put under the command of Lieutenant John S. Strange. At one stage Strange bound up the wounds of Private Charles Mew who had been injured by an exploding shell, sending him back out of the wood for further treatment.

Strange himself was wounded in the right shoulder by shrapnel and after treatment in the field he was evacuated back to Britain. He survived the war, being awarded the Military Cross and the Distinguished Service Order by the King in 1921.

After reorganisation took place, they advanced to the northern edge of the wood. Lieutenant Yorke's Company seized a heavy howitzer but the machine guns were concealed in pits and these caused casualties. 'The men were highly tried but were capably led and responded well to the demands made of them.'[38] Fighting patrols of the 14th Welsh, led by Lieutenant Strange and Lieutenant D. Yorke bombed up a portion of a German communication trench leading out of the wood. Yorke was subsequently awarded the Distinguished Service Order.

Second Lieutenant Rosser was killed in an enemy trench near the northern edge of the wood, the furthest point reached during the day. His men were about to be surrounded so he ordered them to run to safety while he stayed on to hold back the Germans. His body was never identified and he is commemorated on the Thiepval Memorial. He was killed aged 19 and received no gallantry award for his sacrifice.

Arthur Rosser was the only son of Mr and Mrs Rosser of Penrhyn, Eaton Grove, Swansea. The official news was given in a letter to his mother from Lieutenant-Colonel J.H. Hayes:

Dear Mrs Rosser, I am very sorry to inform you that your boy was killed in action on the evening of the 10th. Throughout the day he behaved in a most excellent manner, and had he lived would doubtless have received recognition from the king for his bravery. Boy as he was, he was a man's man, and as such a leader. To him and his like, the country and the new armies owe an eternal debt.[39]

Rosser had joined the Pembrokeshire Yeomanry as a Private from Swansea Grammar School.

The local newspaper wrote of him:

He was a most fearless officer and received numerous congratulations on the field for his gallant conduct. Among the numerous letters of sympathy received by Mr and Mrs Rosser is one from Captain Milbourne Williams in the course of which he says, 'It is so terrible to think that we have all got off so comparatively lightly while he was fatally hit. There was no keener officer in the battalion and certainly no one who was more popular. The night before the attack I saw him, and he was as cheerful as anyone could possibly be, and was looking forward confidently to the next day.'[40]

The headmaster of Swansea Grammar School wrote to the parents to say:

Arthur was such a fine, manly fellow and did his share so frequently in every way at the school that everybody, masters and boys, are deeply moved by the news. The price we have to pay in the best manhood of England is a very high one, and Arthur was one of the very best who went out to fight on our behalf.[41]

Captain Wilson of the 14th Welsh distinguished himself by 'bayonetting in solitary combat at the head of his Company a burly German, and then bringing down with a shot a sniper in a tree. Lieutenant Hawkins did equally good if not better work by charging down on two separate machine guns, both of which he captured though unfortunately he was wounded the second time.'[42]

Frank James Hawkins was originally from Wiveliscombe in Somerset. A blacksmith by trade, he moved to south Wales and joined the Glamorgan

Frank Hawkins

Constabulary. After marrying the daughter of the owner of a public house, he left the police and became a publican himself. He played rugby for Wales on two occasions in 1912, against Ireland and France, and continued to play for Pontypridd as club captain.

During the second attack on an enemy machine gun position on 10 July, he suffered severe injuries to his right leg, which led to him being invalided out of the Army. He was also suffering from gas poisoning. For his courage he was awarded the Military Cross. His citation read: 'For conspicuous gallantry in action. He attacked a hostile machine gun and killed the man working it. He showed great bravery till severely wounded.'[43]

The *Cambria Daily Leader* of 12 October 1917 reported:

Second Lieut. Frank Hawkins, Welsh Regiment, Porth, was on Saturday decorated by his Majesty the King at Buckingham Palace with the Military Cross. Lt. Hawkins was one of the survivors of the terrible battle of Mametz Wood. The immediate gallantry which gained him his distinction was that, finding his company being shot at from behind, he went back about a mile and a half and discovered an officer and some German soldiers with a gun. By the aid of a few explosive bombs the men were killed, and after a fierce trial of strength Hawkins strangled the officer. On returning to the wood a bayonet charge was ordered, and, with his men, the lieutenant was in the thick of the fight and rendered unconscious.[44]

James Bolt of the 14th Welsh Regiment was one of hundreds of soldiers who attacked the Germans in Mametz Wood on the morning of 10 July. They left their trenches and walked forward, a survivor describing what happened next: 'Machine gun and rifle fire was trained on us. Words fail me to adequately describe this stage of the attack. Many of the shells hit the trees above us, detonated and caused more casualties.'[45] James Bolt was one of the 388 casualties sustained by the battalion that day.

Mr and Mrs Lloyd of Lamb Street in Swansea had already

suffered the death of one son on active service and of another being wounded. Then came the news that a third son, Sergeant James Lloyd, was missing. Writing to the parents, Lloyd's captain stated: 'He has been missing since 10 July. On that day the battalion was very heavily engaged, and the sergeant was seen entering a wood which his men had to capture. Since then nothing has been heard of him.'[46]

James Lloyd's body was never found. He is one of the many from that day who are commemorated on the Thiepval Memorial.

Also serving with the 14th Welsh was Private Charles Henry Johnson. Born in Swansea 31 years before, he lived in the Hafod area of the town. On 22 August 1916 his wife Florence received a letter from an officer of the 19th Manchester Regiment who wrote: 'I can tell you that the nature of his wounds were such that death must have been instantaneous. We were only able to reach those poor fellows who had paid the great price during the lulls in the German bombardment, and even then

Private Charles Johnson

at times we had to run for cover.'[47] Johnson's body was buried in Mametz Wood but afterwards was unable to be located. He is therefore listed on the Thiepval Memorial to the missing.

However, when Charles Johnson's personal effects were returned to his wife, the Testament enclosed was not his. Sensing some hope of mistaken identity she wrote to the Army.

Chaplain Stanley Keen of the 19th Manchester Regiment wrote in response to Mrs Johnson's query:

I am very sorry to be unable to give you any information with regard to how your husband died. My Division relieved his and I had to do the best I could to identify the dead who were left. I took special care that no mistakes should be made, and in the case of your husband, the articles I sent you were found on his body which I buried. Death must have been instantaneous, and I am afraid there is no room for doubt. I should be glad if I could send you better news, but I am simply telling you what I know.[48]

His wife received a letter in June 1917 from the British Red Cross and Order of St John in response to her enquiry as to the circumstances surrounding her husband's death. It stated:

I deeply regret that our only news of your missing husband is from Pte. George Richards 14th Welsh Regiment, Highfield Hospital, Liverpool, who cannot tell us any details of your husband's casualty, but states that when the Battalion were forming up for a second attack at Mametz Wood on July 10th, he came across the body of Pte. Johnson lying in the wood. He and several other men carefully examined him, and were perfectly certain that life was extinct.

Richards describes him as tallish, rather dark, clean shaven, a middle weight man, and thinks he was in some Works in Swansea before joining. You will know whether this latter point is correct. In any case, I strongly recommend you to write to Richards in hospital, enclosing your husband's photograph, to make sure whether he is speaking of the right man.[49]

She did as requested and the reply when it came only served to increase her uncertainty. In his letter of 12 June 1917 Richards wrote:

It's quite possible it may not have been him after all, as in the heat and excitement of a battle of that sort you may guess we could not be sure of anything. There were a lot of mistakes of that sort made and I know quite a lot of chaps who turned up after. Some had been taken prisoner and some had got mixed up with other battalions.[50]

At the start of August 1917 she received another letter from the British Red Cross stating that another two witnesses had been found. Private Berry of the 14th Welsh had been told by his brother, Sergeant Berry of the same battalion, that Johnson had been wounded by a shell fragment, either in the head or chest on 10 July, and lived for only an hour. He stated that all the men killed that day had been buried in a large grave outside Mametz Wood.

In addition, another unnamed man stated that he had been killed alongside Johnson's own brother, Lance Corporal Bert Johnson. Bert Johnson was later wounded at Mametz Wood by the bursting of a bomb thrown by a German officer at close quarters, pieces of which entered his leg just above the knee, and also his shoulder. This was the third occasion on which he had been wounded. Prior to the war he had worked as a copper-tester at the Hafod Copper Works.

Still Mrs Johnson did not give up hope. Later in August 1917, she received another letter from the same source which they said finally 'settled the question'. It was a statement from Signaller F. Evans who wrote from a hospital in France:

> I knew Charles Henry Johnson of 'A' Company IV Platoon. It was during the attack on Mametz Wood on the 10th July 1916, that I saw Johnson's body in a trench just inside Mametz Wood, lying close to that of a man called Simpson. I did not stop to examine the body, but I am perfectly sure both men were dead. We advanced a considerable distance beyond the bodies, and we retained our ground. If these men had been alive they would have been brought in.[51]

Sadly, one of the ironies of this war was that Charles' and Bert's grandfather was a German of Prussian descent. When he emigrated to Swansea in the 19th century he anglicised his surname from 'Johansen' to 'Johnson'.

Private Samuel Thomas Gammon from Oystermouth in Swansea was also killed on 10 July, aged 29. He left a widow, Gladys, and three sons and is commemorated on the Thiepval Memorial.

Charles Johnson (left) with his brother   Private Samuel Gammon
Bert Johnson (right)

Also killed on the same day were two other men from the Mumbles area in Swansea. Private John Charles Thomas, aged 22 from Blackpill, was last seen by his sergeant entering the wood and being badly wounded in the legs by a German bomb thrown towards him. His body could not afterwards be identified and he is also recalled on the Thiepval Memorial.

The other man was Private George Herbert Franklyn Walters and he is remembered on the Thiepval Memorial.

Private Gwilym Charles served with the 14th Battalion of the Welsh Regiment. At the time of the census of 1911, the family lived together at 28 Twynybedw Road, Clydach, Swansea. Gwilym was then 16 years of age and worked in the local tinworks where, according to the census, he was a 'helper in the rollermills'. By that stage his father's occupation was given as 'colliery blacksmith'. The family were all Welsh speakers.

Gwilym received a serious gunshot wound to the stomach at Mametz Wood. He was taken to the 36th Casualty Clearing Station at nearby Heilly where he died some days later. There are discrepancies as to the date of his death. The Commonwealth War Graves Commission records give it as 22 July, which is the date which appears on the headstone of his grave. However, his death certificate gives the date as 28 July, as does *Soldiers Died in the Great War 1914–19*.

After his death there were references to him in the south Wales newspaper *Llais Llafur* [South Wales Labour Voice]. On Saturday, 5 August 1916, the paper reported:

> At the evening service at Hebron on Sunday last, references were made to two soldiers brought up in this church who had fallen in battle – Private Archibald Morgan, of the 4th Canadians, and Private Gwilym Charles, of the Welsh Regiment. Mr David Jones and Mr George Williams, two of the deacons, expressed the sympathy of the church with the bereaved families, and the high respect in which the young men were held. The organist, Mr G. Grove, played the 'Dead March in Saul', while the congregation stood with bowed heads. The service was a most impressive one.[52]

The residents of Twynybedw Road wished to remember Gwilym and collected money to have a photograph of him enlarged and framed and which was put on display in the village.

On Saturday, 21 October 1916, the newspaper recounted this mark of respect:

> On view this week in the shop window of Messrs Ellis Bros, the enterprising drapers etc, of the Square, Clydach, is a reproduction which attracts the eye of passers-by, and reminds them of what the taking of that strong German entrenchment known as Mametz Woods has meant to Clydach. It is a very good photographic enlargement by Chapman, Swansea, handsomely framed of Pte Gwilym Charles, of the Welsh Regiment, son of Mr and Mrs Richard Charles, of Twynybedw Road, Clydach, a gallant young soldier who died of wounds in France after participating in a memorable charge, and who thus nobly sacrificed his life. The enlargement is a sympathetic gift to the bereaved parents by their immediate neighbours, and bears upon it the inscription: 'Presented by his friends of Twynybedw Road, Clydach in loving memory of Gwilym Charles, who died from wounds in France on July 22nd, 1916, gallantly fighting for his King and country. Aged 21. Toll for the brave, the brave that are no more!'[53]

Private Gwilym Charles

Then on Saturday, 28 October, the same newspaper carried poems in Welsh in tribute to Gwilym and another resident of Twynybedw Road, Corporal Willie Davies, who had died of wounds in France in April that year. The poems were by a Mr John L. Jenkins also of Twynybedw Road. One is translated here:

Tired world of disturbances and cries,
Is this one full of disappointment,
World full of troubles and concerns,
World of the heavy cross,
I weep with the family,
Somber grief,
For their longing of Gwilym,
Tears…
Young and modest,
He lived an unassuming life,
He loved walking in the way of heaven
Once you knew Gwilym,
Who could not love him,
With his cheerful smile and attitude,
His strong willed intentions,
One of Twynybedw's heroes,
One of the volunteers,
Honest, he had integrity,
Enemy of every fraud,
He gave his life to his King and country,
He believed strongly in his God,
Despite the horrors of the sound of the battlefield.
He came across to France quietly,

With his brilliant brothers,
No longer can he hear the sound of cannons,
You'll be free of every guardian,
We will no longer get drunk again,
Nor see his smile or feel his hand,
He is across in France 'somewhere'.
A downbeat sentence for the family,
He suffered far from Wales
United in his own bravery,
His host far from town,
We remember the warm wishes,
For his young sacrifice.[54]

Gwilym is buried in the Commonwealth War Graves Cemetery at Heilly Station, Méricourt-l'Abbé. His grave is one of those containing the remains of other soldiers: Private 12865 T.E. Simcox of the North Staffordshire Regiment who died on 23 July 1916, aged 25, and Private 5271 C. Keenan of the Royal Scots who also died on 23 July. That part of the headstone which refers to Gwilym has on it the inscription: 'Os yw'r bedd yn Ffrainc o'i golli, nid yw hiraeth wedi oeri.' [If the grave in France is lost, the longing will not cool.]

15th Welsh (Carmarthenshire)

At 5.45 a.m. two platoons were sent forward to carry material for the Royal Engineers. At 6.15 a.m. one platoon was sent forward to replenish bombs, and another to collect the prisoners that were starting to be taken in the wood. At 6.50 a.m. the battalion was ordered to occupy the north-eastern corner of the wood and to be prepared for an enemy counter-attack.

As the battalion moved forward in compliance with this order, they came under enfilading machine gun fire and an artillery barrage. Casualties were slight. However, at Headquarters the artillery fire meant the loss of most of the signallers and runners.

On entering the wood the companies reformed and pushed forward and met little opposition except for the occasional sniper. Twenty-five enemy prisoners were taken. There was no sign of the 13th Welsh, so most of 'B' Company was sent forward to search for them but at 8.05 a.m. it was reported that contact could not be made so another company was sent forward on the same mission.

Five minutes later, reports came in that the Germans were gathering for a counter-attack in the Sunken Road. At the same time some enemy machine gunners had got in the rear of 'B' Company and opened heavy fire on them. Only four other ranks returned out of the two platoons who had been sent forward.

This fire from the rear affected the moral of the men and in addition it was estimated that 20 marksmen were causing numerous casualties in front of the battalion. It was at this time that Major Anthony was killed. And Second Lieutenant Clifton Malet Lucas was shot dead by a sniper.

Lucas had served with the 4th South Wales Borderers at Gallipoli, having enlisted in Canada where he was working as a land surveyor. His body was never identified after the war.

The effect of this German fire was that at 8.20 a.m. the forward troops fell back, though about two platoons under Lieutenant J. Evans and Second Lieutenants P.H. Davies and W.J. Richards still held a position on the south-eastern edge of the wood. The main position gradually became untenable and a further retirement was ordered and the battalion entrenched.

At 10.30 a.m. the men of the 15th Welsh were in touch with those of the 13th Welsh for the first time that day. German machine guns and snipers were still causing a large number of casualties at this time. This went on for over two hours.

At 3 p.m., with the attack of the 15th Welsh stalled, two companies of the 10th South Wales Borderers went through their line and penetrated the wood before they too were held up by machine gun and rifle fire. The battalion moved forward at 7 p.m. but owing to congestion at the ride it was difficult to move any further forward by 8 p.m. At this time an officer of the 14th Welsh arrived to say that he had come to guide them to their position. At that moment heavy machine gun fire opened up on the men on the ride. Some working parties 'retired hastily' as the War Diary puts in and 'for about 10 minutes there was a great deal of confusion.'[55] The battalion was kept in check though and ordered to face north and west.

At 9.15 p.m. orders were received to relieve the 14th Welsh and to support the 15th Royal Welsh Fusiliers. Things then settled down and nothing of note was recorded until the following morning when two platoons were sent to reinforce the 11th S.W.B. at the south-east corner of the wood.

There is some confusion in the War Diary of the 15th Welsh as to the death of its Commanding Officer, Major Christian Gibson Phillips. Phillips had joined the battalion as a Captain with the King's Own (Royal Lancaster Regiment), being promoted Major. He must have died before 8 a.m. on 10 July as at this stage Major Percy Anthony had taken over command before he too was killed. Phillips was 36 years old and is buried in Caterpillar Valley Cemetery.

A party of the 15th Welsh broke through the Germans but eventually had to retreat. One company, under Captain Lewis returned with only seven survivors.

Major Percy Anthony of the 15th Battalion Welsh Regiment fell on 10 July, aged 36. His body was never located and he is commemorated on the Thiepval Memorial.

A notable cricketer, he played for the Worcestershire 2nd XI and for the Wanderers of Johannesburg. He was the son of the proprietor and editor of the *Hereford Times* and a cousin of Lord Robert Baden-Powell. He volunteered for service while in the Malay Straits in October 1914. On being accepted he resigned his appointment and was granted Temporary Captain in the Welsh Regiment. He served as a lieutenant in the contingent of Herefordshire Volunteers attached to the 2nd Shropshire Regiment during the South African War, and was awarded the Queen's Medal with five clasps.

One of the youngest casualties was Second Lieutenant John Reginald Hall who fell leading his men in the attack. The youngest son of Captain Edward Hall and Mrs Hall of Cardiff, he

Major Christian Gibson Phillips   Major Percy Anthony   John Reginald Hall

was educated at the Cathedral School, Llandaff, and at Felsted School in Essex. He was subsequently employed by Messrs T.P. Thomas and Co., Cardiff Docks, before enlisting in the 5th Battalion of the Monmouthshire Regiment in September 1914. He rose to the rank of sergeant before obtaining his commission in the 20th Welsh in August 1915. Posted to the 15th Welsh on 7 June 1916, he joined the battalion at Heilly in the Somme Valley. Hall was just 19 years of age. His body was never identified and he is named on the Thiepval Memorial.

Brothers James and John Jones from Llandovery had enlisted together at Ammanford and were killed on 10 July. John, aged 24, was a corporal in 'B' Company. His brother was 21 and served in the same company. Neither of their bodies could be identified so their names are listed on the Thiepval Memorial.

Private Thomas John Bowen of the Post Office, Kenfig Hill, Glamorgan, was killed on 10 July, aged 21. His death was reported in the local newspaper on 15 September.

One of the most popular young men that Kenfig Hill has given to the Army has made 'the great sacrifice'. 'Jack', as he was known to his many friends, was a universal favourite, his quiet, winning manners endearing him to all. He was a regular attendant at St Theodore's Church and was also a member of the Y.M.C.A. Prior

131

Private Thomas 'Jack' Bowen

to enlistment he acted as town postman at Kenfig Hill. His commanding officer wrote: 'I regret to say Pte. T.J. Bowen was killed in the great fight in Mametz Wood. Please accept my deepest sympathy in the loss of a man who was a credit to his platoon and who fought a good fight.'[56]

His body was never identified and he is listed on the Thiepval Memorial.

115th Brigade

17th Royal Welsh Fusiliers (2nd North Wales)

At 8 a.m. on 10 July the 17th R.W.F. marched off to Queen's Nullah to support 113th Brigade who were attacking Mametz Wood from the south. At 12.30 p.m. the men were moved up in artillery formation from Queen's Nullah over the ridge and entered the south-easterly edge of the wood. 'A' Company entered on the left of the main ride, 'B' Company entered in the centre to the right of the ride and 'C' Company on the extreme right, in touch with the 10th Welsh of 114th Brigade. On the edge of the wood the battalion was extended into line and advanced into the wood, which by now had been cleared by 113th Brigade as far as the first cross-ride. They arrived here at about 2.30 p.m. and, as the War Diary notes, 'fought their way forward with magnificent spirit'[57] as far as the second cross-ride.

At 4 p.m. they were then ordered to advance to the edge of the wood. They got within 30 yards of the edge of the wood by about 6.30 p.m. and they started to dig themselves in. Patrols were pushed forward and they reported the ground to be clear of the enemy.

The War Diary does not stint in its praise for the conduct of the men of the 17th R.W.F. at this point:

> It may be mentioned that a definite clearing of the enemy out of the centre of the wood and its complete occupation was carried out solely by the 17th R.W.F. Several Officers bear testimony to the splendid behaviour and courage of our men and to the brilliant and determined way in which they succeeded to advance in spite of the density of the undergrowth. During the latter part of the advance some of our men in their tremendous eagerness to get to close quarters with the enemy pushed so far forward that they reached our own barrage. Between 60 and 70 prisoners were taken in the course of the afternoon.[58]

It was during this advance that the Commanding Officer and six other officers were wounded.

Lieutenant Algernon Stuart Edwards of the 17th Royal Welsh Fusiliers was leading his platoon in a charge when he was struck by shrapnel, which inflicted a bad head wound and concussion, though without the protection of his helmet his injuries might have proved fatal. He was evacuated back to Britain and recovered in hospital in London. Before enlisting as a private in December 1914, he had worked for the London and North Western Railway. After being invalided home, he remained there until March 1917. Once recovered, he was again sent to the Front and was killed on the first day of the Battle of Passchendaele on 31 July 1917, aged 20. He is commemorated on the Menin Gate. He left a widow, Kathleen, at their home in Achnashean, Bangor.

His brother Kenneth Grenville Edwards was a talented singer, rower and cricketer who joined the 16th Royal Welsh Fusiliers in November 1914. He quickly gained his sergeant's stripes and in February 1915 was gazetted Second Lieutenant. He married in August 1915 and went to France in April 1916 with the 13th R.W.F. Surviving the fighting at Mametz Wood, he was killed on 8 May 1918 when a shell burst in a communication trench he was in. He was 24 and left a widow and two children. Edwards was buried by his friend W.F. Crosthwaite, in Harponville Communal Cemetery.

Private Richard Henry served with the 17th Royal Welsh Fusiliers and was killed on 10 July. Born in Manchester in 1895, he had been an apprentice joiner in Royton, Greater Manchester, but spent time in the Fylde Farm Reformatory School in Poulton le Fylde, Lancashire. He then moved to London and was a labourer when he enlisted on 18 May 1915 (his brother Thomas was killed the following day while serving with The King's (Liverpool Regiment). Like Richard, his body could not subsequently be identified.

After holding this position, the battalion was forced to retire to a position 250 yards from the edge of the wood owing to the British bombardment which was falling on their positions. They remained here through the night, pushing patrols out in front to ensure they were not caught by surprise by a German counter-attack. Around midnight two officers were killed. These were replaced by officers from the reserve, and the Adjutant left the wood suffering from shellshock. The total number of casualties was 180.

Early on the 11 July the battalions reorganised, which left the 17th R.W.F. holding a line from the central ride to the railway, with the 11th S.W.B. on their right and the 16th Welsh on their left. At noon orders were received for an advance to commence at 3 p.m. This was delayed for 30 minutes, so at 3.30 p.m. the battalion advanced and was in action until early the following morning when they were relieved. During this fighting in the wood, five officers were killed and four wounded, while 30 other ranks were killed and 197 wounded. One man was accidentally wounded and a further 37 men were missing.

Captain Hywel Williams was reported missing on 10 July and is assumed to have died some time between that day and 12 July. His body was unable to be identified and he is remembered on the Thiepval Memorial. He was 22 years of age and had joined the King's (Liverpool) Regiment as a Private at the start of the war; he was appointed Captain at just 22. His brother Hugh served with the 14th R.W.F. and had been killed a month earlier.

Second Lieutenant James Victor Sinnett-Jones was nineteen and the son of a clergyman. Born in St Brides, Glamorgan, he had attended the Cathedral School, Llandaff, and King's School, Worcester, before being commissioned as a Second Lieutenant with the 3rd Battalion of the Royal Welsh Fusiliers in September 1915. His elder brother, Captain Gilbert Lloyd Sinnett-Jones, had been killed, aged 23, on 9 April 1916 while serving with the 8th Battalion Royal Welsh Fusiliers in Mesopotamia. A tribute was paid to him in his school magazine:

> Victor Sinnett Jones was the second and surviving son of the Reverend J. Sinnett Jones, formally Vicar of Mountain Ash and now of Caerwys, N. Wales. He entered the School House in September, 1912, with a King's Scholarship from Llandaff Cathedral School. He took a high place and left in July, 1915, in the Upper Sixth to take a temporary commission, hoping later on to enter at St John's College, Oxford, and to take Holy Orders. He was a most public spirited and helpful School Monitor [prefect], a member of the School Cricket XI, Secretary of Cricket, 1915, and in the 2nd Football team; also School Librarian. But he will be remembered most as a singularly loveable and attractive character, maintaining a very high standard of unassuming attention to religious duty. He was much appreciated by his fellows during his training with his regiment at Liverpool, and to the great grief of all who knew him fell a few weeks after he had crossed to France in the fighting on the Somme at the early age of 19.[59]

The other three were: Second Lieutenant Thomas Oliver Thomas, aged 22, who was also the son of a clergyman, this time from Llanberis, Merionethshire; Lieutenant William Clifford Wright, aged 24, whose parents lived in Cottingham in Yorkshire; the fifth officer, recorded in the War Diary as Second Lieutenant Ll. Lewis, is not listed on the Commonwealth War Graves site. All four of the known casualties are recorded as having died sometime between 10 and 12 July as their bodies were never recovered and all are commemorated on the Thiepval Memorial.

Also reported missing on 10 July was John Ellis Roberts from Aber in Caernarvonshire. A poem dedicated to him appeared in *Yr Adlais* [The Echo] newspaper of 24 October 1917. His body could not be identified later and he is remembered on the Thiepval Memorial.

Death of Private Jack Ellis Roberts by a friend

I'll tell you of a friend I lost
The best man I ever had.
He died for his King and Country
Tho' he was just a lad.

We fought in Flanders side by side
The whole long winter through.
It was our way to share alike
Whatever we may do.

On listening point or sentry go
We'd always work together;
And many an awful night we spent
Through that rough wintry weather.

We shared each other's troubles
We shared each other's joys;
And when the news would come from home
Together we read as boys.

At Mametz Wood I lost my pal
You surely must have heard
Of the glorious attack that took place
By the gallant 23rd.

Midst choking fumes of luddite
And the roar of a thousand guns
How from that line we strove all night
To drive the away the Huns.

We charged their trench at midnight
On the 10th day of July

And ne'er will I forget the sight
Of that eventful day.

The gates of hell had opened it seemed
And with our battle cry
'Kitchener – you dogs –
We want to avenge or die.'

We beat them back, but the price we paid
Caused many bitter tears –
To flow for the lads that fell that day
From the Royal Welsh Fusiliers.

That pal of mine was killed outright
By a shell as we left the trench;
He now is sleeping his last long sleep
In the blood sodden soil of the French.

And when my prayers I say at night,
To him my thoughts go back;
And I pray that God may rest in peace
The soul of my good pal Jack.[60]

10th South Wales Borderers (1st Gwent)

On 8 July the battalion was in trenches until 1 a.m. and then returned to their bivouac until noon on 10 July when it left for the trenches to take part in the second attack on the wood. They captured a portion of the wood and took three field guns and two heavy guns.

Second Lieutenant Maryon Jeffreys Everton and Second Lieutenant Ralph Paton Taylor and 21 other ranks were killed, while nine officers and 120 other ranks were wounded. Six men were reported missing.

Everton was 31 and his father lived in Birmingham. He is buried in Flatiron Copse Cemetery.

Taylor was 20 and his parents lived in Northampton. After leaving school he had joined his father in the firm of Malcolm Inglis Limited, a leather and hide importer. He had tried to enlist early in the war but was rejected on the grounds of fitness. He eventually joined the Northamptonshire Regiment in the spring of 1915 and was commissioned and sent to France in 1916. He was attached to the 10th Battalion of the South Wales Borderers. A letter to his parents stated: 'With great bravery your son led his platoon into action, and unfortunately he was hit. He was carried out of action and buried on the field of battle... His last resting place is near Mametz Wood.'[61]

Ralph Paton Taylor is now buried in Dantzig Alley British Cemetery, Mametz.

The soldiers of the 10th South Wales Borderers were then subjected to a heavy bombardment by the German artillery during the night of the 11/12 July, before returning to their bivouac at 9 a.m. the following morning.

Second Lieutenant Trevor Thomas Taylor served with the 10th South Wales Borderers at Mametz Wood. Later that year, on 6 October, he was part of a fighting patrol that entered a German sap trench, killed all six occupants, and after collecting their identifications they set off back to their own lines. After a hundred yards or so they lost contact with the officer commanding and another soldier. Taylor sent his men back to their lines and, with another man, turned back to search for the two missing men in the face of enemy fire. They saw the officer being taken away by the Germans on a stretcher but could find no trace of the other man. Taylor was then wounded by machine gun fire and they were forced to return to their own lines. For his actions that night Taylor was awarded the Military Cross.

11th South Wales Borderers (2nd Gwent)

On 10 July 'C' and 'D' companies held Caterpillar and Marlborough Woods and 'A' and 'B' companies attacked Mametz Wood.

Nine men from the battalion were killed on this day. Lance Corporal Walter Williams was born in Birkdale, Lancashire, and had enlisted in Liverpool. He was one of the original members of the battalion and was reported as missing on 10 July. His body could not subsequently be identified and he is

Lance Corporal Walter Williams   Richard Yapp

recalled on the Thiepval Memorial.

Private Albert Yapp was born in Bullingham in Herefordshire. In 1908 he had married Mary Rowlands and pre-war was living in Sebastopol in Monmouthshire. He had enlisted, aged 30, in 1914 and was killed on 10 July. His elder brother Richard had enlisted in the 10th South Wales Borderers and had been killed in action on 19 April 1916.

16th Welsh (Cardiff City)

At 3 a.m. on 10 July the battalion stood to and acted as a reserve that day to the brigades involved in the second attack. At about 9 p.m. orders were received to enter Mametz Wood to reinforce the attack. They reached the wood at about 11 p.m. and reported to Brigadier-General Marden who was in command until Brigadier-General Evans arrived the following morning.

The battalion now took up position along the railway which ran through the western edge of the wood, with their right flank about 300 yards from the northern edge of the wood. To the right of the battalion were the 17th Royal Welsh Fusiliers, and on the left the 15th and 13th R.W.F. On the eastern side of the central ride were the 10th and 11th South Wales Borderers. Some reorganisation took place at this point and the 16th Welsh held a position parallel with the northern edge of the wood, about 300 yards in from the open ground. The 17th R.W.F. were on their right as far as the central ride and the 10th Welsh came into the line on their left. The 16th R.W.F. relieved the 15th R.W.F. The men then dug themselves in.

Orders were received for the line to advance at 3 p.m. on 11 July but 20 minutes before they were due to set off, the British artillery opened fire, their shells dropping into the British line. The battalion again suffered numerous casualties amongst its officers and other ranks, and the battalion was 'rather shaken' according to the War Diary.

The 10th Welsh moved forward later in the afternoon but, owing to the weakness in numbers of the 17th Royal Welsh Fusiliers, the 16th Welsh were ordered to hold the line and proceed to use the time to improve their own position in preparation for a counter-attack.

At 6 p.m. the German artillery began to pound their position with 5.9-inch guns and kept this up for some time. The German artillery now bombarded the line with gas shells, 5.9s and Minenwerfers. This lasted incessantly until the battalion was relieved at 6 a.m. by a battalion of the Northumberland Fusiliers, and returned to their bivouac under heavy shellfire.

The casualties during this second period of action were: two officers wounded, three officers suffering from shellshock and 67 other ranks killed and wounded.

Sergeant Frank Blackmore of Cogan died while serving with the Cardiff City Battalion on 10 July. He was an ex-Penarth Rugby Club forward. In a letter received by his widow from the company officer it stated: 'Sergeant Blackmore was an honest N.C.O., a very fine soldier and could always be trusted.'[62] Prior to the war he had worked at the local cement works. He left behind a pregnant widow and six little girls. His body was never identified.

Private Joseph Bailey from Cardiff joined the 16th Welsh in Cardiff and was killed in action on 10 July, aged 24. He left £7 6s 9d, including a war gratuity of £6, to his widow, Hannah, and two sons. His grave was lost and he is remembered on the Thiepval Memorial. Before the war he had been a farm labourer.

19th Welsh (Glamorgan Pioneers)

The battalion received orders on the afternoon of 9 July to follow the attack of the units assaulting Mametz Wood and to consolidate designated points in preparation for the anticipated German counter-attack. Accordingly, Headquarters and two companies were attached to 114th Infantry Brigade and two companies to 113th Brigade. They were to accompany soldiers of 151st Company of the Royal Engineers and were allocated rendezvous points. Two platoons of 'C' Company were given the task of digging a communication trench from Caterpillar Wood to Mametz Wood.

All the platoons were engaged during the night of 9/10 July in carrying Royal Engineers' material and forming dumps in

Sergeant Frank Blackmore

Private Joseph Bailey

141

the vicinity of White Trench and Caterpillar Wood. The three platoons of 'B' Company followed the 14th Welsh into Mametz Wood and set to work consolidating the captured positions and setting up barbed wire. They also took an active part in the fighting in the wood.

It was a different picture for the two platoons of 'C' Company. German artillery shelling and machine gun fire prevented them from leaving the shelter of the ravine north-west of Caterpillar Wood. The digging of the communication trench to Mametz Wood had to be abandoned in the face of this hostile fire as considerable casualties were sustained.

Around 1 p.m. on 10 July orders were received to support the attack on the wood. The Company Lewis Guns were brought into action from the north crest of the ravine and were ordered to keep the northern part of the wood under fire.

The Battalion War Diary notes that at this point 'the situation in the wood was very obscure... and more definite orders could not be given for fear of hitting our own men.'[63]

One platoon was ordered to enter the wood from the east in order to create a diversion, but as soon as they left cover, the officer and six men were immediately shot at and the platoon was ordered to retire. By 8 p.m. attempts to get into the wood from the east had to be abandoned, and the men were ordered to return to their bivouacs for rest and rations at Minden Post. At 10 a.m. on 11 July these platoons were in the wood in relief of 'A' and 'B' companies.

The companies under orders from 113th Brigade had rendezvoused at 3 a.m. on the 10 July and by 7 a.m. had advanced form Dantzig Alley Trench to Queen's Nullah. They were ordered to dig a communication trench from Cliff Trench to Strip Trench. Two platoons were allotted this task with two more assisting the infantry in digging trenches at the cross-ride inside Mametz Wood. At 4 p.m. that day the companies received orders to garrison the cross-ride in preparation for an attack. Further orders were then received to fall back and dig in again. After this there was another retirement, 'owing to confusion' according to the War Diary. Two companies were then ordered back to the cross-ride. At 10.45 a.m. on 11 July they returned to their bivouacs at Minden Post, having been carrying, digging and fighting continuously since 6 p.m. on the evening of 9 July.

'D' Company had dug trench mortar emplacements at Queen's Nullah during the night of 9/10 July, complete with dugouts and ammunition pits. At 8 a.m. on 10 July two platoons were sent to Halte for ammunition but none was to be found. Instead, the battalion's reserve ammunition was brought up from Minden Post. The two platoons in Queen's Nullah were moved into the wood and commenced work consolidating the strongpoints at the junction of Wood Trench and Strip Trench. Later the whole Company undertook wiring duties.

The total casualties for the 19th Battalion during this period were: one officer killed and three wounded, 12 other ranks killed, a further two dying of their wounds, 106 wounded and 15 missing. The battalion left Mametz Wood at 9.30 p.m. on 11 July and were moved with the Battalion Transport to their bivouac at Citadel Camp.

The officer killed was Second Lieutenant Walter Tessier Newlyn, who died, aged 32, on 11 July. He was the husband of Maude Newlyn, of 3 Hambledon Road, Southfields, London, and he left two sons. His body was unable to be identified and he is commemorated on the Thiepval Memorial.

Royal Engineers

151st Field Company

At 4.45 a.m. on 10 July, after the first waves of infantry reached the edge of Mametz Wood, one section, accompanied by one platoon of the 19th Welsh, were sent forward to make a strongpoint near the eastern end of the cross-ride. At 5.15 a.m. the remainder of the section, with another platoon from the 19th Welsh, went forward to the wood to build another strongpoint at the junction of the southern cross-ride and the main central ride.

On the right, owing to there being no contact with the Liaison Officer, all the consolidating parties in Caterpillar Wood were in the dark as to the progress of the attack inside the wood. Numbers 2 and 3 Sections under Second Lieutenant Carroll, with two platoons from the 19th Welsh, were sent forward to construct strongpoints in the wood, but on emerging from the ravine they immediately came under heavy rifle fire from the German Second Line or from Mametz Wood itself. They were obliged to make a detour through Caterpillar Wood and approached Mametz Wood from the south.

123rd Field Company

On 10 July at 7.14 a.m. they moved forward to Queen's Nullah and Lieutenants McLean and Lethbridge were ordered to reconnoitre the front line and, if conditions were favourable, to arrange with the infantry for a covering party to enable them to wire the line at once. At 7.46 a.m. they duly went forward with the Company Sergeant-Major to see what work could be done. They proceeded up the trench on the west side of the wood to a point 150 yards to the rear of the front line. They found the infantry there retiring, having lost all their officers. They reorganised them and took command until relieved at 9.30 a.m. by Major Bell of the 13th Royal Welsh Fusiliers.

At 2 p.m. around 60 Germans gave themselves up as prisoners of war. One of them admitted to speaking English and when questioned he informed the officer that the enemy troop, which were very few, were completely demoralised. He was taken to more senior officers who decided, on the basis of this evidence, to attack once more. At 5.15 p.m. reconnaissance parties were sent out to report on the feasibility of wiring the new front. It was decided not to proceed with this as another advance was intended. Consequently, the company carried material to the cross-ride instead.

Shortly afterwards, the company was ordered to make a strongpoint, but owing to heavy rifle and machine gun fire this was abandoned. Wiring continued the following day until they were ordered back to their billets on the evening of 11 July.

Three members of the 123rd were killed during their two days in action, and one died of his wounds. The men killed were Corporal David Robert Masters, aged 24 from Mountain Ash; Sapper Albert James Brooks and Sapper Herbert Bellis. Masters and Brooks were killed on 11 July, and Bellis on 10 July. None of the three men has a known grave and they are all remembered on the Thiepval Memorial.

Sapper R.T. Williams, also of the 123rd, from Menai Bridge, Anglesey, died of his wounds on 11 July, aged 26. He is buried in Morlancourt British Cemetery Number One. A lieutenant wrote to the bereaved parents that their son was struck in the leg by a piece of shell and died of his wounds. When wounded he was acting as a dispatch bearer and was exposed in one part of his journey to the enemy shellfire. Men from his section also wrote to the parents: 'His courage was never found wanting and it was with a smiling face that he endured the hardest of hardships and thus he faced the greatest ordeal (and last) in which he was ever called to take part.'[64]

124th Field Company

At 5.45 a.m. on the morning of 10 July the company received information that the southern portion of the wood was clear of the enemy. Second Lieutenant Cowper was instructed to reconnoitre the wood and to find out the exact position of the units engaged. This was done and Pioneers began construction of a strongpoint at the junction of Wood Trench and Strip Trench. At 9 a.m. it was found that the infantry were not making sufficient progress in consolidating the new front line so the officer commanding withdrew the Pioneers from the communication trench running from White Trench to Strip Trench and moved them on to consolidating the new line. At 4 p.m. the Engineers and Pioneers had to man the new trench to enable the infantry to advance to clear the remaining part of the wood. At 9 p.m. the infantry retired to the central strongpoint at the cross-ride where they were steadied up by the Royal Engineers manning the strongpoint. During the night both infantry and engineers stood to.

The only man of the unit killed on this day was Sapper Charles Johns whose body was never identified and is commemorated on the Thiepval Memorial.

The artillery barrage was causing many casualties at this time and some sections were withdrawn. At 3.30 p.m. the infantry was formed up for the advance to clear the north and west of the wood but were disorganised by the artillery firing onto them. The Royal Engineers were withdrawn as further consolidation was not required at this stage. Their casualties from the 6 to 11 July were two N.C.O.s killed and 24 men wounded.

Lieutenant Cyril Arthur Charles Aitkens, Special Section, Special Brigade of the Royal Engineers was wounded on 10 July and died later the same day, aged 23. A marine engineer, he had volunteered at the outbreak of war and had arrived at the Front on 24 June. He was originally buried in Queen's Nullah before being moved after the war to Dantzig Alley British Cemetery, Mametz. In his pocketbook was found a receipt made out for 12 prisoners, dated 25 June.

Captain H. Livens R.E. wrote: 'This officer behaved with very great gallantry in some of the hottest phases of the fighting at the commencement of the offensive. He was also able to save the lives of some of his own men, and of several other units, by skilful dressing in the field, and thus preventing them bleeding to death.'

Lieutenant Cyril Aitkens

A Sapper from his unit wrote to Aitkens' parents of his conduct a few days earlier:

> It was a grand sight; I shall never forget when he led us out of the British trenches on 1 July under heavy shell and machine gun fire. He took the lead and cheered us on; his words were: 'Remember, boys, we can only die once, and better heroes than cowards.' We had got as far as the third line of German trenches when I was wounded; I was shot through the arm and shoulder. He did my wounds and got me safely back into the dressing station. He also carried a wounded sergeant of another regiment across. I shall never forget him covered with blood. Your son died a hero, and one of the best of gentlemen. I thank him for my life.[65]

Aitkens was also Mentioned in Dispatches for 'valuable and courageous work in connection with wiring'.

119th Brigade Royal Field Artillery

By 11 July the guns were registering on the enemy's wire at the second line in front of Bazentin-le-Petit Wood.

The brigade had one man killed on 11 July and three on 12 July as the wire cutting continued. The casualty on 11 July was Bombardier Stephen Temblett of A Battery who has no known grave. On the following day the casualties were: Gunner James Slater Nuttall of C Battery, aged 19, from Manchester who was buried in Ovillers Military Cemetery; Gunner J. Davies of A Battery who was buried in Gordon Dump Cemetery, Ovillers-la-Boiselle; and Sergeant Thomas Jones Lloyd, also of A Battery, a married man of 47 from Trehafod, Pontypridd, who is buried in the same cemetery.

121st Brigade Royal Field Artillery

On 10 July fire was directed at Pearl Alley and during the night B, C and D batteries moved forward and took up a position 1,000 yards south of Mametz Wood to Queen's Nullah. On 12 July they bombarded the German front line and the support line. At 5.15 p.m. information was received that the Germans

Sergeant Gus Taylor

were advancing over the crest towards Mametz Wood so the batteries fired on targets in front of Bazentin Wood.

Sergeant Gus Taylor of Penarth served with D Battery 121st Brigade of the Royal Field Artillery. He was born in 1893 and was a keen sportsman who swam for Cardiff Y.M.C.A. and the Penarth Swimming Club. He played rugby for Cardiff in the 1913/14 season and worked for the Taff Vale Railway. He was awarded the Military Medal and bar for gallantry and survived the war, being heavily involved in organising annual reunions of old comrades for many years afterwards.

130th St John Field Ambulance

On 10 July they were ordered to the forward areas once more. Soon after the attack was launched, the casualties began to grow and additional bearers were soon required. By 8 a.m. 52 stretcher cases were lying at the Triangle awaiting evacuation to the Advanced Dressing Station. The total number of casualties assessed between 9 p.m. on 9 July and 9 p.m. on 10 July was 463. From 9 p.m. on July 10 to 9 p.m. on 11 July the figure was 377 and in the next 24 hours it was 190.

131st Field Ambulance

By 4.15 a.m. on 10 July it was reported that there was a great demand for stretchers and all the medical reserves were called forward by 6am. The War Diary records: 'All ranks worked splendidly, especially the bearers Private Cunningham and Private B.E. Thomas who were recommended to the A.D.M.S.

for official recognition for their gallantry and devotion to duty.'[66]

The same six dressing rooms were used as on 7 July, and by 12 July the unit had seen 3,059 wounded men pass through its hands – 112 officers and 2,947 other ranks.

Captain David of 131st Field Ambulance was wounded while reconnoitring the ground from Rose Cottage to Mametz. He was struck by a piece of shell and his right scapula was fractured and he had blood spitting. He was subsequently evacuated to the 21st Casualty Clearing Station. Captain Lawrence of the R.A.M.C. and three others were killed at the same time (see above).

One of these officers was Lieutenant Raymond Jones who had taken a medical course at Victoria University and completed his degree. He had established his own practice in Cardiff before enlisting not long after the outbreak of war. Serving with the 129th Field Ambulance, he was killed on 10 July and was buried in Carnoy Cemetery.

His batman, Private J.R. Jones, wrote to Raymond's brother, Major Edgar Jones:

> It was not long before the wounded came pouring in. Your brother took charge of the stretcher-bearers and attended many cases. After going across the open to within 20 yards of the wood, where he fell with bullet through the right lung and one through the left thigh. I bandaged him up and with help carried him to the shelter of the wood, where he died in about 20 minutes. We failed to carry the body from there until the following day, as there was such a large number of wounded.
>
> He is buried in a British cemetery in a little village behind the line, the name of which you may soon learn. There is one consolation the whole family may derive from his death and that is he gave his life for others nobly and fearlessly. We all mourn his loss greatly, he was so kind and thoughtful to all of us especially myself as I had served him as a servant from the time we were in England. Accept my sympathy in your great loss.[67]

Lieutenant D.A. Taylor wrote:

Could here be a fine example of self-sacrifice? A soldier goes
forwards to kill or be killed – the doctor usually stays behind to
dress the wounded who are brought back to him, but Raymond
deliberately went forward to face death – that perchance he might
be able to save a life – or to ease some tortured soldiers' suffering.
I saw him after he was killed and his face was quite peaceful and
calm, as though he knew he had done his duty and was content to
pay the terrible price. I saw afterwards the cross, which was the
most beautiful cross I have ever seen out here – I have seen many
alas! How many! Everyone that could get to his funeral went to it. I
regret that I could not go owing to most urgent work and everyone
misses him, but no one misses him more than I do – for I have lost
a kind friend who was indeed one of the heroes of England.'[68]

Another letter from an unknown writer stated:

Lieutenant Raymond Jones
(standing)

You might tell him (Major Edgar Jones) how popular his brother was with all ranks and how gallantly he met his death. Our stretcher-bearers came into our advanced post with the news that hundreds of wounded, serious cases, were lying in the wood and could not be brought in for some time. As soon as Jones heard this, at about 4.30am, he filled his pockets with bandages and went to find them. Over a small ridge and down to the edge of the wood across about 40 yards of open, in which it seemed impossible for anything to live.

He never found his goal, he was killed before he reached the wood. I am going tomorrow by motorcar to the little wayside cemetery where we buried Jones, to stick up an oak cross, suitably inscribed on his grave:

'Lieut. Raymond Jones, R.A.M.C. Formerly of Cardiff, Practising here.'[69]

His chequebook, with a bullet hole through it, was sent back to the family, as was his cigarette case, which was untouched. The family could not but wonder what might have resulted had the two items been in opposite breast pockets.

CHAPTER 6

11 July – The Third Movement

AT 5 A.M. Brigadier Evans (115th Brigade) took over the command of all the troops in Mametz Wood, establishing his H.Q. on the junction of the central ride with the first cross-ride. He was slightly wounded, while his Brigade-Major was severely wounded by a British shell which burst among the three brigadiers whilst they were conferring.

Evans ordered into the wood the 16th Welsh and the remaining companies of the 11th South Wales Borderers who relieved some of the battalions of 113th Brigade and 114th Brigade. He established a line from the west of: 16th Royal Welsh Fusiliers, 16th Welsh, 17th Royal Welsh Fusiliers, 11th South Wales Borderers and 10th South Wales Borderers.

Having consolidated a presence in the wood the task now was to drive the Germans out of it. Accordingly, an attack was planned for 3 p.m. using the 16th Welsh, 17th Royal Welsh Fusiliers and 11th South Wales Borderers. At 2.45 p.m. a British artillery barrage commenced and as the 18 Pounder guns were firing at the limit of their range, shells began to fall short into the British troops. This continued until 3.30 p.m.

When the bombardment ceased the attacking battalions rose from their positions and began their advance. By 5.40 p.m. the 11th S.W.B. had reached the north-east corner of Mametz Wood but the 16th Welsh and 17th R.W.F. had met sterner resistance and were held up amidst fierce fighting.

By 9.20 p.m. all the battalions had retired to their starting positions.

At this stage the Germans realised that another attack the following day would see them driven out of the wood so they began their retirement to their second line under the cover of darkness, leaving just a few patrols on the edge of the wood.

The following morning, 12 July, units of 62nd Brigade of 21st Division relieved the battalions of the 38th Welsh and moved forward to occupy the northern edge, meeting only sporadic resistance.

113th Brigade

13th Royal Welsh Fusiliers (1st North Wales)

The War Diary for the battalion records: '11 July 7.00am: Three patrols were sent forward to reconnoitre the ground up to the railway line, on their returning the line advanced, our right being in touch with the 16th Welsh. Patrols were sent out to extreme edge of wood.'[1]

At noon the battalion retired. At 3.30 p.m. a British shell fell short and wounded the Commanding Officer, Major Bell, and the Adjutant. Captain Hardwick assumed command. Bell also suffered a gunshot wound to his left thigh.

At 5.37 p.m. the battalion moved forward again, with a further advance taking place at 7.25 p.m. They formed up either side of the 14th Royal Welsh Fusiliers and were now in the very front line in the wood.

At 10 p.m. orders were received from Brigadier-General Evans to evacuate the new line and to take over the second line held by the 11th South Wales Borderers on the right of the central ride with three companies, and to place a further company on the left of the central ride.

At 1 a.m. on the morning of the 12 July the battalion was relieved by the 12th Northumberland Fusiliers from 21st Division and they bivouacked for the night at Minden Post. At 5.30 p.m. they marched out of the area and their experience of Mametz Wood was over.

153

Shortly afterwards Mr and Mrs Morse of 116 Barry Road, Cadoxton, received news from the War Office that their son, Private Frederick Augustus Morse, of the 13th Royal Welsh Fusiliers, had been seriously wounded in action. His left leg had been amputated just below the knee. He was also suffering from 14 gunshot wounds in his right leg and both arms. He was discharged from the Army in April of the following year.

14th Royal Welsh Fusiliers (Caernarvon and Anglesey)

The War Diary relates:

> About noon the General Officer Commanding 113th Brigade ordered us up as a reserve at first cross-ride to an attack that was being organised that afternoon. About 4.00pm we had orders to reinforce the 11th S.W.B. 200 yards to the north east of the second ride running east and west across the wood.
>
> At this time we were subjected to our own artillery fire. The 11th S.W.B. had pushed on to a point mentioned and our men were moved in file in parallel columns to reinforce. The parties on the right met the 11th S.W.B. retiring but they moved up to a line 50 yards from the front edge of the wood. There they dug themselves in and a line was held including from main ride to the east for 200 yards, the flanks being protected by Lewis Guns. About half an hour later the 14th R.W.F. under Captain Wheldon who had been awaiting the order to reinforce just south of the wood came up and extended the line on the right and a few minutes later Captain Hardwick and men of the 13th R.W.F. arrived and held the line on the left and still further extended it on the left. A good supply of ammunition and bombs was brought up.
>
> About 10.00pm Captain T. Glynn Jones reported the situation to G.O.C. 115th Brigade and he ordered the line to retire to the south to the first cross-ride in the wood. This was done and we stayed there until relieved by the Warwicks at midnight. During the whole period there was a heavy barrage on the south of the wood by the enemy and on the north of the wood by our artillery.[2]

The 14th Royal Welsh Fusiliers were relieved and the following morning marched back to Mametz village.

Lieutenant J.B. Martin of the 14th Bn. Royal Welsh Fusiliers, formerly of 95 Main Street, Cadoxton, was admitted to the 8th General Hospital in Rouen on 12 July with gunshot wounds in both thighs. His brother, Private F.H. Martin of the 1st Monmouths, had been killed at Ypres in April 1915.

Lieutenant James Venmore was born in Walton in 1869; he later studied architecture at the University of Liverpool. His occupation prior to the war was as an architect. He had been awarded the Military Cross for his conduct earlier in the war. On the night of 30 January 1916, Venmore was on duty as a patrol officer in front of the British trenches in France, when a sentry in the firing trench reported that three men in an advanced listening post had been wounded. Two of these men were just able to crawl back to the British lines over the barbed wire, but the third man was too seriously wounded to follow, being shot through both legs. Venmore volunteered to go to his assistance, and took with him a non-commissioned officer (Corporal William Williams, a Caernarvon man), who was later awarded the Distinguished Conduct Medal.

They went out under heavy fire over the parapet and, after great difficulty, successfully brought in the man over the wire and two ditches. This brave action was succeeded by a further gallant act on the following morning. When a message was received that a man had had his arm blown off at another listening post, practically unapproachable by daylight, Lieutenant Venmore again undertook to go to his aid, once more taking with him Corporal Williams. They crawled across the open ground in the face of heavy machine gun fire.

Lieutenant James Venmore

The casualty was reached, his wounds tended to, and he was subsequently brought to safety.

Venmore enlisted as a private in the 3rd Battalion of the Liverpool Regiment. He was commissioned in the 14th Royal Welsh Fusiliers in December 1914 and proved himself a capable and popular officer. He was 28 when he was killed on 11 July and is buried in Dantzig Alley British Cemetery.

15th Royal Welsh Fusiliers (London Welsh)

At 10 a.m. on 11 July they were relieved in the wood by the 16th R.W.F. and withdrawn to Queen's Nullah.

16th Royal Welsh Fusiliers

On 11 July the battalion moved back into Mametz Wood and relieved the 13th R.W.F. and 15th R.W.F. During the day the battalion consolidated the northern and north-western edges of the wood. They were due to be relieved at 10 p.m. by the 10th Northumberland Fusiliers but they went through the 16th's lines, attacking the German second line of defences instead. This delayed their relief until noon the following day.

Fred and William Arthur Phillips, from Whitchurch in Shropshire, died while serving with the 16th Battalion. The

The Phillips Brothers – Sidney (left), William (centre) and Fred (right)

brothers have no known graves and are commemorated on the Thiepval Memorial to the missing. Their brother Sidney Phillips served in the same battalion and was invalided home with neurasthenia in May 1916. He was eventually discharged but never fully recovered and died in 1956. The sole remaining brother, Norman, was later called up and served in France in the 17th Battalion of the Royal Welsh Fusiliers and survived the war.

Private Emrys Elwyn Hughes was killed aged 19 on 11 July. Pre-war he was training to be a commercial artist in London, and his fellow soldiers always knew where he had been as he had left sketches in the various camps.

Born in Walworth in London, Emrys had enlisted in November 1915 in Holborn, initially joining the ranks of the 18th Royal Welsh Fusiliers. He was soon transferred to the 16th Battalion and was in France by April 1916. He had lied about his age on enlistment, giving his age as 19 years and 11 months when he was actually a year younger.

His other brother, Hubert, served with the 15th Royal Welsh Fusiliers (London Welsh), and was present during the fighting in Mametz Wood. He was wounded and discharged from the Army on 3 December 1918. He died soon afterwards of his war wounds.

Hubert had joined up early in the war and entered France on 3 December 1915. It appears that his younger brother was anxious to join and thus gave a false age to the recruiting office. The family story was that Hubert found Emrys dying in the wood and stopped to cradle him as he died. His body was never subsequently identified and he is remembered on the Thiepval Memorial.

Private Emrys Elwyn Hughes

Lance Corporal William Lawson Holgate was born in Darwen, Lancashire; his father was a blast furnace manager. After three years as an apprentice he enrolled on a course in Mechanical Engineering at the Municipal School of Technology in Manchester. He was twice recommended for a commission while serving in France and was killed in action on 11 July. His commanding officer wrote:

> The battalion was joining up to attack the German position when a shell burst close to him, killing him instantaneously. He was one of the very many brave soldiers who fell that day, but there is none whose loss will be more keenly felt by his comrades or by myself personally. His bearing throughout his period of service, especially in France, was invariably that of a true and loyal soldier.

A comrade stated: 'He led his section over the top with the greatest coolness and bravery. He was first wounded in the cheek by a bullet and soon after a shell burst just in front of him, killing him instantaneously.'[3] His body was later unable to be identified.

The Common War Graves Commission site wrongly gave his battalion as the 7th Royal Welsh Fusiliers. I wrote to them in 2015 and this was changed. His Thiepval Memorial listing will be altered too after nearly 100 years.

Private Wilfred Brown of the 16th Royal Welsh Fusiliers was 20 when he was killed on 11 July. Born in Llandudno, north Wales, his body was never identified.

Corporal Thomas Fergusson was also killed on 11 July. He left behind a widow and a baby girl. There was no identified grave for him and he is remembered on the Thiepval Memorial.

The 16th Battalion R.W.F. lost Second Lieutenant Henry Hugh Tregarthen Rees when he was killed on 11 July, aged 24. From Caernarvon, he is remembered on the Thiepval Memorial. When the war broke out he was the second officer on an American liner, and he immediately resigned his position to join the Army as a Private. He was commissioned the following

March and had been home on leave a few weeks before his death.

Major F.R.H. McLellan wrote to Mrs Rees:

I deeply regret to have to tell you that your son was killed in action on the 10th of this month. He was in command of a party of bombers, detailed to attack a trench in a wood, and while carrying out this duty he was shot at close quarters, and died almost immediately. His loss is keenly felt by us all, for he was a fearless young officer and a fine leader. His men would have followed him anywhere, and the work they did on that day is sufficient testimony to the power of his example. Had he survived he would have been recommended for decoration. Besides this, his loss is a personal loss to me. In all the time of his service I felt that he was a man on whom I could rely, and a friend who would never fail me. Eighteen months of comradeship had led to a very real affection between us, and the parting is a bitter one for me. May God comfort you in your bereavement.[4]

Captain J.H. Davies also wrote stating:

It is with very great sorrow that I am writing to tell you of Hugh's death in action... I knew him personally, for we were together in the same company from January 1915 until I left the company in March of this year. We were personal friends, and one would

Lance Corporal William Holgate

Private Wilfred Brown

Corporal Thomas Fergusson

159

not wish to meet with a nicer lad. You will be comforted in your
sorrow to know that he died bravely, leading his men into action. I
saw some of his men yesterday, and they all told me that they had
the utmost confidence in his leadership, and they missed him more
than words can tell. In your sorrow you have the sympathy of all
officers and men of his battalion.[5]

Mr and Mrs William Thomas of Borthyn, Ruthin, received
information on 19 July that their sons Harold David Thomas
and John Frederick Thomas were both officially reported as
missing. Harold was serving with the 17th R.W.F. and John
with the 16th R.W.F.

Shortly afterwards the parents received a letter from a
friend of the brothers:

I suppose you have already heard about your son Harold being
amongst the missing. Our division was given the task of clearing
the Huns out of the woods where all the recent fighting occurred.
As we had severe casualties, a party of men were told to carry the
wounded to safety. The last time I saw Harold, he was helping a
wounded man to a dressing station, and we don't know whether he
was hit carrying the wounded man out, or whatever happened to
him.

I have been looking for Fred. I hope he is all right. Harold told
me if a parcel should come and anything happen to him for me to
share it with the boys. The parcel has arrived and I have shared
it and I have possession of the safety razor, and I will keep it for
Harold. Hoping to hear from you very shortly,

I remain your sons' Pal,

Pte. W. Nicholas[6]

John was killed during the fighting on 11 July, aged just 17.
His body was never recovered and he is commemorated on the
Thiepval Memorial. Harold died on the 14 July, aged 19, and
lies in London Cemetery and Extension, Longueval.

114th Brigade

In the early morning of 11 July the 13th and 14th Welsh were relieved in Mametz Wood and marched back to the Citadel. The 10th and 15th Welsh remained in the wood. Marden sent a Special Order of the Day to the 114th Brigade on 13 July which was in complete contrast to that which Price-Davies was to write. In it he congratulated all ranks on their achievements on 10 and 11 July. He went so far as to appreciate the difficulties the soldiers faced in fighting this form of warfare:

'Wood fighting is recognised as the most difficult form of fighting and it reflects the greatest credit on all engaged that at the end of the day all units in the Brigade were under their own commanders.'[7]

The second part of the sentence could be what irked Price-Davies so much in his report on his own brigade, as his units were mixed with units of the 114th, as above. Marden made reference to the casualty lists which to him showed an acknowledgment of the severity of the fighting.

He named several officers and commended them for their actions, not least in assuming command of battalions, companies and platoons where their leaders fell – something quite different to Price-Davies' report of the behaviour of some of his officers. Marden ended 'With such a splendid start, the 114th Infantry Brigade can look with confidence to the future, and with pride to the past.'[8]

10th Welsh (1st Rhondda)

Mr and Mrs Sherlock of 18 Amherst Crescent, Barry Island, received word that their eldest son, 20-year-old Private Frank Sherlock of the 10th Welsh had been killed in action on 11 July. A comrade, Corporal S.A. White (who later wrote a poem about Mametz Wood) had written home to express his sympathy. However, a week later the parents received a postcard from their son informing them that he was in fact a prisoner of war at Dülmen in Westphalia. He wrote asking for a parcel of food.

Needless to say, according to Mr Sherlock, his wife made the journey from the island to the town Post Office in about three steps to dispatch the parcel to their son.

13th Welsh (2nd Rhondda)

At 4.30 a.m. on the 11th Captain Johnson received orders for the battalion to withdraw.

14th Welsh (Swansea)

Private Oliver James Loosemore of the 14th Welsh died on 11 July, aged 21. The son of James Loosemore from Penrhiwceiber in Glamorgan, he had enlisted in Caerphilly in November 1915. Posted to the Army Service Corps on account of his poor eyesight, he was sent to the Packers and Loaders Station at Aldershot but in January 1916 he applied for a transfer to the Welsh Regiment and was sent for training at Kinmel Park, after which he was posted to the 14th Welsh. He was wounded during the attack on 10 July and was taken from the battlefield to the large field hospital at Heilly Station near Corbie, first by stretcher-bearers and then probably by train. Sadly, he died the following day and is buried at Heilly Station Cemetery in

the same grave as two other soldiers.

Returned to the family with his personal effects was an unopened letter from his mother that was written six days after he had died. In it she wrote poignantly: 'Just a few lines to you hoping it will find you quite well. We have

Private Oliver Loosemore

been waiting to hear if you had our parcel. Dad has sent you 3 shillings and hopes that you will be able to buy some things to eat. I hope that I shall hear from you soon.'[9]A hairdresser by trade he was a local preacher and his ambition was to train as a minister.

The battalion was brought out of the line at 1 a.m. on 11 July, having lost 376 men killed, wounded and missing out of the 676 men with which it had begun the attack. About 100 of these casualties were killed or died later of their wounds.

15th Welsh (Carmarthenshire)

At 2 p.m. the battalion moved out to attack the north-west corner of Mametz Wood at 3 p.m. However, the British artillery barrage was falling short and in the very thick undergrowth they made slow progress and did not reach their starting position until 4 p.m. The attack was then further delayed to allow the 16th Welsh to get into position.

At 6.25 p.m. the attack began, with the 16th R.W.F. on their left and the 10th Welsh on their right. There was by now no sign of the Germans and they entrenched 60 yards from the north-east edge of the wood. At 9 p.m. the German artillery commenced its bombardment of the wood and this heavy shelling continued throughout the night. This chiefly consisted of the fire of 5.9-inch guns, and some trench mortar fire, which it was thought was coming from Pearl Alley.

By 2.30 a.m. on 12 July this position had become untenable and the battalion was withdrawn to the railway line, but the shelling followed them so they were ordered forward to the original line, leaving the 10th Welsh, 16th Welsh and 16th R.W.F. to hold the line in the rear.

The battalion was relieved in the wood at 9 a.m. and the total casualties in the fighting for Mametz Wood were 228, including eight officers. Of these, 46 were killed, 59 were reported missing and 123 were wounded.

Two brothers from Ferndale died on 11 July while serving with the 15th Battalion of the Welsh Regiment. Harry and

Thomas Hardwidge were buried in adjacent graves in Flatiron Copse Cemetery, Mametz.

A local newspaper reported:

> Confirmation of the official news has been received of the death in action of the two brothers Hardwidge, in a letter from their officer to the two widows. Corporal Tom Hardwidge, the eldest of the two, was wounded by a sniper's bullet. Henry went to his assistance, and whilst giving him water was himself killed by a sniper's bullet, both dying in each other's arms. The officer writes – 'I had known them for nearly 12 months, for they were in my platoon. More cheerful, willing, and capable soldiers I do not think it is possible to find, and their presence is greatly missed by everyone in the platoon and by myself.' They were members of a well-known Ferndale family, and all were enthusiastic supporters of all kinds of sport. Another brother is still serving in France. Tom leaves a wife and three children at 17 High Street, and Henry leaves a wife and one child at 13 Lake Street.[10]

Their other brother, 16172 Private Morgan David Hardwidge, was killed in action on Christmas Day in 1916 whilst serving with the 2nd Battalion of the Welsh Regiment.

The Hardwidge brothers lie alongside each other

In a postcard to his wife Annie in Ferndale, Tom Hardwidge wrote:

My darling wife, A p.c. [postcard] in answer to your loving letter, which I've just received this morning with the first post. Haven't time to write more now, but will write you a nice long letter after I've finished work tonight and perhaps will hear something sure by then about my leave. I'm only dropping you this card now because I can see that your letter has been delayed somewhat, and I thought that you may be anxious about me, but I'm alright love. Hoping that you and the little ones are the same and you shall have a letter from me later.

Tom[11]

The brothers' obituaries in the *Rhondda Leader* read:

The Hardwidge brothers – Tom (left) and Henry (right) with their wives

HARDWIDGE – In loving memory of Lance Corporal Henry Hardwidge, the beloved husband of Jennie Hardwidge, who fell in action July 11th at Mametz Wood, Sadly missed by Wife and Children.

Your last faint whispers I should have liked to have heard,
And to breathe in your ear just one loving word,
Only those who have suffered are able to tell
The pain of the heart of not saying farewell.

HARDWIDGE – In loving memory of Corporal Tom Hardwidge, the beloved husband of Annie Hardwidge who fell in action at Mametz Wood, July 11th 1916, Sadly missed by Wife and Children.

Some may think that we've forgotten,
Some may think the wound is healed,
But out minds are always wandering
To his grave on the battlefield.[12]

Private John Robert Noyes was the son of John and Mary Noyes of 37 Taff Street in Pontypridd. He was also killed in the wood on 11 July, aged 21. He has no known grave and is remembered on the Thiepval Memorial.

John Noyes was born in 1895 and educated at the County School for Boys in Pontypridd. His father ran the family

Tom Hardwidge, front left, and other men of his battalion

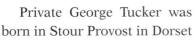

John Noyes' Medals and
Memorial Plaque

George Tucker

business, a fruiterer, in Taff Street. At the start of the war John was working in the Pontypridd Workhouse Guardians' offices. He enlisted in the 20th Welsh (3rd Rhondda) around July 1915 and underwent training with them at St Asaph. He was sent to France in early 1916 and joined the 15th Welsh there.

Private George Tucker was born in Stour Provost in Dorset but was living in Arabella Street, Roath in Cardiff when he enlisted in the 15th Welsh. He was killed during the fighting in the wood on 11 July and his body is still there. Tucker was 37 years of age and left a widow, Mary, to mourn his passing. He is remembered on the Thiepval Memorial.

115th Brigade

The battalions of the 115th were not in action again until the afternoon of 10 July when at 2 p.m. the two companies of the 10th South Wales Borderers in Pommiers Trench and Montauban Alley were in action under the 114th Brigade, and the 17th Royal Welsh Fusiliers under the 113th Brigade.

Two companies of the 11th South Wales Borderers, the 115th Trench Mortar Battery and four machine guns of the 115th Machine Gun Company were holding Caterpillar Wood, leaving just two companies of the 11th S.W.B. and the 16th Welsh to move into Mametz Wood to relieve the 113th and 114th Brigades, as ordered. This they did at 5 a.m. on the morning of 11 July.

The War Diary reports that at this time the front line was not as advanced as had been thought, the northern edge was still being held by the enemy's machine guns and infantry had been seen entering the wood from the west. The men were tired and the morale of some units was shaken, and numbers were weak. The line was straightened by Evans and Brigade Headquarters moved to the southern cross-ride. Patrols were sent out to gauge the enemy's strength and the soldiers were instructed to dig in. Five German prisoners were taken.

A message timed at 11 a.m. from Major-General Watts indicated that the German second line was being shelled and it was his opinion that the Germans could not be present in any strength in the northern sector of the wood. The 115th Brigade was ordered to attack without delay.

Staff Officer Lieutenant-Colonel Gossett arrived and gave orders that an attack to the north and west was to be carried out. Evans disagreed, pointing out that the defensive position was not completed and that some of his units were still too disorganised to be formed up for an attack. He also wanted to reconnoitre the wood beforehand. However, he eventually agreed to launch the attack at 3 p.m.

The 11th South Wales Borderers were formed up on the

right, the 17th Royal Welsh Fusiliers on the central ride and the 16th Welsh along the railway on the left. Evans wished to catch the Germans by surprise, so he ordered a bayonet attack and no artillery bombardment. Patrols were sent out to ascertain the enemy's strength and location. None were located to the west but to the north it was another story; the enemy had a strong presence with several machine guns.

Despite Evans' request, at 2.45 p.m. the British artillery opened fire, making it impossible for the infantry to advance. It lasted until 3.30 p.m. and could not be stopped as the enemy shelling had cut the communication wires once more. When it ceased Evans ordered the battalions forward. At 4.25 p.m. the officer commanding 16th Welsh stated that he was to the left of the 17th Royal Welsh Fusiliers who were unable to advance owing to heavy machine gun fire. Fourteen prisoners had been captured from the 77th Regiment, 2nd Guards Reserve Division and the 122nd Regiment of the 3rd Guards Division, who said that a thousand men had been moved into Mametz Wood during the night of 10/11 July. Colonel Frank Smith of the 16th Welsh also reported that in his opinion his men were too tired to stage a successful attack but that they had captured one enemy machine gun.

On the right, the 11th South Wales Borderers, in spite of heavy machine gun fire and stubborn resistance, had captured the north-eastern corner of the wood by 5.40 p.m., but by this time the other two battalions, having also taken casualties from their own artillery, had withdrawn to their original positions. By 6 p.m. the 11th S.W.B. had been reinforced by two companies each of the 10th S.W.B. and the 10th Welsh. The 17th R.W.F. and 16th Welsh were ordered forward again to assist.

By 8 p.m. the officer commanding the 11th South Wales Borderers reported that he was unable to move west along the northern edge of the wood as the enemy had been strongly reinforced. Meanwhile the 17th Royal Welsh Fusiliers and the 16th Welsh had been driven back by the Germans to nearly their starting positions. Evans saw at once the exposed position the 11th S.W.B. were in and ordered the commanding officer to use his own initiative as to whether to hold the ground gained or to retire to his starting position.

In the meantime, the 16th Royal Welsh Fusiliers and the 15th Welsh had seized the western edge of the wood and were digging themselves in. One platoon was sent to bomb down the northern trench towards the centre of the northern edge of the wood.

By 9.20 p.m. the 11th South Wales Borderers had been compelled to return to their original starting position, owing to the lack of support on their left. At 10.50 p.m. heavy artillery fire and trench mortar fire drove the two battalions on the western edge back to the line of the railway. The Germans tried to locate the British troops in the north of the wood by opening rifle fire at 11.20 p.m. but the British soldiers were ordered not to return fire. The Germans then searched the whole of Mametz Wood with 5.9-inch and 8-inch artillery shells throughout the night, causing considerable casualties.

The 115th Brigade was relieved at 3 a.m. on 12 July and they returned to their bivouacs. Their casualties from 6 to 12 July had been: 17 officers killed and 53 wounded; other ranks: 167 killed, 709 wounded and 162 missing.

11th South Wales Borderers (2nd Gwent)

At noon on 11 July 'C' and 'D' companies in Caterpillar and Marlborough Woods were relieved by the 8th Devonshire Regiment. 'A' and 'B' companies in Mametz Wood were also relieved. Captain Lewis and Second Lieutenant Fletcher had been killed, with Second Lieutenant Miller-Hallett being reported missing.

Captain Lawrence Reddrop Lewis was killed on 11 July, aged 34, and is listed on the Thiepval Memorial. His next of kin was a brother living in Finsbury, London.

Second Lieutenant Arthur Stanley Fletcher was killed on 11 July, aged 26, while advancing with the 11th Battalion of the South Wales Borderers. His body was never located and he is remembered on the Thiepval Memorial. He had joined the Honourable Artillery Company at the outbreak of war and had received his commission twelve months before his death. He had been at the Front for about three months. Before joining the colours he worked at Cardiff Docks with Messrs Stewart and Lloyds, iron tube manufacturers. Major T.H. Morgan wrote to his parents at 155 Mackintosh Place in Cardiff: 'His brother officers desire me to convey to you their deepest sympathy in your sad loss. Your son was nobly leading his platoon in battle with the enemy when he was struck down, and he was doing his duty well and nobly.'[13]

Second Lieutenant Stewart Alexander Miller-Hallett was 25 and married. His body was never recovered and he is commemorated on the Thiepval Memorial. A talented cricketer, he had played for Rugby in the 1908/09 seasons, and was a member of the M.C.C. since 1911. He was killed in action by machine gun fire inside Mametz Wood while carrying an important verbal message from Brigadier-General Evans, accompanied by a runner who was badly wounded but escaped.

His Colonel wrote to his parents in Chelsfield, Kent: 'I cannot tell you how much I sympathise with you on the loss of your dear boy; he had a charming personality which endeared him to us all, and was in addition a splendid Officer. Not long ago I picked him out to join our General's Staff, and I know how much he appreciated him.'

Second Lieutenant Stewart Miller-Hallett

Brigadier-General Evans wrote: 'May I add my sincere sympathy in your grievous loss? Your son was attached to my Staff. He was a gallant lad, always cheery, bright and willing, and had endeared himself to us all. He was a son I should have been proud of, and his absence causes a great blank here.'[14]

Private Arthur George Battle of the 11th Battalion South Wales Borderers was killed on 11 July. He is remembered on the Thiepval Memorial. Aged 29, he was born in Somerset but lived in Cwm, Monmouthshire.

16th Welsh (Cardiff City)

Captain Lyn Arthur Philip Harris was the only son of Mr and Mrs A.J. Harris of Llanishen in Cardiff. The commanding officer of the 16th Battalion wrote to his young widow:

> It is a very painful duty that compels me to tell you that your husband and my friend was killed on the 11th inst. He was struck by an enemy bullet and quickly passed away, but was conscious to the last. His last thoughts were of you, and his ring (which he particularly requested Dr. Pettigrew to send to you) is in the care of Captain Angus. His brother officers who survive are deeply grieved at losing a splendid comrade, whom we all admired. He was buried under heavy shellfire, and I was present with Dr. Pettigrew at his burial. The doctor, with his stretcher-bearer, after your husband died, carried him a long way to the rear of a big wood in which we were at the time of fighting to ensure he should not be lost.[15]

It was reported of him:

> The deceased officer was married in October last to Miss Mary Grant Gardiner of Llanishen. An engineer, he had every promise of attaining a high position in his profession. Captain Harris was born in 1892, and received his education at the Cardiff Intermediate School, and later at Denstone College, Staffordshire, where he served in the Officers Training Corps. At the time war broke out he was serving his apprenticeship under Mr Riches at the Caerphilly works of the Rhymney Railway Company, and had already passed the intermediate examination

Officers of the 16th Welsh: L.A.P. Harris (left) W.M. Stewart (second left)

in London for the B.Sc. degree. He joined the Public Schools Battalion of the Royal Fusiliers, and was afterwards granted a commission as second lieutenant in one of the battalions of the famous 41st Regiment. At the time of his death he was acting as adjutant of his battalion.

A pathetic incident is recorded by a correspondent, who states that a local resident received from the deceased officer a letter written before his death. When the letter arrived at its destination, however, Captain Harris had been killed.[16]

Harris was just 23 years of age and had lived in the same road in Llanishen as Frank Gaskell. He now lies buried in Dantzig Alley British Cemetery, Mametz.

On 11 July the Germans used machine guns and a flame-projector to drive the 16th Welsh back.

19th Welsh (Glamorgan Pioneers)

Serving with the 19th Battalion Welsh Regiment (Glamorgan Pioneers), Private Alfred Rich, after being reported missing on 10 July, was presumed dead on 11 July, though his body

Alfred Rich

was never recovered. Born in Bridgwater, the family had moved to Cardiff and he was educated at Grangetown School. He was 43 years of age and had volunteered for service in May of 1915. His company officer wrote to his widow:

> He was a company stretcher-bearer and along with his mate did splendid work for the company. They worked like heroes, and in spite of very heavy shelling carried wounded men to the Field Ambulance. Private Rich was a most unselfish worker, and I have mentioned him to the commanding officer on three occasions for his good work. He was very much liked by both officers and men.'[17]

Prior to the war he was for 17 years in the employment of the Cardiff Gas Light and Coke Company at Grangetown. He was a keen athlete and won several prizes in walking matches.

Private Ernest Joseph Jenkins was killed on 11 July, aged 22. He left a widow, Gertrude, at Cathays, Cardiff. He was a keen footballer and cricketer and is remembered on the Thiepval Memorial.

124th Field Company Royal Engineers

On 11 July the 124th spent time constructing strongpoints on the western flank of Mametz Wood, at the junction of the bottom edge of the wood and railway and also at the junction of Wood Support Trench with Mametz Wood. They also continued consolidating the new front line, losing six other ranks in the process before being withdrawn on 12 July.

Lance Corporal Peter Lowe Currie was a married man from Musselburgh in Scotland and was 33. He was buried in Flatiron Copse Cemetery. Sapper J. Tamplin, aged 20, was buried in the same cemetery, as was Sapper T.J. Harris.

The body of Sergeant Horace Frank Anderson was never identified and he is recalled on the Thiepval Memorial, as is Corporal John Morgan Davies, aged 19 from Treorchy, and Sapper Henry Cox, aged 33, who was a married man from Aberavon. Frank Anderson was at first reported as missing and it was not until May 1917 that it was announced that he had been killed on 11 July. Originally from Aberdare, he had joined the Royal Engineers in December 1914 and rose rapidly to the rank of sergeant three months later. He had been home on leave the previous month and was killed on his 23rd birthday. Before enlisting he was in the employment of the Powell Duffryn Steam Coal Company as a draughtsman at Aberaman.

CHAPTER 7

12 July – Coda

THE DIVISION WAS relieved and their part in the fighting for Mametz Wood was now over. The Germans had withdrawn and the wood was now in British hands but there were yet more casualties.

113th Brigade

13th Royal Welsh Fusiliers (1st North Wales)

Lieutenant-Colonel Oswald Swift Flower, the commanding officer of the 13th Royal Welsh Fusiliers, died of his wounds on 12 July, aged 45, and was buried in Morlancourt British Cemetery Number 1. He was born in Stratford-upon-Avon in 1871 and grew up in Broadway, Worcestershire. Educated at Wellington College and Jesus College, Cambridge, Flower initially joined the Royal Warwickshire Regiment but transferred to the Royal Welsh Fusiliers in 1892, serving in Crete, Malta, China (the Boxer Rebellion of 1900), Burma and India before retiring from the Army in 1913 as the result of ill health. He was twice Mentioned in Dispatches. In June 1916 he had returned home on leave and it was apparent to his family that he was ill once more. Nevertheless he insisted on returning to the Front.

Captain Leonard Stuart Ayer was the son of a draper from Holywell. A clerk with the London City and Midland Bank, He had received his commission in October 1914 and landed in France in December. Leonard died of his wounds, aged 25, on 15 July and was buried in Heilly Station Cemetery. He left a widow, Alice, residing at The Cottage, Strand, in Holywell.

114th Brigade

10th Welsh (1st Rhondda)

Captain David Jones of the 10th Welsh was killed in action on 12 July. Aged 23, his body was unable to be located and he is remembered on the Thiepval Memorial. His parents lived in Llanio, Cardiganshire. He was reported to have been buried in Mametz Wood so it is likely that his body is still there today.

A fellow officer wrote to Jones' mother in response to her query re Jones' kit:

> I don't know whether Dai had his pocket book on him or not when he was killed but most likely he had left it behind before going into action. As to his revolver and field glasses, he was wearing them when he got killed so I am very doubtful whether you will ever get them. I should have taken them off him, but seeing him dead and having been wounded I completely lost my head and forgot to search him.[1]

Lieutenant-Colonel Oswald Flower

Captain David Jones, second row, centre

Mrs Jones also sought information as to her son's last days and the manner of his death to which he replied:

As I told you in my last letter he was undoubtedly the best officer we had, and of whom the colonel had a very high opinion. To go into action he was taken away from his company in order to act as second in command of the battalion, a position filled in all other battalions in the brigade by a major. He was simply delighted at the thought of going into action. Before all our battalion had left the trench to attack, the colonel was wounded, hence the word of commanding and directing the whole battalion devolved on Dai. The trust shown in him was amply justified during the two days we were in the wood. He was everywhere, seeing to everything with spirits that cheered every officer and man who came in contact with him. We got into the wood about 5am Monday morning July 10th and remained in our first position until 2pm when the 10th were given orders to attack again. We went but had to come back owing to the fire of some hidden machine guns. At 4pm they attacked again but I was left behind as a support with a few men. Dai went on. I did not see him until 6am Tuesday morning. When talking together that morning he said, 'You didn't mind me leaving you behind yesterday Ifor did you; you are married and I am not.' That was all but what more could any one wish for from a friend who was willing to risk his life in order to leave another in comparative safety. I shall remember those words as long as I live. At 3pm Tuesday afternoon we had to deliver another attack. Dai and I went forward together and from that moment onward we were not parted for one minute until death itself parted us forever on this world. Oh what a terrible night that Tuesday night was and how well he bore up under such an ordeal. We were relieved about 7 o'clock on Wednesday morning. Dai sent all the other officers and men out of the wood. I stayed behind with him while he gave some information to the new officers. In about twenty minutes' time we started off through the wood together and were nearly out of it when that shell burst killing him and wounding me. He did not live one second, death being absolutely instantaneous. Not one groan did he utter.[2]

His mother wrote asking for the return of his personal effects and when these and the money she thought he had on his person were not immediately forthcoming, she received a brusque official response.

> Personally Mrs. Jones I think you are laboring under a false
> impression regarding the amount. Let me tell you that no
> officer is allowed to draw more than 125 francs at a time from
> the field cashier – that is a little under £5. Besides for weeks
> before the Battle we had no opportunity of visiting the cashier
> and your son was in the same boat as the rest. I am very sorry
> that you should have cast such insinuations – but I suppose
> your grief at your sad loss made you write words you did not
> intend to.[3]

Jones wrote home regularly to his parents in Welsh, though in an early letter, written in English, he wrote: 'I am very sorry I cannot write to you in Welsh. I am afraid the people in authority are not too willing because they can read all letters if they like to. Of course, they do not read letters coming out so you can go on writing in Welsh.'[4]

A letter dated 19 July was sent to his mother by an unnamed soldier of the battalion:

> I hope I am not breaking this news too sudden to you. As I
> was taking a part in an advance on the Mametz Wood I saw
> Captain Jones fall. It was a German shell that bursted very
> close by and a piece of shrapnel hit him in the side. Later on
> that day I was passing him and I found a few cards in a pocket
> case lying close by. On one of them I saw this address so I have
> sent this letter.[5]

A letter written on 26 August to Mrs Jones stated:

> The battalion went into action with the rest of the division and
> did marvellous work. As you may imagine the cost was heavy.
> Our colonel was seriously wounded – so were the company
> officers – in fact in your son's company, he alone escaped without

wounds. However, after the gallant work was done and the position consolidated, the division, covered with glory, came out of action. Your son was the last officer to come out of the wood. On his way out however he was struck by a shell and killed instantaneously. But being in such a position the burial of the body had to be left to the incoming division. Your son's body, as well as scores of others who so gallantly died for their country, was buried at Mametz.[6]

His mother's cousin wrote to her:

I viewed him as being related to the best class of boys that are on the battlefields. He had an excellent education, and on top of this, he was a religious boy in the education and attorneyship of the Lord. I'm thankful for this last point, the virtue that we do not die today, but live, yes, and live in a healthy and heavenly world.[7]

Private Llewellyn Morgan was also killed on 12 July. He was 19 years old and was a bomber, his company having twice been Mentioned in Dispatches. On one occasion he became entangled in barbed wire and came out of it with his uniform ripped to shreds. Prior to enlisting in March 1915 he had been a miner at the Aberaman Colliery and a goalkeeper with the local football team.

Second Lieutenant Thomas Yale Lloyd was also killed in action on 12 July while serving with the 10th Welsh. He was 20 and originally from Liverpool. He was buried in Flatiron Copse Cemetery.

Hiram Davies from Maesteg of the 10th Welsh fought at Mametz Wood. He later became a sergeant and was awarded the Distinguished Conduct Medal in November 1918 for skilfully organising and leading a bombing party which silenced three German machine guns.

13th Welsh (2nd Rhondda)

George Mervyn Stothert from Dinas Powys served as a Second Lieutenant with the 13th Welsh at Mametz Wood. The following year, while on patrol at Boesinghe, he was wounded by a shell

Second Lieutenant Thomas Lloyd	Hiram Davies	Second Lieutenant George Stothert

burst and died the next day at No. 12 Casualty Clearing Station. His senior officer Colonel Kennedy wrote:

> He had served under my command for 11 months and I had the greatest admiration for him. He was a very excellent and capable young soldier, and was very much liked by officers, N.C.O.s and men of the battalion. He was ever ready to do whatever was required to be done, and of late had done some very useful patrol work in his usual capable manner.[8]

Another officer wrote: 'He was such a gallant fellow and had done so splendidly previously in patrol work, and had he come through this show would have undoubtedly got the Military Cross.'[9] Stothert was Mentioned in Dispatches for gallant and distinguished service in the field.

14th Welsh (Swansea)

Private David Thomas was killed on 12 July. A communication of 6 October 1916 informed his parents that he was buried in a grave in a trench inside Mametz Wood about 50 yards on the right side of the road one and three-quarters miles north-east of Mametz, four and three-quarter miles east-north-east of Albert. Sadly, even with this information, his temporary grave could not be found, or perhaps the body identified post-war, and he is remembered on the Thiepval Memorial

The parish magazine of Cheriton and Llanmadoc carried the following article on him:

> Quite a gloom was cast over the village when it became known from the War Office that Private David Thomas had fallen in action. A previous communication to his parents stated that he was missing and possibly a prisoner of war, and we were hoping that such might prove to be true and tidings would come that he was safe. Hope dies hard. It was not to be. The rain came and wiped out the landscape. He fell at the Sergeant's side at Mametz Wood where the Swansea Battalion suffered severely. Sorrow is finding its way into quiet peaceful homes in hamlet, village, town and city. Bright lads, their parents' joy and comfort go out to the plains of France, to ancient Greece or Egypt, they go out in thousands never to return. No one when the call comes to die, can die better than a soldier's death. We were looking forward to the welcome home when the heroes of the day would recount and relate their thrilling experiences round the old kitchen fire. But for some other lips have shouted the welcome home. These are the tragedies of life that lead us through the valley of tears. The country can count upon its thousands of Rachels weeping for their children because they are not. But the boys who have never come back must be borne in remembrance. Some memorial, either in our Parish Churches or Churchyards should be erected at the end of the War to perpetuate the memory of those who have fallen. Private David Thomas was an honourable lad, trusted by all the Lieutenants in the Swansea's. When at home he was a most faithful churchman and a communicant. He has left behind him very pleasant memories in the parish and in the home. Our sympathy goes out to a sorrowing household and a large circle of relatives. A memorial service was held in Cheriton Church, when a large and reverent congregation met with manifest signs of sorrow to pay a tribute of respect to one who had endeared himself to a large number of friends, and died a noble death.[10]

Private William Henry Jones served with the 14th Welsh and was killed on 12 July. Originally from Swansea, he left a widow and was 31. He has no known grave.

Private William Jones   Private Edward Evans

15th Welsh (Carmarthenshire)

Sergeant Edward Evans, a miner from Salop, served with the 15th Welsh. He survived the war and was awarded the Distinguished Conduct Medal for 'fearless courage' at Chateau Angles in October 1918 when he and two other men captured a German officer and 40 other ranks. He never discussed this with his family and the award of the D.C.M. only came to light after his death. After the war ended he emigrated to Canada to work on the railways and when he returned to south Wales he went back to work underground – in his 50s.

115th Brigade

10th and 11th South Wales Borderers (1st and 2nd Gwent)

A number of officers of the 10th and 11th South Wales Borderers were brought to the attention of Brigadier Evans for good work. Among them was Captain Evan Thomas Rees, who before enlisting had been a schoolteacher at Cadoxton School in Barry. Rees was awarded the Military Cross for his gallantry. He had enlisted in the Army as a private in

September 1914, aged 31, and after a course of training at Sandringham he was appointed to a commission with the South Wales Borderers in 1915, obtaining his captaincy and majority in rapid succession in 1916. In December 1917, Rees was promoted to Lieutenant-Colonel, gazetted to the command of the 7th Battalion Norfolk Regiment and was mentioned by Haig in his dispatches. Rees was wounded and taken prisoner by the Germans during their spring offensive of 1918, winning the D.S.O. for his courage in holding a post against the enemy.

Other 10th Battalion officers mentioned were: Captain Arthur Galsworthy, who was wounded as well as being commended, and Lieutenant and Adjutant Edgar Francis Orford, who was awarded the Military Cross and later the Distinguished Conduct Medal.

From the 11th Battalion: Colonel J.R. Gaussen who had previously been Mentioned in Dispatches and was later to be awarded the Distinguished Service Order, Captain E.F. Browning, Second Lieutenants T.H. Davies and Richard Mortimer Heppel.

Evan Rees, second from left standing, as a teacher at Cadoxton School, Barry, pre-war

16th Welsh (Cardiff City)

George Osborne was a collier who enlisted in the 16th Welsh in November 1914. He had previously served in the Gloucestershire Regiment so was quickly promoted to Company Sergeant-Major. After surviving the fighting at Mametz Wood, his health began to deteriorate due to the conditions at the Front. By 1917, aged 43, he was reported to be suffering from several muscular and bronchial ailments, which left him 50 per cent disabled. He was discharged in August 1917 and attended army medical boards in 1918 and 1919. He died on 13 February 1920 and was buried in St Woolos Cemetery in Newport, with a Commonwealth War Graves' headstone as his death was brought on by his military service.

Ernest Errington King was commissioned as a Second Lieutenant into the 16th Welsh in December 1914 and first went to France at the end of the following year. He took part in the attack on 7 July and remained on regular frontline duties with the battalion until early 1917 – latterly as second in command in the rank of Acting Major – when he was posted to Brigade H.Q. for Staff Officer duties. He was awarded the Military Cross for his actions during the Battle of Passchendaele in 1917. His citation read:

> For conspicuous gallantry and devotion to duty. He displayed untiring energy in his efforts to maintain forward dumps by means of mule convoy, repeatedly passing through the enemy's barrage to bring up fresh supplies. It was due to his initiative and fearlessness that the forward brigade dump was able to meet all demands of units throughout the operations.[11]

Frederick Tyler enlisted in the 16th Welsh in December 1914 and was wounded at Mametz Wood, suffering shrapnel wounds to both legs. He was treated in Radyr Hospital and then sent back to the Front. He was later transferred to the Shropshire Light Infantry and is pictured here in the last year of the war.

Ernest King

Private Frederick Tyler

113th Siege Battery Royal Garrison Artillery

This battery provided supporting fire for the infantry attacks. Frank Peachey Lewis from Penarth was a dental mechanic who joined the 113th Siege Battery pre-war, as it was then a local Territorial unit, based on the coast at Lavernock near Penarth. Frank was killed, aged 25, on 18 July 1916 at Montauban. He is commemorated on the Thiepval Memorial as one of the missing. His brother John was killed in October 1916 while serving with the 89th Company Machine Gun Corps.

Henry White was part of the same unit and went to France in June 1916. He was killed at the end of August 1916 on the Somme, possibly near Delville Wood, aged 18, and was buried in Peronne Road Cemetery, Maricourt.

38th Signal Company Royal Engineers

Pioneer Horace Edward Hall was born in Penarth. He was killed on 12 July, aged 20, while serving with the 38th Signal Company. He was buried in Flatiron Copse Cemetery.

131st Field Ambulance

Private Thomas David Williams, from Coity near Bridgend, was 21 and serving with the 131st Field Ambulance when he was killed on 12 July after helping wounded men for 72 hours under heavy shellfire. Killed alongside him was Private William J. Lewis and they are buried in the same row in Carnoy Military Cemetery, close to each other.

An officer wrote to William Lewis' parents in Merthyr describing his fate:

> He died nobly while carrying a wounded man from the trenches, and you have one consolation that it was while succouring others he met his own death. His death was instantaneous and he suffered no pain. He was always so cheerful in all circumstances. Will was always singing and joking and I used to find that his singing cheered us all up. I always regarded him as a perfectly straight boy, who never shirked his duty, the soul of brightness and lightness of heart.[12]

The parents of Thomas Williams received a certificate of honour commemorating the devotion to duty of their son. His Sergeant-Major wrote:

> It may comfort you to know from the nature of his wounds he must have died at once, and without pain. He was killed while in the act of attending the wounded under heavy shellfire. When all are heroes it is not well to make exceptions, but your boy was as good as the best. On hearing of his death I asked that, if possible, he should be brought in, and some of his comrades at considerable risk to themselves succeeded in doing this.[13]

It is important to also recall those men who were wounded during the various assaults on Mametz Wood but who never recovered from their wounds. Some were to die months afterwards. Some were disfigured for life; some suffered the horrors of shell shock. Private Stanley Smale of the 14th Welsh was severely wounded at Mametz Wood and brought home to

Britain for treatment. Unfortunately, he never recovered and died of his wounds on 23 September 1916. He was laid to rest in Cockett Cemetery, Swansea, in the presence of his family, including his fiancée. Before the war he had worked for the South Wales Transport Company.

Private William Henry Peters of the 15th Welsh was wounded in his left scapula by shell shrapnel. On repatriation, his mother was summoned to the hospital. As he had lost so much blood it was feared he would die; the shrapnel embedded in his left shoulder was consistently severing an artery. He survived and the shrapnel was finally removed whereupon he had it made into a key ring. Peters' left arm was paralysed and his left hand, which had withered, was eventually amputated. He was discharged in November 1917 from the County of Middlesex War Hospital in St Albans.

Private William Peters, seated left, with fellow soldiers of the 15th Welsh

CHAPTER 8

The Aftermath

THE FIGHTING FOR Mametz Wood was now over. The 38th (Welsh) Division had incurred nearly 4,000 casualties – about a third of its infantry strength. The constituent battalions were now moved out of the line for rest and refitting. Despite the difficult task they had been set they had accomplished it, and in a relatively short space of time. But the ramifications and accusations rumbled on, and the legacy of Mametz Wood is that it is often deemed that it was not until the Battle of Passchendaele, or Third Ypres, specifically the capture of Pilckem Ridge, that the division was to have its honour restored.

The losses of the 38th Division were:

Killed	46 officers	556 other ranks
Wounded	138 officers	2,668 other ranks
Missing	6 officers	579 other ranks
Total	190 officers	3,803 other ranks[1]

Some 400 German prisoners were taken from five different regiments, the 114th Brigade capturing half of these and two artillery guns. The battalions of this brigade were observed to be carrying many German pickelhaubes.

Captain J.C. Dunn of the 23rd Royal Welsh Fusiliers reached the area on the 12 July and commented:

Some of us went exploring in Mametz Wood, where the Welsh Division was so mishandled, and there were nasty sights… There was angry complaint that our artillery support was poor and misdirected, and that messages to Division went unheeded. As the scraps were put together a local disaster took form. The German

189

guns were splendidly served, the machine guns were sufficient and artfully placed.[2]

Captain Llewellyn Evans of the same battalion wrote: 'I was a unit in the 13th R.W.F. of the 113th Brigade. We attacked en masse from the south-east, and fought for yards of ground thickly held by an enemy with no thought of retreat... On our immediate front were only courageous rearguards, well supported by artillery, covering their retreating main body.'[3]

Captain A. Radclyffe Dugmore of the King's Own Light Infantry passed through the battlefield some time after the fighting had ceased. He wrote:

> The scene around the outskirts and edge of Mametz Wood was simply indescribable. The whole place was literally carpeted with bodies, the enemy having put up an especially vigorous resistance in the attempt to hold the Wood. Considering that he was most thoroughly entrenched and had the protection of the wood, it struck me as marvellous that our men had succeeded in winning. They had had to rush over a wide stretch of absolutely open country without a particle of shelter except what was afforded by the shell holes, and it was uphill all the way from the road. What terrible execution they wrought among the enemy was very evident, for the trenches were in many places piled three and four deep with bodies.[4]

Captain Rowland Feilding of the Coldstream Guards witnessed the wounded being brought back from the ground in front of Mametz Wood on 8 July: 'The wounded were being carried back in streams, all covered from head to foot with the mud in which they had been fighting, slimy and glistening like seals. It looks more and more as if Hell cannot be much worse than what our infantry is going through at the present moment.'[5]

Private J.E. Roberts of the 2nd Battalion Royal Welsh Fusiliers was a pre-war soldier. He wrote: 'We got to Mametz Wood – many of our dead were lying about. Mametz Wood was full of Germans and ours – dead and blown up like balloons.'[6]

Samuel Williams entered the wood on 13 July: 'Walking

through the middle of land that had been churned up by the bombardment – and bodies of soldiers killed in the forces around us... I remember seeing a German soldier had been chained to his machine gun.'[7]

More famously, Francis Philip Woodruff, writing under the pseudonym 'Frank Richards', of the same battalion, arrived in the area a few days after the battle had ended and wrote:

We arrived on the Somme by a six days march from the railhead, and early in the morning of the 15th July passed through Fricourt, where our First Battalion had broken through on 1st July, and arrived at the end of Mametz Wood which had been captured some days before by the 38th Welsh Division which included four of our new service battalions. The enemy had been sending over tear-gas and the valley was thick with it. It smelt like strong onions which made our eyes and noses run very badly; we were soon coughing, sneezing and cursing. We rested in shell holes, the ground all around us being thick with dead of the troops who had been attacking Mametz Wood.[8]

Second Lieutenant Charles Pritchard Clayton of the 2nd Welsh Regiment advanced past the battlefield in front of Mametz Wood in August. For over a month the bodies of the dead lay unburied owing to artillery and machine gun fire from the German lines. He wrote:

Mametz Wood is for the most part a mass of stumps and mangled branches. The track [to the wood] has been made by throwing faggots and branches across a narrow opening which has been cleared, and throwing earth and stones into the spaces between. As we climb to higher ground we find a deep hollow running up on our left. The slope on the opposite side of the hollow is bare and there, lying in rows, each a few paces from the other, we can see the dead bodies of men who fell in the earlier attack. They were evidently caught by machine gun fire which probably came from the wood we are now passing through. On the ground right in the track lies the body of a young British officer, sprawled face down. He has been dead some time, but his uniform seems spotless and a perfect fit. His spick and span appearance seems to bring death closer.[9]

The writer Gerald Brenan who was serving with the 5th Battalion of the Gloucestershire Regiment described his visit to Mametz Wood:

> What seemed extraordinary was that all the dead bodies there lay just as they had fallen in their original places, as though they were being kept as an exhibit for a war museum. Germans in their field-grey, British in their khaki lying side by side, their faces and their hands a pale waxy green, the colour of rare marble. Heads covered with flat mushroom helmets next to heads in domed steel helmets that came down behind the ears. Some of these figures still sat with their backs against a tree and two of them – this had to be seen to be believed – stood locked together by their bayonets which had pierced one another's bodies and sustained in that position by the tree trunk against which they had fallen. I felt I was visiting a room in Madame Tussaud's Chamber of Horrors, for I could not imagine any of these bodies ever having been alive. Yet the effect in its morbid way was beautiful.[10]

Luther Morley of the 11th South Wales Borderers later drew a stark diagram of the location of the burials.

Luther Morley's diagram showing where the dead were laid out after the fighting moved on

192

An unnamed Irish soldier wrote:

The bodies of the Welsh soldiers that were killed fighting for the
woods were so numerous, and the amount of remaining men to
bury them so few, that it meant a large number were lying on the
ground the entire time I was there. Rigor mortis had begun, with
the scorching sun further speeding the terrible process. No longer
can anyone claim that war is romantic who has been testament to
the sight of rotting bodies that have been neglected without care and
understanding that what remains is a person that was once loved.[11]

In his 1918 work on the war, Arthur Conan Doyle wrote of
the difficulties facing the attackers:

It is impossible to imagine anything more difficult and involved
than some of this fighting, for apart from the abattis and other
natural impediments of a tangled wood, the place was a perfect
rabbit-warren of trenches, and had occasional land mines in it,
which were exploded – some of them prematurely, so that it was
the retreating Germans who received the full force of the blast.
Burning petrol was also used continually in the defence, and
frequently proved to be a two-edged weapon.

Some of the garrison stood to their work with extraordinary
courage, and nothing but the most devoted valour upon the part
of their assailants could have driven them out. 'Every man of them
was killed where he stood,' said a Welsh Fusilier, in describing the
resistance of one group. 'They refused offers of quarter right to the
last, and died with cheers for the Kaiser or words of defiance on
their lips. They were brave men, and we were very sorry indeed
to have to kill them, for we could not but admire them for their
courage.'[12]

The official history of the Welsh Regiment spends some
time deliberating on the Division's failure to capture the whole
of the wood. It begins with the failure of the 13th Welsh to
capture The Hammerhead owing to their loss of direction;
113th Brigade is cited wholesale for its failure to capture their
first objective on 10 July.

A failure of leadership inside the wood was due to the heavy casualties amongst officers and N.C.O.s, and nowhere more than wood fighting is leadership necessary, for men lose their way and become disorientated. Officers alone had compasses and without their leadership the men lost direction and cohesion.

There was nothing wrong with the fighting spirit of the men but it was important to remember the strength of the enemy. Lieutenant-Colonel Hayes wrote that he saw many German machine gun pits, each with dead Germans and he paid tribute to the courage of the enemy resistance. 'Among the troops in the wood were two companies of the Lehr Regiment, an instructional depot for the Prussian Guards, composed of men of big stature, who fought splendidly.'[13]

> There is no doubt that the Germans were at this period our superiors in wood fighting owing to their large number of trained officers and N.C.O.s. The 38th Division had carried out a few raids but had never been exercised in such manoeuvres as wood fighting. The numbers of enemy dead, especially on the southern and eastern edges of the wood were very great.[14]

Brigadier-General Evans of 115th Brigade criticised Divisional Orders for not taking into account the difficulties of wood fighting and being too rigid in their timings and too ambitious in their expectations, given the dense nature of the undergrowth, even if no opposition had been encountered. He reiterated his earlier concern that he had not been closely involved in the preparation of the artillery support. He criticised the method of communication between the brigade and the artillery via Divisional Headquarters as being too slow and not responsive enough. The bad weather had played its part too, making the ground heavy for the advancing troop and clogging up the communication trenches.

Evans also highlighted the difficulties of communication and the delay caused when telephone lines were cut and he had had to rely on runners. He stated that, as an example, it had taken him 45 minutes to go from the Advanced Brigade Headquarters to the front line, a distance of about 2,000 yards.

The orders issued to his brigade were also criticised as, although the orders made clear the 115th were to relieve the 113th and 114th brigades, they gave no intimation that an immediate attack was to be carried out. His men had been in action for most of the previous day and night. The units they were relieving were scattered and disorganised, and there was no clear line from which to mount the attack. Re-organisation, collection of units and the establishment of the line were the first prerequisites, followed by a through reconnaissance of the German positions. Only then could an attack with the possibility of success be launched.

He wrote that Lieutenant-Colonel Gossett seemed unaware of the arrangements for the artillery barrage, and, even worse, may have failed to inform the General Officer Commanding that if the artillery barrage went ahead it would fall on the brigade's line, which caused considerable casualties. It shook the survivors and caused the attack to be postponed until the men could be rallied. Further, the artillery support that Evans did ask for did not materialise and this, coupled with the denseness of the undergrowth, impeded the progress of the advance.

Despite these obstacles, the battalions did succeed in taking the north-eastern corner of the wood but could not hold it owing to exhaustion and lack of reinforcements.

Evans suggested improvements for the future. He stated that if an immediate action was required, then the fullest possible information as to the other arms involved in the operation be given to the commander ordered to carry out the attack, so that he could make the appropriate dispositions. He even went so far as to name the officers and men, down to private soldier level, whom he considered worthy of mention for services during this period – an attitude in complete contrast to that of Price-Davies.

His concerns are supported by the official history of the South Wales Borderers when it states:

> Mametz Wood had been an exhausting and searching trial for
> the two Gwent battalions. In their six months of trench warfare
> neither had had to go over the top and it was hard to have to
> carry out their first attack in a wood of such thickness and
> magnitude, in bad weather, when rains had made communication
> trenches impassable and going over the open difficult. There
> was much delay over getting and directing artillery assistance,
> communication between headquarters and the units in action was
> more than usually uncertain and slow, and little time was given to
> reconnoitre or to prepare for each successive operation.[15]

The attack by 115th Brigade is described as a small attack to test the enemy's strength. On the other hand, the attack on 10 July is described as 'one of the most magnificent sights of the war. In the words of officers of a neighbouring division wave after wave of men were seen advancing without hesitation and without a break.'[16]

Despite Price-Davies' somewhat less than enthusiastic evaluation of his brigade, and in particular of the 14th Royal Welsh Fusiliers, and repeated reference to 'panic' in the wood without an understanding that wood fighting is the most nerve-racking form of combat, the Commander-in-Chief had no hesitation in sending this message to the 113th Infantry Brigade on 11 July: 'The C-in-C desires to express his appreciation to all ranks of the 38th (Welsh) Division for the splendid response made to his appeal for a special effort yesterday.'[17]

On 16 July, Price-Davies was even more critical of the actions of his own soldiers than he had been in his report of 14 July. While continuing to praise the gallantry shown in the advance across open ground to the wood, he wrote:

> By the time the first objective was reached the sting had gone from
> the attack and a certain degree of demoralisation set in. The desire
> to press on had vanished and it was only by the most strenuous

efforts on the part of a few officers that it was possible to make progress. The demoralisation increased towards evening on the 10th and culminated in a disgraceful panic during which many left the wood. Whilst others seemed quite incapable of understanding, or unwilling to carry out the simplest order. A few stout-hearted Germans would have stampeded the whole of the troops in the wood.[18]

This is a curious interpretation of events inside Mametz Wood. The lines of soldiers of the Royal Welsh Fusiliers had advanced towards the wood without cover in the face of heavy fire which makes it all the more incomprehensible why their courage should have deserted them when they reached the cover of the undergrowth and trees. The survivors' accounts give no indication of such a malaise and one wonders how much of this was misrepresented to Price-Davies. In his own words he only saw a party of men leaving the wood, not as many as he alludes to above.

During the night when shadows, noises and movement would be exaggerated, the soldiers were naturally nervous of any perceived attempt by the Germans to creep up on them or to launch a full-scale counter-attack. They would, of course, fire rounds off at any such disturbance and, as it is easy to lose one's sense of direction in a wood, it is perfectly feasible that they would have fired into groups of men on their own side. They are criticised for this, yet there is little official criticism of the British artillery, which killed a fair number of men on their own side.

Price-Davies then wrote that while he wished to give credit for successes, failure should be faced and he instructed his battalion commanders to tell all ranks that they must make a more determined effort in the future and make greater sacrifice.

One glance at the casualty figures for the 113th Infantry Brigade shows up the nonsense of this statement. The 13th Battalion lost nine officers and 218 other ranks; the 14th 17 officers and 299 other ranks; the 15th six officers and 235 other ranks, the 16th eight officers and 280 other ranks and the 113th Machine Gun Company two officers and 28 other ranks. This represents a total of over 1,000 men who were killed, wounded or missing – a huge sacrifice equivalent to over a battalion in itself.

Price-Davies then criticises the battalions N.C.O.s for not backing their officers and failing to ensure their men obey orders but the source of this misinformation is unclear.

Moving on to the treatment of the wounded he states that only stretcher-bearers should be allowed to take wounded men out of the firing line, not able-bodied ordinary soldiers. Even the escorting of prisoners is reviewed, with a recommendation of one armed soldier to every ten German prisoners, the implication being that the soldiers of the Royal Welsh Fusiliers were happy to escort a mere handful of prisoners to the rear in order to remove themselves from front-line action and the danger it held.

Then came the threat: 'In future battle police will be established to take the names of all such shirkers who will be tried by Court Martial.'[19]

Reading his interpretation of the events one would have imagined that the battle had been lost and Mametz Wood not taken after days of bloody fighting, with the commensurate loss of life on both sides. This was not Price-Davies' viewpoint, though as he went on to belittle the efforts of the soldiers to take the wood: 'After the wood had been entered no very serious opposition was experienced, and there was very little hostile artillery fire. Moreover, the Brigade was not called upon to repel any serious consequences.'[20]

His praise was however reserved for the dead senior officers:

In particular the names of Lieutenant-Colonel Flower, Lieutenant-Colonel Carden and Major Wills should ever be remembered by us as officers who have set us a glorious example, an example we should all endeavour to copy. Such officers can never be replaced but it is hoped that their courage and self sacrifice may long act as an inspiration to those who witnessed their gallant conduct.[21]

This message to the battalion commanding officers had obviously generated a hostile response as, on 20 July, Price-Davies wrote a confidential document to the headquarters of 38th Division, prompted, one suspects, by criticism of his earlier memorandum.

He began by giving the sources for his original interpretation of events in Mametz Wood – the accounts furnished by the battalion commanders themselves and from his own personal experience. He then backtracked, claiming to have subsequently heard accounts of gallantry performed by officers and other ranks. This had led to a change of mind and now he feels 'that possibly I may not have given my Brigade full credit for what they did.'[22]

He claimed that this erroneous impression was also created by 'the discreditable behaviour of the men of the Division who fled in panic at about 8.45pm on July 10th.'[23] He then stated that he did not wish to brag about the success of his Brigade in capturing field guns in the wood, the number of German machine guns they took as well as the difficult task they faced, and overcame, of attacking through thick wood in the presence of enemy snipers and machine guns. Citing the difficulty of the soldiers who faced a similar challenge in High Wood and Trônes Wood, he concluded by admitting he had painted a gloomier picture of the behaviour of his troops than he should have done.

By this time though the damage to the reputation of the division had been done and for that Price-Davies' irresponsible report must take the blame. Not that this was the end of the damning analysis. On 23 July, Captain Bentley, who had signed Price-Davies' 16 July document, put his signature to another document. This time the focus was on two perceived deficiencies of the Brigade.

Firstly, that when the initial objective was taken the position was not maintained by digging in and consolidated with Lewis Guns. Then Bentley turned his attention to those retiring from the front line.

> The danger of ANYONE, even officers, leaving the front line once he has arrived there cannot be too strongly emphasised... You should make a serious effort to instil into your men that the word 'retire' is not to be used and that any man using it is liable to be shot on the spot... Officers must deal with all cases of indiscipline of this nature which can only be stamped out by the most dramatic action. All ranks must realise that there will always be someone who will make use of the word 'retire' and they must, therefore, be prepared to disregard it.[24]

Clearly the focus had now shifted to the underperformance of the junior officers and their apparent lack of discipline. This appears to be at odds with Price-Davies' earlier missive and one wonders upon what evidence Bentley was basing his conclusions, or why this criticism of the battalions persisted when the objective had been won at such great cost of life, with several references to the gallantry of the men concerned. Was this due to criticism levelled at the Brigade, or at Price-Davies by the other Brigade Commanders?

In *Wales: its part in the War* (1919) it was stated: 'It must be left to the military historians of the future to record the doings of the Welsh battalions in the Battle of the Somme, where the newly-formed 38th (Welsh Division), which was recruited with men from every part of Wales, covered itself with glory in the famous attack on Mametz Wood.'[25]

However, the damage had been done, and while amongst the officers and ordinary ranks there was huge pride in their achievement, at higher levels doubt had been cast on the ability of the 38th (Welsh) Division and its perceived underperformance. This erroneous perception still lingers.

CHAPTER 9

The Survivors' Accounts

Contemporary Published Accounts, 1916

The newspapers were thirsty for accounts of the battle and were quick to interview survivors, many of them now in hospital beds in Britain. On 20 July 1916, *The Western Mail* published accounts by unnamed wounded officers:

IRRESTIBLE RUSH OF THE WELSH
Thrilling stories are told by wounded Welsh officers new in hospital in London of how the Welsh, whose raising was the result of Mr Lloyd George's Queens-hall idea, acquitted themselves in the tremendous struggle for the woods after the 'Great Push' had started. They were able to capture important positions and to lay the sure and certain foundations for the great victory. All the battalions concerned received the highest praise for the skill and tenacity with which they carried out operations of the most difficult kind. I had tonight a graphic description of the fighting from an officer who belongs to the London battalion which has already been mentioned in dispatches, and which had the honour of leading the great attack upon the woods last Monday week. [10 July]

'On the Monday morning,' he said, 'we went forward on the greatest adventure we had undertaken since our arrival in France. Everybody knows that Sir Douglas Haig wanted the woods, whatever effort might be necessary to secure them. It was a glorious opportunity for the Welsh to distinguish themselves, and the men went forward determined to strike hard for the glory of Gwalia.

'We attacked soon after dawn under the cover of an artillery fire which was in every way splendid. Our troops rushed forwards like one man – no one hesitated, but clenched his teeth as he went forward to use his last ounce of strength so that no defection of his might cast additional burden on any comrade. It is in this spirit the Welsh troops have been trained. It was not lacking when the great test came. Brave officers, many of whom have paid the greatest sacrifice of all, led the attack, and the troops responded to their call in a mighty irresistible rush down an embankment and across the little plateau, which narrowed considerably before the entrance to the woods was reached.

'The enemy was strongly positioned, and the moment the troops reached the steep bank a merciless machine gun fire opened up on every point – many times more severe, it seemed, than that to which we were subjected as we left the shelter of the embankment. But, though comrades went down right across the line, the general body of troops never wavered, and position after position in the woods was captured and consolidated.

'Fighting continued without a break from half-past five that morning till late at night. Nor did it cease altogether even then, for not a single position did the enemy yield without persistent counter-attacks, some of which were violently made under the cover of darkness. When dawn came fighting re-commenced in all its fury, and the Welsh troops continued their successful effort, which enabled the reinforcements to resume the attack on the enemy with a more certain prospect of success, for when the Welshmen had done their work and the time for a retirement of a well-nigh exhausted battalion came, the Germans now languishing under the strain of so persistently violent an onslaught, had to meet the attack of fresh and eager units, with what results the world by this time knows.'[1]

This was underlined by another article in the same edition:

A WELSH BATTALION 'BEHAVED SPLENDIDLY IN PRESENT BATTLE'
The commanding officer of a well-known Welsh battalion, writing to the Lord Mayor of Cardiff, states:-

'The battalion were engaged on the 7th, 10th, 11th and 12th of July in the heavy fighting now in progress. The men behaved splendidly. We have lost a number of officers and men, but that, of course, must be, much as we deplore their loss.

'Our men took a German machine gun, which I hope to be spared to hand to you for the city. I cannot go into details, for obvious reason, but our men are second to none.'[2]

The same edition also noted the fate of Ivor Philipps:

Major-General Ivor Philipps, D.S.O., M.P., is now at home on leave at his Pembrokeshire seat, Cosheston Hall, near Pembroke. General Philipps, who assisted in raising a division, was for some months Parliamentary and military secretary to the Ministry of Munitions, but at the special request of Lord Kitchener relinquished the post to resume command. He had been some months in the fighting line.[3]

Philipps gave an interview to a reporter:

Major-General Ivor Philipps appears to have stood the rigours of the campaign extremely well. He told an interviewer that his services were now, as they always had been, entirely at the service of his country.

Referring to the Welsh Division, he said that he thought everyone in Wales should be proud of this fine body of men, who had acquitted themselves splendidly in the battle of the Somme, during eight days of which he was present. 'The Welsh Division is absolutely splendid,' he said enthusiastically. 'It is a splendid division with a splendid spirit right through it. The men are in excellent health, cheery and bright. Although the rain and mud were for a time beyond description, the men, in spite of all hardships, were never depressed, and when the time for action came they acquitted themselves in a manner beyond all praise.'[4]

The wounded continued to be brought back:

One hundred and forty-three wounded men who have been taking part in 'The Great Push' reached Cardiff by ambulance train on Tuesday, and were taken to the local sectional hospitals of the 3rd Western General Hospital, of which Colonel David Hepburn, M.D., is the directing chief. The percentage of badly-wounded was the largest in any single convoy so far received at the Welsh

Metropolis, stretchers having to be requisitioned for no fewer than 138 of the arrivals.[5]

Private Trevor Chowles wrote to his brother from the military hospital at Stratford-upon-Avon:

Just a few lines to let you know that I am one of the lucky ones to come out of a place in France called Mametz Wood. I expect you have read about it; it was terrible. My left leg is fractured, and my right leg slightly wounded. I think myself very lucky to come back alive. We started charging at 4 am. I got hit at 4.45am. I was lying wounded for 37 hours before anyone came near me. We drove the enemy out alright and captured about 250 prisoners, but a lot of our chaps got killed and wounded. I thought I was going to Cardiff Hospital but it was full up.[6]

By August 1916 there was no doubt that in addition to the dozens of photographs of the fallen from other theatres that appeared in each newspaper, a large number of Welsh casualties had occurred at Mametz Wood.

HEAVY TOLL OF WELSH REGIMENTS
The official lists recording casualties among officers issued on Monday include 21 names associated with Welsh regiments. One of the most striking features of the rank and file casualties… is the considerable number of men of Welsh regiments who have been killed or wounded. Right nobly have they "done their bit" in the recent great advance.[7]

The press was still keen to focus on the gallantry of the individual soldier though and later carried a report of a conversation between royalty and a wounded soldier:

After attacking the Mametz Wood, on which occasion both bones in one of his legs were injured, Private Thomas J. Price of the Welsh Regiment, son of Mr T. Price, stationmaster, Dowlais, was removed to Hampstead General Hospital, London, and the best hopes are entertained of saving the limb. Whilst in hospital Private Price had the honour of a visit from their Majesties the King and

Queen, with whom was the Grand Duke Michael of Russia, and they greatly cheered the wounded by their free conversation and encouraging words.

King George, addressing Private Price, put the question:-
'Where did you get wounded?'
'At Mametz Wood, your Majesty,' was the reply.
'It was warm work there,' continued the King.
'Yes, your Majesty, but our division drove them out,' was the confidential utterance of Private Price.
'Yes, the Welsh did right well!' was King George's delightful response.

Before the King and his party went to another room in the hospital and bid the wounded a pleasant adieu, the Grand Duke Michael presented each of the occupants with a splendid, massive pipe, which they greatly cherish.

Young Price, who had only just turned his sixteenth year when he enlisted in May last year, was previously engaged by the Brecon and Merthyr Railway Company as booking clerk at Dowlais, and later at Aberbargoed and Pengam Stations.[8]

Tom Price was later instrumental in raising the profile of a campaign to have a permanent memorial to the 38th Division erected in honour of his fallen comrades.

This letter appeared on 1 August from an unknown writer from Clydach in Swansea:

Just a few lines to let you know that I am back in England. I got wounded on July 10th at Mametz Wood, and I have been here for four days. I got a bullet through the top thick part of my left arm and it came out through the back. I don't think it has touched the bone, as it is not very painful. I also had a bit of shrapnel hit me in the hand and one finger and bruised my back, like a falling tree, but these are only small things and the leg is the worst. Have you heard from Oscar and Frank? The last I saw of Oscar he was dressing Willo Cole's feet. I never saw Frank after we went over the top. We lost a lot of men going over, as we had 600 yards of open ground before we entered the wood. Major Dyson Williams had it badly in the right arm and side, but he put his revolver in the other hand and shot about six Boches after. It wasn't half exciting and the boys went over singing and laughing and smoking, and were all glad to get into the wood and start slinging bombs, as we carried bags full of them. Fred Moss had about six of our men blown up near him and they fell on top of him and buried him but I think he is all right. There is one consolation – we took the wood all right.[9]

Major Dyson Brock Williams survived the war and was subsequently awarded the Distinguished Service Order by the King at Buckingham Place to add to his Military Cross. A Swansea cricketer, he had helped form the Swansea Battalion of the Welsh Regiment. He was wounded in the lung but recovered to take part in the fighting at Third Ypres in 1917. In 1919 he marched through Swansea at the head of his battalion but his experiences on the Western Front left him a changed man.

Shortly after his mother's death in 1921 Williams told a friend he felt 'desolate' and was soon bankrupt. Not only had he business losses, but he also had interest on loans and gambling debts. He vanished soon after the bankruptcy hearing but his brother managed to trace him and sheltered him in his Maidenhead home. Soon afterwards Williams worked with an old army friend, Major Arnold Wilson, to promote the George Carpentier-Kid Lewis World Light-Heavyweight fight, but Brock Williams then suffered another relapse. He resumed gambling and his cheques bounced, including one for £200. He

sailed for Belgium and began playing the casinos but on 18 April 1922 he committed suicide in London. The cleaner found his room filled with gas and his body on the floor. Major Wilson later blamed the war for his friend's sad decline.

Major Dyson Brock Williams

An impression of the nature of the fighting was given by Lieutenant W.R.M. Gwynne, Royal Engineers, who was wounded in Mametz Wood on 11 July. Recuperating at home in Swansea he was interviewed by a reporter in August:

'After the British had taken the wood,' he proceeded, 'we constructed two "strong points", and were out there for 28 hours. We had just been relieved, and were going to the back of the firing line when a shrapnel shell burst over us and two of my men and myself were hit. I was struck in both legs by shrapnel bullets which went clean through the flesh. Had it not been for the shrapnel-proof helmets we were wearing, I believe we should have all been finished off. I walked a distance of about 100 yards, and then became semi-conscious, having lost a good deal of blood.'[10]

From the casualty clearing station Lieutenant Gwynne was conveyed to a base hospital, and later to the 3rd London General Hospital at Wandsworth, where he remained for seven weeks. His recovery was hindered by complications and he was only able to take limited exercise.

Questioned as to his feelings in the midst of an artillery bombardment, the young lieutenant – he was only 21 years of age – said:

It is a most peculiar effect on one. You cannot really adequately describe the sensation felt at the continued deafening roar of the guns and the incessant rain of shells. At Mametz the British artillery set up an intense bombardment, and shells were being poured into the German positions at the rate, I should think, of 100 to 150 a minute. The Germans were in a terrible funk about it, and gave themselves up in droves.

Two days before the British took Mametz Wood the Boches peppered Mametz with 'weeping' shells and we had to put on our goggles. These lachrymatory shells give off a rather sweet smell, but they make tears come to the eyes and eventually, if you don't resort to your goggles, you get so bad that you cannot see.[11]

Writing to a friend at Fforestfach in Swansea from his hospital bed in Cheshire, Private D. Jones said:

> I was one of the first to be on top of the Huns in Mametz Wood, planting bombs among them as quickly as my fingers could pull the pins out. It's a miracle how I came out alive as my clothes were torn by bullets and shrapnel. I was hit three times and think I came out alive through not being broad. I well remember one of the Bosches who fired at me at only seven yards' range. He missed the mark, and before he could reload I hit him full in the chest with a bomb and up he went. That enchanted wood was a fair hell, what with the rifle firing, bombs, mortars, high explosives. Together with the groans of the wounded and dying, and the Huns shouting for mercy and firing at every opportunity, and the Welsh cursing, blinding and strafing them. All at once something exploded near me, hit me in the arm, and blew me up a few yards. Falling into a deep shell hole I lay low awhile and then started on my way back to the R.A.M.C. The Germans were sniping them and also the wounded, and I had to make sharp sprints from one shell hole to another like a rabbit. In these holes I saw some pitiful sights. There were men who had legs and arms blown off, and others who, having been shot in the stomach, had crawled in from machine gun fire, but only to die.[12]

A dramatic account of his escape from death at Mametz Wood was supplied by Sergeant Vincent Watkins of the machine gun section, Welsh Regiment, from Cadoxton, Barry, when writing to his wife from Halesworth Hospital in Suffolk:

> I was turning to see where the other gun was when I was shot in the chest, and I had quite a lively time getting away. I rolled into a shell hole, but I hadn't been there long before a big howitzer shell dropped about a yard away on the left and buried me completely, and I said 'finish' then. Two of our boys, advancing to the attack, saw what had happened and dug me out with entrenching tools. One of them, Corporal Northdale, while kneeling to pull some stuff off my chest, was shot through the face. I should like to know what became of him. I hope he got back. He deserves the V.C.; also Private Leigh, for after Northdale was shot he got me out and

helped me into the hole made by the shell that buried me. It took me until nightfall to crawl 500 yards back to a hollow where the battalion bivouacked the previous night. The doctor saw me and sent me forward. Whilst the stretcher party was resting a shell dropped in the midst of them, killing two and wounding two, and they fell on top of me in the stretcher, but I wasn't hit. It rained all night and all next day, and I didn't get to the dressing station till after midnight on the Saturday. They sent me on to the clearing station, where I was not expected to live. Now I am almost well, and hope to be home within the next fortnight.'[13]

Sergeant Eli Hollyfield of the 10th Welsh left a vivid account of the attack on Mametz Wood. A former collier and bandmaster of the Bargoed Silver Band and the Ystrad Mynach Brass band, he was wounded and sent to East Leeds War Hospital.

We went forward over the ground which had been tilled up in fine style by the artillery of the Huns (they can give our artillery best). The Germans were shelling the wood in form, which we never expected. All praise, they worked very hard. We landed next in a chalk trench on top of a hill which we had to go down. This portion of the ground was a special mark for the Huns' artillery and machine guns. The order came for us to advance down the hill and up the slope to the wood, which our lads did in fine style. Going down the hill, several of our battalion got hit, including the colonel. The other battalions in advance of us were lying under cover as well as they could near the edge of the wood.

As soon as we reached the edge of the wood my captain gave the order to go through the wood in single file, and I can assure you we had a hard task to get through. After the artillery had done its work in front of us it was more like a maze than a wood. We got to

a road going through the centre of the wood. Here we had orders to dig ourselves in. We got to work and dug a trench alongside of the road while the artillery traversed the position in front of us.

Sergeant Vincent Watkins

After we had completed digging our trench, we advanced further in the same formation. After some work when we captured 22 Germans and one officer and a machine gun, we got near the end of the wood. The order 'Dig yourselves in' was given again, and as soon as we finished this line of trench, we were told to keep good lookout for an attack, because we had a battery of theirs, as well as a large bomb stores: but they did not come.

The Germans shelled us heavily that night, and the following day and night, when we were relieved by the Northumberland Fusiliers. On the 14th of July we came out of the ordeal less in number than when we started; but the colliers of South Wales took the position and held it for 48 hours, and consolidated it, not withstanding the fact that three previous attempts had been made and failed by other units. I was the only non-commissioned officer left, with six men, out of my platoon. My superior officer was killed.[14]

Eli Hollyfield was subsequently transferred to the Labour Corps, and when the war ended he enlisted in the Chinese Labour Corps to stay on and work in France.

Sergeant John Charles Rowlands of the 17th Royal Welsh Fusiliers wrote:

At dawn, we with weapons were ready. Then the artillery started. We saw the branches of the trees through thick clouds of smoke. What part would my fellow soldiers play? This was a worrying time. We did not consider our success, but wondered which of us would cross the horizon. At last, we were in the wood, halfway through, and we were supposed to help to finish the job. Many looked to the wood for a respite from the fighting, but here it was at its most fierce. Wrecked trees fell around us, artillery behind us and machine guns spitting cruelly. The wounded and dead around us – friends falling never to rise again, us without time to neither help nor cherish. 'Forward' was the order. We moved forward until we got to a path crossing the wood. It was now or never. We saw the enemy and that was enough. Welsh blood was boiling in us. We pushed through the bushes. It was now our turn. Man against man – until he fell. And more often than not it was him that fell. The Welsh fight by laughing; there is no mystery in the woods now.

Officers and soldiers at their best, success smiles on them. Having finished our work, with the wood now in our possession, we left it, under a cloud of smoke, its ground stained by the blood of our friends, but we had won this sacred land with precious blood – the purest and best Welsh blood.[15]

Lance Corporal William O. Hughes of the same battalion of the Royal Welsh Fusiliers wrote:

I raised my head to have one look at the valiant boys and the sight that I saw will remain in my mind for the rest of my days – every one with fixed bayonet and in extended order with one knee on the ground. The wood was on the other side, Mametz Wood, without one enemy soldier to be seen, but everyone felt that somehow the place was full of snares and that Death himself had stirred.[16]

Hughes later became a casualty: 'After dodging every sniper for over 40 minutes, Fritz had his chance to pay me back. As I was about to jump down into the trench a bullet shot through my right arm.'[17]

Lance Corporal William Jones Edwards of the 19th Welsh recalled his time in the darkness of Mametz Wood:

When we strolled from place to place without having a clue where we were during the night, I saw a beam of light coming from a dugout. I crept towards it and eventually plucked up the courage to ask, 'Who's there?' I must have spoken with a Welsh accent as the answer was 'Dewch i mewn [come in].' I've never heard three words sounds as sweet in my entire life. After getting used to the darkness I saw that it was one of the South Wales Borderers that I was with. There was a smile on his cheerful face and he asked, 'Where do you come from?' 'Aberystwyth,' I answered. 'Well, well,' he said, 'I am from Lampeter.'[18]

Private Timothy Richards of the 130th (St John) Field Ambulance wrote the following letter home after the battle:

I am quite safe and A1 at present. No doubt you have heard of the great advance that we have made. Our Division has done excellent

211

work in the advance. I should like very much to tell you where, but I cannot.

We went into action last Friday week, and was in for 36 hours without a rest. It has never been known before for the R.A.M.C. to take up the position we took, as we were right up against the infantry in the front line. It was Hell upon earth, and the way we worked is a credit to our unit. We had the name of being the best field ambulance out here before and had not been in action, and now we have proved it in action.

We started out with some cases. We had to come through the old German communication trench, and what a hole it was! We started at 6 a.m. up the trench, and we were knee deep in mud. There was an inferno of fire while we were in this place, and it is marvellous how any of us came out alive. It took us 12 hours to go 400 yards, with high explosive and shrapnel bursting all around us.

One of the boys shouted, 'Over the top, boys, and take our chances,' and we were ready for it. Beat to the world as we were, over the top we went. An Officer waiting to pass us shouted 'For God's sake come back.' Of that we took no notice, as it was the only chance we had to get the boys back.

On and on we went, the mud weighing us down. We stuck to it like heroes, every one of us, and got back to the hospital safe. We were very fortunate in only having two killed and two slightly wounded – a shell hit one and a sniper had the other. We had 16 hours rest after that, and in again for 60 hours.[19]

Private Ieuan Phillips of the same unit wrote a diary of his experiences at Mametz Wood:

7th Morlancourt. Terribly busy no sleep. Wounded coming down in mournful numbers. Covered with clay from head to foot. Mud and clay knee deep in the tranches, very awkward carrying stretchers. Working again tonight, wounded still arriving. Lce Cpl West & Pte Houston killed in action.

8th Morlancourt. Slept till 12 noon then came on duty. Plenty of work doing. Walked to the end of (?) & saw the battle for Mametz Wood. Great though pitiful sight. Wounded arriving continually our stretcher-bearers called back tonight for rest.

9th and 10th Morlancourt. Kept busy in Hospital until 4.30pm when I was ordered to rest until 9pm. 9pm fall in & marched to trenches arriving 12.30am, rest until 2am then the attack commenced. Great numbers of wounded coming (Short rations) down. I did three trips from the Happy Valley in front of the wood to the Dressing Station close by Carnoy. Then I commenced dressing wounded in Caterpillar trench and carried the patients to a row of Dugouts for the night. Turned in on the fire step for the night. Short rations.

11th Trenches. Commenced carrying again today at 4pm. Walking all day. Rested at 6pm. Germans shelling very heavily. Called out at 9pm. Then went to the dug outs to carry in 4 patients. Only safe to carry in the night. Short rations.

12th Trenches: Still carrying. Rest at 7pm. Relieved at 12 noon then marched down to Morlancourt arriving at 3pm. Unit left at 4pm for Edgehill, those from trenches to remain here over night. Had my first wash & shave for 3 days. Short rations. [20]

Ieuan Phillips died of wounds on 1 September 1918 and is buried in Bagneux British Cemetery, Gezaincourt. By this time he was a lance corporal and had been awarded the Military Medal. His parents ran the post office in Six Bells, Abertillery. He was 23.

On 21 October 1916 further information as to the death of Private Henry Hasell of the 14th Welsh was reported in the local newspaper. A letter from Captain Milbourne Williams to Hasell's parents said:

I was so sorry to see in the paper that your son was killed in the attack on Mametz Wood on July 10th, and would like to offer you my sincerest sympathy. I was in charge of the company in which your son was on that date, and you have no doubt heard how well our men advanced against a very strong position. I saw your son after I was wounded, and he helped to bandage my wounds and until I saw the account of his death in the paper I had hoped he might have come through safely.[21]

The parents also received a letter from Captain R.O. Lloyd, a Church of England chaplain, who said that he himself buried the body behind the British lines, and that a cross was erected

Private Henry Hasell

over the grave. It was reported that his death was instantaneous, as he was with a comrade at a listening post when he was killed by a bullet.

In fact, Henry Hasell was killed in action on 18 August 1916, aged 21, in the manner Captain Lloyd described. He is buried at Essex Farm Cemetery.

In the same newspaper an amazing story of an escape from death was related. Private Austin Rees from Clydach in Swansea took part in the attack on Mametz Wood and while crossing the exposed ground was knocked unconscious by a shell burst. Later, some members of the field ambulance arrived on the scene and found his apparently dead body. After examination they came to the conclusion that he was dead and consequently took one part of his identification disc and other personal effects. They then placed the body in a shell hole until such time as it could be buried, but he regained consciousness some 15 hours later and found himself alone. He picked up a German bayonet that was lying nearby and made his way back to the British lines.

An article in the *Cambria Daily Leader* on 18 October 1916 bemoaned the unequal coverage of the Somme offensive:

> Mr. Lloyd George yesterday spoke of the capture of Mametz Wood as one of the finest things in this war, and of the daring courage and skill of the lads from Wales who captured it. Yet it is irritating to think what little recognition the Welsh troops have obtained in the war. Out at the Front, it is a matter for wonder among the soldiers why the correspondents, eager enough to record brave deeds on the part of the sister nations, going out of their way to

write up the work of the Londoners, should have missed or ignored this.[22]

This was supported by a letter in *The Aberdare Leader* of 28 October 1916 in which an unnamed Cwmavon soldier wrote: 'From what I noticed in the papers very little was said about the glorious deeds of the Welsh regiments. It's a shame that some regiments are given all the praise and others not mentioned. The Welsh have done well, and perhaps the reason they were not praised is that the newspaper correspondents don't hail from Wales.'[23]

Contemporary Published Accounts, 1917

These sentiments were still in evidence the following year when it was reported that:

> In June 1917 at the monthly meeting of the Abergele Urban District Council Mr W. Pierce Morris criticised the way in which the English Press was ignoring the work of Welsh troops at the Front. He stated that the reports of the English correspondents and even the reports by commissioned officers were very scant regarding the efforts of Welsh troops. Wales was a small nation, but had contributed a great deal in the war. Mr Edward Williams agreed with Morris and said that it was not long since Mr Lloyd George had spoken to troops at Kinmel Park of the splendid work of the Welsh soldiers at Mametz Wood and urged the men in front of him to follow their example. 'The Mametz Wood engagement was one of the greatest lights of the war, and it was the Welsh troops who cleared the wood when other regiments failed.'[24]

A Welsh-language account of the fighting appeared in *Y Clorianydd* [The Judge] on 24 January 1917 with this introduction: 'After listening to my friend, Private O.T. Jones, Llanerchymedd relating the story of the Battle of Mametz Wood.' It was written by D.C. Herbert, Park Hall Camp, Oswestry. It is translated here.

All through our night-watches came urgent dispatches
To get ourselves ready as soon as we could;
The order was given: 'The foe must be driven
Away from his lair in the depth of the wood.'

The darkness ascended and daylight descended,
And the strangest day dawned on us there as we stood,
And on that strange morning we awaited the warning,
The word to advance and capture the wood.

Our officers shouted: 'The foe must be routed,
You Welsh must be brave,' and we all understood;
'Pray, as the storm gathers, to the God of your fathers;
You must fight unto death – you must capture the wood.'

And the lads started singing a hymn that went ringing
Around the whole trench, as the singing was good;
And it was the finest, and, yes, the divinest,

Singing yet heard, before taking the wood.
The bloodshed was endless, the slaughter relentless,
But we fought on as hard as anyone could;
The foe was defeated, but our ranks were depleted,
Leaving many a grave at the edge of the wood.[25]

A year after the battle for Mametz Wood a writer under the pseudonym 'Fred Ambrose' wrote a series of sketches entitled *With the Welsh*. In the work there is a chapter entitled 'First Aid Post at Mametz' which carries an informed account of the treatment of the wounded.

One of our first cases was a 'walking case', a bit of shrapnel in his jaw, a 'pickelhaube' on his head, and a cheerful grin on his face. The effect was extremely ludicrous. He would talk. The charge of the Swansea was the greatest thing of the war.

Machine gun wounds poured in (they were not men; they were wounds), clean wounds, and for the most part easily healed – kill or cure wounds – a fine 'blight' or eternity. Then came the shell wounds – hideous and ghastly wounds – wounds which depressed our souls.

Our world – and we smiled – our world was now a hollow in a

hell of mangled, torn bodies. 'Pan na fydd rhyfel mwyach' [When war shall be no more] – the words came from my old world to my brain. And what I heard as a meaningless, void phrase, became a passionate yearning – 'Pan na fydd rhyfel mwyach.'

There was little time for reflection for the communication trench continued to pour forth its stream of maimed, mutilated men. As one party of exhausted bearers laid their burden down, I saw a man rush forward with a basin of soup, and lift the blanket from the motionless form. It had no face! He laid the blanket gently back, and threw himself on the ground and burst into tears of pity for the form still pitifully alive.

Towards noon, when the attack upon the wood was developing, and the stream was greater than ever, two lads, with whom I had played in my boyhood in that faraway village upon a Welsh hill, were brought in.

As evening wore on our patients became fewer, and for the first time the bivouacs were empty. Climbing over the ridge with the O.C., I watched the German 'evening hate'. And our guns reply. Over Mametz and Fricourt Wood, the Johnsons burst persistently, seeking, sometimes not in vain, the British batteries and British men. A steel-blue sky, with a hand of red in the West, provided a fitting background for the bursting shells and the blinding flash of the guns.

Through the twilight, the ration parties stole up the communication trench, bearing provisions for their comrades lost to sight in the darkness of the wood. Suddenly the Boches shelled the communication trench and the crest of the ridge before us, judging with exactness the time when the ration parties would cross. Very soon we were busy again. Transport men, Pioneers and Engineers were brought in. The bearers were again treading by the light of a faint moon the devious and dangerous track to the Advanced Dressing Station.

Relieved of my work at the Aid Post, I joined the bearer parties. All through the night we toiled, bearing our stretcher-burdens across the shell-pocked ground. We toiled, silent but dogged, until arms, neck, and legs were on combined ache. We toiled until our hands were blistering and bleeding. As if in a dream, we crossed and re-crossed that ground. We would have sold our souls for one hour's rest on the ground, anywhere; but still the wounded came in to the Aid Post, and still we bore them to the advanced dressing

station. We were just one little link in the chain which bound
Mametz to England, and we did not break.

I helped to carry a big Sergeant-Major – a thigh wound. He had
'taken it' in the charge at daybreak, and had lain for sixteen hours
in a shell-hole. His chief anxiety was that he was too heavy for us;
he weighed sixteen stone. We assured him that we could easily
manage. He was proud of the boys. He had trained them and damn
they were a credit to the Army. There was not a better battalion in
the whole British Army than his.

The darkness in the East became grey, and a new day dawned
on our world. For a second there was a hush – a strange
expectancy. No gun was heard. Then all at once the iron chorus
opened again, belching death into the German lines.

All day long the stream of wounded flowed into and through our
Aid Post – at times almost submerging it. There was little rest from
the toil. One wound detached itself from the others and became
an entirety – a man, no a boy – a boy of eighteen, lying white and
still on his stretcher. I looked again; his feet had been blown off. A
stretcher party took him immediately to the Dressing Station. And
there I saw him later. He was one of many very still forms wrapped
in their blankets, lying on a green strip of secluded ground. I went
up and looked at him. He was just a boy – just on the threshold of
life. And now he was dead – and all the glorious possibilities latent
in him dead with him.[26]

Sergeant John Jarman from Garth in Powys recalled his
memories of the battle in poetry:

'Twas in the early days of May,
We left Lavantie Town;
Our boys sang 'Tipperary'
Whilst the shells fell all around.

Then we marched each day from morn till night,
But none of us knew where,
That we were taking a part in the great advance,
By digging the Hun from his lair.

We reached a place called 'Mouchey Bretton',
Where we all had a full week's training;
Our boys were all worn out
But stuck it without complaining.

Then close to the line we got,
Where the battle was raging,
But we all had a good night's rest
For orders we were waiting.

Next day in the village our packs we left,
And in the trenches got
Where the shells fell all amongst us,
But we did not care a jot.

There we stood four days and four nights,
Knee deep in water and mud;
Then fresh orders came to leave the ground,
Where our lads had spilled their blood.

Back to a field we went
To have a good night's cot;
For on the following morn,
We had to take a wood which the Huns had got.

At 11 o'clock one night they gave us a feed,
And a small issue of rum;
Then, we marched towards the place,
Where some dirty work was done.

We lined the ridge at 2.30 next morn,
And over the top we got;
Whilst our artillery bombarded the wood,
Which covered our lads a lot.

When the guns had done their bit,
The wood in the distance we could see;
Mametz is the wood I'm speaking of,
With Huns in every tree.

The Huns then opened rapid fire
Which made it simply hell;
But our lads still kept advancing,
For they were doing mighty well.

Over a hill we had to go,
When we faced a hell of a fire,
The officers started shouting,
Stick it boys, 'Wales for ever.'

With teeth set hard we continued the rush,
And in the wood we got,
Hacking away at the Huns,
Which made them retire at the trot.

Yes, hundreds of prisoners we too that morn,
This was in the big battle of the Somme;
Our boys fell like heroes that day,
Some were killed, I'm sorry to say.

We held the wood for two days more,
With all of us that were left;
The Huns then counter-attacked,
Which made it the 'valley of death.'

But our boys stood fast and blazed away
Where no living soul could creep;
And amongst the trees and bushes they came,
Like playing 'hide and seek.'

They retired when it couldn't be done,
To get our lads on the run;
With hearts of steel we fought our way,
For we were out to die, or win the day.

So Wales can awake in earnest,
For we defeated the boasting Huns;
For the hardest task we went through that morn
That's been done by British sons.

May the killed [lie] in peace,
With Jesus by their side;
Then, we shall meet again some day
In 'Paradise.'[27]

Jarman served with the 14th Royal Welsh Fusiliers and survived the war.

On 4 November 1917 Charles Martin, the Secretary of the Cardiff City Battalion Comforts Fund, wrote an ode to the Cardiff City Battalion:

When the martial call to arms resounded,
In our ancient city on the Taff,
There were many noble boys responded,
With buoyant spirit, full of 'chaff!'
Nigh three weary years have now fled,
Since we saw the fine Battalion pass,
With a gallant Colonel at their head,
Through the crowded, busy streets, en masse.

All honour to the name Frank Gaskell,
He who led his troops with pride,
And paid the supreme sacrifice,
Beside his chivalrous men who died.
He who formed the youth and manhood,
From the Office, Bench and Store,
With 'City Boys' – and those who would,
From hills and dales of Wales galore!

They have fought and held the fighting line,
At many a roughish danger spot,
And thanks to all their pluck and grit,
Have helped to push back 'Fritz' a lot.
The day will come for strife to end,
When our 'glorious boys' will gladly show,
Their eagerness for 'Home' to wend,
But we must win their knock-out blow!

For those brave lads who've gone straight West,
We wish with all the heart and soul,
They have received what's deeded best, –
His great reward 'Thou art made whole!'
That soon we all may rest secure,
In Britain's free and lovely isles,
No 'boy' can offer greater gift,
Than pay the supreme debt with smiles.

We wish them 'Rest' with 'God of Love',
From earthly troubles they are free,
To meet their loving friends above,
When the 'Roll Call' comes to you and me!
May many by the 'Grace of God',
Be spared to those whom they adore,
Then soldiers of the 'Cross of Love',
Will 'wax and wane' on earth no more.[28]

Contemporary Published Accounts, 1918

Nearly two years after the battle *The Welsh Outlook* of April 1918 carried an account by 'G.J.' of the fate of the wounded:

We went into Mametz Wood. For hours and days we struggled through the dense undergrowth in search of our hidden enemy, who, after having fired at us, surrendered or bolted. On the second day we had a short pause, which I spent in collecting together the scattered remains of the dear old boys we had trained and lived with for such a long time. It was indeed only a very small handful. We used the pause to search for some of our wounded friends. I knew that our stout stretcher-bearers could never manage to collect the wounded dying in open places for many hours, to say nothing of searching for others. So we set out to collect and take to the side of the paths the men wounded in out-of-the-way places.

We found under trees and bushes many a boy who had lost all hope of being found, and who had settled down in that desolate spot to die.

In one corner, at the foot of a tree, we found Roberts*. From his wounds I could see at once that we could do nothing for him. I got down, undid his collar, took off his cap and put my hand on his clear forehead. Feeling a touch he opened his eyes, and recognising me smiled faintly, and murmured in a gentle voice, 'Captain.' In a hopeless way I tried to do something for him, but he wanted nothing. He was in terrific pain but he looked so mysteriously calm. The precious breath was getting fainter and fainter whilst his face became brighter and brighter, developing at the last a clearness that was well nigh unearthly.

Solemnly and quietly in the midst of the 'strafe' we stood there whilst passed away the soul of our friend and hero – a passing away worthy of any hero in history – something attempted – everything well done.

The only two words he murmured were 'O! Arglwydd' [Oh, Lord], and each word was there and then branded on my soul. We left the place silently and solemnly for it was time to go on with the fight. But we left a sacred spot on which lay a man who was a thousand times better than we.[29]

* This is probably Second Lieutenant A.S. Roberts of the

14th Royal Welsh Fusiliers. Alan Sheriff Roberts was 20 and was from Curzon Park, Chester. He is buried in Dantzig Alley British Cemetery. His brother Henry was killed on 28 August the following year and another brother, Frederick, on 29 August 1918, aged 19.

Accounts by the men of 113th Brigade

Brigadier-General Price-Davies wrote to his wife after the battle. The letter is dated July 1916 and is certainly at odds with the remarks he made about the performance of his brigade elsewhere:

I am very well but a little shaky from lack of sleep, food and drink. You will know by this time of our capture of Mametz Wood. I think it was a fine piece of work. On the 8/9th I was to have carried out an attack on a small scale. It was miscarried owing to a battalion taking too long to reach the starting point. The Divisional Commander had been degummed. I am sorry, as I fear I contributed but the plan I thought a bad one and I was entirely borne out at a conference by the success of the present plan, which was what I advocated. Well, I hadn't much sleep that night and then moved to an advanced H.Q. for our attack which began at 4am but was out most of the night seeing that things were alright. I saw Carden for the last time at 4.30am, a fine gallant soldier. I feel his loss very much.

At 4.15am I felt fearfully hungry and had a cup of tea and a sandwich. About 7am we were told that we had captured the whole wood and prisoners. I went off to see the captured wood. There was a great number of dead Germans and we took some machine guns too. After that it became clear that we had not captured even half of the wood, also things were not going well. That's how I got tangled up in it. I thank God I have come through. Well, I stayed and tried to do my level best as a commander. I think I inspired them. Harry Williams who blows my horn so violently says the men say I saved the situation!! So nice of them. What I lack is power of organisation and I don't suppose I will ever overcome it and I think I shall put it to our H.Q. so as to give them the chance of getting rid of me if they want. Well, we remained in the fighting in the thickest undergrowth all day. Machine guns bothered us a

223

great deal and snipers. Well, tired as we were, the Boche was more
tired and kept surrendering but it was a job to get hold of such a
great wood with tired men. Well-trained fresh regulars would have
found it hard on manoeuvres even!! We had no water up there
and I got so dry. I had nothing to eat but an officer gave me some
jam sandwiches and about 11pm Marden gave me chocolate and
biscuits but still no drink except two tiny sips from a water bottle.

Practically no sleep at night as we were very busy with a
number of arrangements. We took two or three biggish guns
in the wood and a lot of machine guns. Some alterations were
made to the dispositions in the morning and General Evans took
command and I came out. Everyone is delighted at the success
as one's reputation was at low ebb. It was not only my brigade
but Marden was there also. About 4am my servant appeared
with coffee and sandwiches. I got back about 7 but all my kit is
scattered in different places and has to be collected so I cannot
wash or shave but I had a good breakfast and feel fine. I forgot
to say I thought I was wounded. I felt a very violent bang in the
left corner of my tummy and felt a warm feeling like blood. I was
sure I was badly hit (it was a piece of shell) and that I was done
for. I thought I ought to be down and be carried out and so looked
to see where I should lie down. Then I thought I didn't want to
lie down!! My coat was all in shreds at the pocket of my breeches
so I was not cut at all, only burned. I suffered no inconveniences
after a minute or two. I must sleep only a bit as I must watch
my battalions coming in. I don't know the number of prisoners,
probably about 200. I am in a Boche dugout now. Quite comfy
little place and comfy chair. The weather has been fine but there
was a fearful wind in the wood.[30]

On 12 July he wrote:

My staff are so good. I came in yesterday. They fussed about and
got me breakfast as our H.Q. was being shelled. Did I tell you we
took three siege guns in our attack. Our losses are not heavy but
we lost Carden and Flower, both killed. Flower did most awfully
well. I never saw a man with so much go. He was beaten to the
world and actually fainted right off once and fell flat down so
many times it made me laugh. The fighting took place on the 10th
and 11th. I came away as General Evans took over command. It

was late in the day when Flower was killed. I fancy I forgot I told you I was sent all the way back to the wood yesterday afternoon. I was not required as the message had been wrongly addressed. I was rather annoyed as it took two hours and there was a lot of shelling going on. I told you about our prisoners. I hear the total for the Division is about 300. Some of them were delighted to be taken. After dinner I went to see another Division I had been working with. They were very pleased with results. When I got back we had to move again. I had time for breakfast and a wash and shave and then went off to the station. I slept well in the train.[31]

His diary for 13 July stated:

It is difficult to write an account of the next few days. We had several wires along the line. We had orders to undertake several enterprises but in almost all cases the orders were too late to admit to being carried out and troops got tired to no purpose.

On the night of the 8/9th for instance the 14th were to have carried an enterprise but were delayed reaching the place from which they were to start. After this General Philipps was relieved of his command. I felt very guilty about it. On the morning of the 11 July at 4.15am we attacked Mametz Wood. The fight went pretty well but the wood was fearfully thick and communication difficult. Hearing we had captured it I went forward about 7am but found we had only reached our first objective. The men were very tired and morale at a low ebb. Subsequently we made a considerable advance, took some more prisoners and machine guns. In the operation the Division took about 300 prisoners, three siege guns and several machine guns.

The night was very noisy and men inclined to panic but the enemy made no attack. General Evans took over command of the wood (then General Marden and myself had each commanded a portion).

On the morning of July 11th I left three battalions behind. However, in the afternoon I received orders to go back to the wood and did so only to find I wasn't required there when I arrived. We were supposed to be relieved in the evening of the 11th but Bently and I waited in vain and thinking they had found another way.[32]

Private Daniel John Gregory, 13th Royal Welsh Fusiliers, made the following entry in his diary:

10th July: Entered wood and were greeted with machine gun fire. Dense undergrowth made movement difficult – walls of young saplings not thinned for two years. Casualties commenced very soon but we got to positions near centre of wood where we dug in. Our work was to drive and clear wood 220 acres in extent.[33]

Corporal Harold Iball also served with the 13th Battalion Royal Welsh Fusiliers:

I was one of the first to take part in the attack but we had to retreat during heavy losses to the reserve trenches and had to run up and down firing at random to let the Germans think the trenches were well manned.

You would scarcely have thought it was a wood: trees all blown to blazes and wide open spaces; and inside the wood was full of shell holes with very little cover and not much undergrowth. It was not a deep wood and once we were inside we could see the Germans on the other side. As soon as we got in we found several wounded Germans in shell holes. We had to crawl on our stomachs for what little cover we could get from the Germans the other side of the wood. One popped his head up and I was able to shoot him – the only one throughout the war I knew I had shot!

There was no barbed wire to the entrance of the wood. It had been destroyed by the artillery. The 13th Battalion attacked the centre of the wood but before that the first wave was over on our right, which consisted of the South Wales Borderers and another regiment. They were mowed down by machine gun fire, having no cover. When their attack failed we were sent into the attack and just a few of us managed to get into the wood; I think I had about six men left from my platoon. I don't remember the 16th Battalion making the attack on the left.

There was no one more surprised than myself that I ever reached the wood across the open ground. There was no confusion amongst us. The wood was right in front of us on top of an incline and once in the wood we took cover behind fallen trees and in shell holes until we were relieved. I personally took five German prisoners and took them to our headquarters where I was received by Mr Lloyd George's son and told to go and have a meal and a rest until the following morning – being 'all in'.

After I had rested I was asked to give an account of the attack to our Major Hardwick; Mr Lloyd George's son was also a major at headquarters.[34]

Harold Iball was later commissioned but was blown up by a trench mortar and was discharged in March 1918. He was awarded a Silver War Badge in recognition of this.

T.H. Davies served with the 13th Royal Welsh Fusiliers and described the attack of the Cardiff City Battalion on 7 July:

I was a signaller and acting as runner at the time as had no telephone lines from our advance post back to Battalion Headquarters. From where we were stationed in a German dugout [Company Headquarters] we could see the Welshmen going over in line up over the first rise but when they topped the second rise Gerry was ready having come up from their dugouts, machined them down like chaff. I don't remember how many attacks were made but to make matters worse it came on to rain heavily. Those who could crawl back took whatever shelter they could in the Nullah. The light railway was full of dead and dying, as were also the dugouts.

It was my job to carry messages from Company Headquarters to the junction of the communication trench which was a quagmire. On one of my journeys I spoke to a Red Cross corporal. What a mess – when I returned he was lying decapitated. I recognised him by his stripe. He was the only Red Cross man left.

After the attack was called off it took me over an hour to get back to Battalion Headquarters.

On the morning of the 10th we followed in single file along a sunken road, covered by German machine guns. I can remember the rain in between bursts. Some were lucky and others were left where they fell. Such was our indifference to death and destruction.

We arrived at the edge of the wood and I can remember lying there waiting for the whistle to advance, kicking my legs up hoping for a Blighty one. I carried a haversack, rifle and telephone. I didn't notice other men carrying anything other than rifle ammunition in bandoliers, rifles, bayonets and entrenching tools strapped to their backs in leather cases. The grass was fairly short and not disturbed to any great extent. The open ground didn't appear to be cut up.

We advanced in small groups between bursts of machine gun fire. This was more troublesome than anything else. There was the noise from the guns and shells from both sides.

We went in and relieved our 16th Battalion in a trench full of dead bodies, mainly German. On the top we could hear the cries of the wounded calling for help and we were helpless to respond. So indifferent were we that when a friend of mine in the 16th passed me we were standing on a fat German but we did pass a few remarks.

When we got into the wood we were ordered to dig in. This we did and after a time on taking stock Sergeant Jackson, Private Billy Brown and myself were in a corner and I remembered a discussion we had in the Y.M.C.A. in Winchester. Did a man go mad in a bayonet charge?

Lying out there in front of the wood, waiting for the whistle, I had a feeling of tension and my stomach turned over. From then on all thoughts of home and family faded. The main interest was of self-preservation. It was kill or be killed.

The wood itself was just a wilderness of tree stumps and I can remember calling on the unseen Germans to come into the clearing. We saw none alive.

There was no panic. There was confusion as most of our officers were put out of action when we went to a clearing in the wood for rations. Here the trees were taller and bigger than previously seen. Salvoes of shells came over which I understand later were our own. Such was the confusion and you must remember we were told of nothing beforehand except that the German wire would be breached by our bombardment. We were told that we would have little opposition. If we had been briefed, as we were in latter battles e.g. Ypres in July 1917, we would know what to expect. I can say from experience that the British soldier is dependable to the last man if he knows what the position is and what is expected, not false information like we had on the Somme.

I noticed what I thought was a German observation plane plotting for their artillery, but this turned out to be British.

Strip Trench and Wood Trench had already been taken as shown by the bodies lying around. Our job it appears was to follow on into the wood. Here we were ordered to dig in, then move to the left and dig in, then move to the right and dig in. By then we had lost all sense of direction. Bullets and shells were coming from all directions.

I do not remember any wire in front of us as we travelled in single file towards the wood which had already been occupied by our other battalion. In the wood, after the heavy shelling about midday, we were led by N.C.O.s who as far as I remember had no compasses.

I saw no defences except for the trenches. It was just stumps or short trees, shell holes, bodies and an unseen enemy. No doubt there must have been others in front of us, adding to our confusion. We were fighting an invisible enemy; if there was an enemy, I didn't see one.

Our artillery could not have known what part of the wood we occupied, hence those shells dropping on us in the clearing at midday. I saw no heroic action except to be shot at by unseen Germans or our own guns. We came out about midnight again in single file led by some N.C.O. who had more information than the rest of us.[35]

T.H. Davies had previously won the Military Medal for his conduct during the battle of Neuve Chapelle in 1915. He was later promoted to sergeant and survived the war. In April 1960 he placed a memorial plaque on a German blockhouse captured by the 38th Division in August 1917 near Langemark. It is still there today.

Private Edward Morris Edwards of the 14th Battalion Royal Welsh Fusiliers left this account:

We attacked at 4.00am on July 10th 1916. We were led by Lieutenant Venmore, whose last words before going over the top were 'Don't forget the regiment you belong to!' He was the first man to be killed – shot through the head. We penetrated approximately half way into the wood, suffering heavy casualties. Captain Glyn Jones, Pontypridd, mustered only forty-eight men out of the original one thousand, when preparing for the German counter-attack. This duly came and we held the position until midnight. Our rifles were red hot and the machine guns were bursting in the magazines. The 19th Welsh Pioneers laid down barbed wire between us and the Germans. We piled the Germans up as high as this room, stacked up on the barbed wire, during this counter-attack. Eventually we were relieved by the 12th Division, known as the Ace of Spades (flash on arm). Our heaviest casualties were suffered in the dipped fields leading to the woods, which were on a rise. The Germans just pumped their shells into this area.[36]

Edward Edwards survived the war, even attending a sniping course to hone his shooting skills, and was demobilised in April 1919.

Tom Phillips served with the 16th Royal Welsh Fusiliers as a signaller and kept a diary of his time at Mametz Wood:

5 July: Left Ribemont at quarter of an hour's notice. Found ourselves in the line after 7 miles march. Quite hell upon earth all night.

6 July: In action. Intense artillery activity. Vacated the line at 4pm and came back to OB lines to bivouac. Had good night in the open. All sorts of lights about.

Private Edward Edwards   Second Lieutenant Tom Phillips

7 July: Terrible duel. Hell fire going over Hun lines. Feel quite safe in God's hands and am quite steady though all. Left our bivouac for the line. Terribly hard time – no sleep and wet through. Quite cheerful though.

8 July: Terrible inferno. Lived on biscuits all day. Fine and warm. Hun having warm time. Laid cables to Corps. Attack to be made at 2am. Heavy bombardment. Communications splendid. No sleep. Feel quite fit. Received 2 letters from Lill. Much cheered.

9 July: Received 2 letters from Lill again. Quite a new man. Rations better. Shan't be sorry to get out to have some rest. Feel quite fit trusting God implicitly.

10 July: 2.20am. Laid out of trench ready for attack. Terrific bombardment. Reeled out cable and kept up communications. Horrible sights. God has protected me. Retired to Queen's Nullah 5pm. Had hit on right thigh. Our Colonel killed.

11 July: Terrific bombardment going on. Shelled our headquarters. Had narrow escape from death but God has kept and protected me. Hit on right chest by piece of shell. Went to ADS. Was inoculated.

12 July: Arrived at CCS at Darcourt. Passed restful day. Went to Hospital at Rouen. Worrying a lot about my dear Lill. Hope she is alright.[37]

He later paid tribute to the bravery of the men around him:

Seconds seemed like minutes, and minutes like hours. In due time, we saw the Bosch, but alas, unarmed with hands up, and escorted by one or two Tommies. These prisoners had been taken by 'B' and 'D' companies. One of the escort waved his arm as a signal to go forward again, and out of the trench everyone leapt without waiting for definite orders from superior officers. It displayed the instinctive valour of a British Tommy and individual determination to gain the objective.

At this juncture, the enemy put up a heavy barrage of incendiary shells that burst 100 yards or so short. The sudden burst of flame which extended from the point of bursting 200 feet high to the ground had a demoralising effect, as no-one in the Battalion had previously heard of them. Colonel Carden was mortally wounded within 20 yards of the wood.

At this point, the Bosch had three machine gun posts which momentarily checked the entrance. These machine gunners were dealt with.[38]

Tom Phillips was commissioned as a second lieutenant in October 1916 and in April 1917 was Mentioned in Dispatches 'for gallant and distinguished services in the Field'. A member of the Cardiganshire Volunteers before the war, he joined the Army in August 1914 and served in France from 1915 to 1918. In November 1918 he was admitted to the officers' convalescent hospital at Nannau, Dolgellau, until his release to civilian life once more in July 1919.

Arthur Hope Bury recalled his time with Number 8 Platoon, 'B' Company, 16th Battalion Royal Welsh Fusiliers. He enlisted in Manchester in December 1914 and after training in Llandudno and Winchester he arrived on the Somme in 1916.

I was at a small village called Fricourt where I remember a Salvation Army hut which supplied us with smokes and tins of salmon, and that was my last meal before going into action on the 10th July 1916.

On route I had divested myself of my underclothing and had a swim in the River Somme. It was a really hot summer's day. By this time I was a fully blown sergeant (promoted whilst on leave in England, when I married).

I well remember the approach to the wood (well wooded). There was an old unused railway track line, minus the rails, and it proved to be a death trap to us. I lost my officer wounded and we had a meeting to decide on immediate plans. I was to endeavour to capture or destroy a machine gun post, when I was wounded in the right arm and shoulder and left the battle scene.

My most unhappy meeting was with an old lady later whose son was in my platoon and was killed.[39]

Aled Parry served with the 16th Royal Welsh Fusiliers:

At 4.15am July 10th we went over the top and the firing machine guns were mowing us down like hay before the scythe. Backwards and forwards then 'smack' – a bullet right through the left lung.

I lay there for hours in the heat, the stretcher-bearers passing me as dead. And then I saw through a haze two soldiers who picked me up and I came to in a Base Hospital with nets around me and boys groaning and dying all around. After two or three months I was sent to Blighty for four further operations.

When I was lying apparently dead, I seemed to see, although hazy, a line of German prisoners coming and one took from under his hat a bomb which fell not far away and some of the shrapnel entered my arm – scars today.

Also on a night raid once, a big German came at me, bayonet fixed, and knocked my rifle from me. All I could do then was to try to hold his rifle from gutting me and in the process I split my finger, which is still broken.[40]

After recovering from his wound, Aled Parry served with the Labour Corps before being demobilised in April 1919.

Private Griff J. Jones, 'D' Company, 16th Battalion Royal Welsh Fusiliers wrote:

I was there July 10 1916. Our battalion left the Ypres Salient, the canal bank. We went through Poperinghe on route for the Albert front. Foot slogging, very dry and dusty. We did not know our objective but arrived on the Somme area. We stopped at a farm billet close to a railway line. Prisoners were passing to the rear in trucks. We rested for the night.

The following morning our packs were taken from us and fell-in in fighting kit. We left the billet, proceeding in platoon formation towards the Front. Going down the hill, we passed companies on side of road, the 14th Battalion. Later, our company bivouacked in marshy long grass hollow. Two of us formed a low tent, ground sheets together and slept for a while. Then torrential rain came on us, water running down from the slope, we were soaked to the skin. Later the hot sun was drying us up. I think it was July 6 in this situation.

Then we moved through the shattered village of Contalmaison, then moving in platoon formation down towards Queen's Nullah on our right, a hollow ravine. Then resting during the night. It was fairly quiet at this time, occasional coal box dropping in and machine gun fire concentrating on ridge above us from Mametz direction. Our company formed up and went up the white chalk trench relieving the S.W.B., I think then, just on day break, about 4.30 we were forming up fixed bayonets and some with grenades. The barbed wire in front was cut and was ordered to file out in wave order on this flat ridge. I think the 14th battalion was forming up behind us not very far back and then the artillery barrage opened up behind us bombarding Mametz Wood.

I laid flat in the grass. The Jerry was concentrating on this flat ridge with machine-gun fire, the bullets was cutting the grass close to me. Smoke screen was forming up. Our formation stayed put for a while. The right flank of our division was held back. Eventually, we, our battalion had to fall back. We had come too quick moving forward.

The white trench we occupied again for a short while, then we attacked Mametz Wood proper through the smoke, shell and bullets. I went down the slope from the ridge, zig-zag. Many were killed and groaning after I got to the bottom. The front of the wood was only about 200 yards. I was given a bucket full of bombs, grenades, as you know the German front line was facing us on the edge of the wood. Myself and three others crept forward through the smoke.

I got stuck in some barbed wire which I found was in front of a sap or listening post. There were two Germans inside it defending some of the retreating Jerries. The two were brave fellows. I threw the grenades in, both were killed. I laid low inside, up to my knees in mud. Saw German helmets passing about ten yards from me retreating toward communication trench left of the wood running upwards.

Our bombardment was so heavy it had blown down many trees across the communication trench, our shells had blown in the side of a pond and water and mud was pouring down towards me. Smoke and shells all around. Many Jerries and ours lay dead in this communication trench, treading on the bodies, I moved up about 200 yards, rifle and bayonet I stuck to, I was called off the trench by Corporal Williams who had a machine gun into a shell hole, covering a footpath leading from us strafing Jerries running across far end of path.

I went back to the trench. Moving up through the mud I came up against a foot-thick tree trunk. I decided not to go underneath, the mud would be up to my neck, so I lifted one leg over it and thought of bringing the other to follow. I was up on it and to my surprise a German behind a bush about 25 yards away levelled his rifle towards me. I threw myself back leaving one leg in the air; I was hit by a bullet in the leg.

Eventually, I got up in the mud and felt burning pain. Saw the mud covered putties red with blood. I took the bayonet off the rifle and used the rifle as a crutch. I trudged along back down the trench. When I came to the open, I fell down exhausted. I was taken away by stretcher-bearers.

I came to fairly on a stretcher in a Red Cross train. I was laying on a bottom stretcher with my head hanging outwards. Coming to gradually I felt something warm dropping on my cheek. It was blood from the mouth of a wounded fellow above. I arrived at Saint Omer clearing station. When I came to I was tucked in a single bed with nice white sheet with two big safety pins holding it down.'[41]

Captain E. Beynon Davies served with the Royal Welsh Fusiliers and wrote an account of his war experiences in 1965. He was a pre-war Territorial and wrote 'psychologists can usually divide soldiers into two types, introverts and extroverts. The Welsh belong to the former. However, when there is an emergency we come out of it uninjured. We realise that we can withstand it.'[42]

He commented too on the conduct of the junior officers '... many young officers were unfamiliar with this type of warfare. They held their ground without surrendering.'[43]

Accounts by the men of 114th Brigade

Private Albert Kelland of the 10th Welsh Regiment (1st Rhondda Pals) was a former miner from Dinas Rhondda. It appears that on 10 July while advancing through Mametz Wood he received a gunshot wound to his right hand which removed the top segment of his thumb. He went down the line to Étaples where he spent a few days before onward evacuation to Leeds

Hospital. He was discharged in 1917, declaring himself to be 'quite incapable of holding a rifle'. Sadly, his brother Walter was killed on 24 June 1917 serving with the 7th Battalion Somerset Light Infantry.

Irving Jones served as a signaller in the 1st Rhondda Battalion at Mametz Wood. 'I was working in the colliery and there were people joining up, you know, and I and my brother in law discussed it and we decided to join up. We thought, well, it will be a bit of a holiday. We would beat the Germans in about six months.'[44]

When he was offered a tot from the rum jar before the attack he refused, as he wanted to keep a clear head. He recalled Colonel Ricketts blowing his whistle for the start of the attack and the order being given not to stop advancing to see to the wounded. Of 54 signallers who went into the attack, only four were unscathed at the end of the battle.

Jones had enlisted whilst still underage but had reached the rank of sergeant by the time he was 17. When his true age was discovered, courtesy of his mother, he was discharged. He returned to work at Bedwas Colliery until he was recalled to the Army.

A keen boxer, he was the battalion champion and put his skills to good use when a bullying sergeant was invited to settle their dispute behind a barrack building.

Corporal Samuel Arthur White enlisted in the 10th Welsh in November 1914. He was born in Penarth but was living in Fryatt Street, Barry Dock and

Corporal Samuel White

working as a labourer. Just a month before he went into action at Mametz Wood, he had been ordered to pay four pence a day to Sarah Morgan of Cardiff for the maintenance of their illegitimate daughter. He survived the war, rising to the rank of Company Quartermaster Sergeant. He wrote a poem describing his experiences entitled 'The Welsh at Mametz Wood':

'Twas in the daily papers, for anyone to see,
How City Clerks like demons fought and won a victory.
The deeds performed were glorious, all honour to their name,
Yet gallant lads from little Wales have helped foul Huns to tame.
This action's unrecorded, their praises all unsung,
But if you pay attention – I'll tell both old and young,
How the Valiant, brave First Rhonddas,
Faced the German's shot and shell,
And helped to capture Mametz Wood,
'Tis a tale I'm proud to tell.
For I am one of the Rhondda boys,
One of the lads who helped to lay the Germans out full length.
Although the Press don't praise us on the pedestal of fame,
We know what we accomplished, we fully played the game.
To get on with my story – 'twas the tenth day of July,
Just before Old Sol had raised into the skies.
The orders came – the Rhonddas will drive the Germans from the wood,
And in spite of deadly gunfire, we made progress slow, but good.
At intervals a comrade would go down with a cry of pain,
Yet look! The Hero tries to rise and struggle on again.
Our brave Heroic Colonel, whilst leading first to fall,
In falling cheered us onwards, with words that thrilled us all.
Although put out of action, would not be taken back,
Until he had seen his gallant boys well into the attack.
Daylight was now upon us, the sun had risen high,
And found the 10th still pressing on, to do their bit or die.
Yes, forward was the watchword,
Though shot and shell fell fast,
Till after fearful slaughter, we reached the wood at last.
We reached the dread inferno,
We stormed the Gates of Hell,

How anyone lived through it is beyond my power to tell.
Machine gun fire assailed us, and shells of every kind,
With the smoke of the burning wood, it drove us almost blind.
'Twas 'Stick it, Welsh' – we stuck it,
We surely made our name.
The miners' bold battalion gained everlasting fame.
In mingled heaps the enemy lay, gasping with our own,
In every sooth and spectacle, which chilled me to the bone.
Daylight waned, grim darkness fell for a fearsome night,
And as the long black hours of night drew on,
We prayed for morning's light.
The night wore on, dawn broke, the sun appeared again,
Discovering many fallen pals, some suffering fearful pain.
And some had joined that Noble Band,
Whose earthly tasks were done,
Victims in the 'Fight for Right', brave heroes every one.
Yet still the Valiant Rhonddas fought and bled in very Hell.
And now we came to grips to fighting hand to hand,
Our bayonets dripped with German blood, shed for the Fatherland,
By fiends who smiled approval for the Lusitanic crime,
And laughed with glee when Nurse Cavell was murdered in her
    prime.
Judge then of our emotions, when we caught the Hated Huns,
Who brutally had crucified and tortured Britain's sons.
Why wonder when I tell you, we all went sort of mad,
But yet took mercy on the Huns crying 'Mercy, Kamerad.'
Although we all remembered the brutal deeds they done,
We deigned to show them mercy, though they had shown us none.
We fought as Britons always, the only way we know,
A clean fair fight, with right as might, no matter who the foe.
So we battered them and shattered them, until the wood was won,
The God of Battles aiding us, while famous deeds were done.
Now what of fallen comrades, who nobly gave their all,
Who fell for King and Country and answered their last call?
'O God in tender mercy,' we cried from the blood-stained field,
'Be kind to those now left to mourn those heroes brave and good.
Sustain the suffering wounded, help them their pains to bear,
Be with those made captives, shield them with Heavenly care.'
My story now is ended, by which I've proved to all,
The miners like the city man, went forth at duty's call.

The lads who delved in gloomy depths have got there just the same,
Right well their master tactics, right well they played the game.
When led by gallant officers, with hearts as true as steel,
Who are ready, ever ready, with their shoulders at the wheel,
To do their best for homeland and forever crush the Hun,
To fight for right and liberty, with bayonet, bomb and gun.
May luck attend the collier boys,
Who rushed from hills and vales,
And worthily upheld the fame of 'Gallant little Wales.'[45]

Tom Price of the 13th Welsh Regiment wrote in a letter in 1974:

The 38th Division, of which we were a part, had marched from Merville in the north down to the Somme. 21 days on the road with a rest of 3 days at a place called Minguval [Mingoval]. The rest consisted of a 5 mile march each day to attack a wood in that area in order to get us used to the job for which we had been earmarked – the assault of Mametz Wood.

We entered the area through Albert, where we saw the Virgin and Child on the church that had been displaced by shellfire and was leaning over at an angle to the tower. We then passed through Fricourt and entered what was known as Caterpillar Trench, through which we waded up to our hips in mud and water to a point directly overlooking the wood. We were on higher ground than the wood and could look down on it. We arrived there on

July 5th. On our way through Caterpillar Trench I saw men fall into the mud and water in sheer exhaustion. We just had to lift them out and revive them as best we could until we got to our allotted position.

I was then not yet 19 years old, as I had put my age on 2 years

Private Tom Price

in order to join up in October 1914, just 2 days after my 17th birthday.

From our position at Caterpillar Trench we used to crawl out each night to see as fine a fireworks sight as one could wish, for our field guns and the French 75s were pouring liquid fire shells on the wood in order to burn it up ready for our attack.

Then on the morning of July 7th for some unknown reason, the City Battalion was sent in against the wood, which had resisted all attempts to capture it from July 1st to that date. We were in a position to see the 16th Battalion being mown down like corn and we had to threaten our men in order to stop them going in to help the 16th Battalion. One half of that battalion suddenly seemed to falter and turn back, whilst the others went on. Anyway, the whole unit was almost wiped out, and the following day those that remained were brought into our various battalions to make up our strength.

When we were resting at Minguval, orders came through that all ranks had to have our hair close cut, probably because of head wounds; anyway, they were like a lot of convicts. One corporal refused and was court martialled and reduced and then had his hair cut.

Then at 4.00am on July 10th we made our attack on the wood under orders to take it at all costs.

No one knew what the costs were to be! Our battalion (13th Welsh) went in over 1000 strong (clerks, cooks and everyone) and at roll call two days later I am told that 136 men answered the call.

We were in the first line of the attack. After going down the embankment and across a road we had a long strip of meadow to cross towards the wood. A heavy artillery barrage preceded us (some shells fell short) and eventually we entered the wood which we had thought would be poorly manned in view of the fire shells and other artillery action, but we were very much wrong.

The Germans met us head on and after hand to hand fighting, drove us out again into the field.

We reformed and attacked again and on the second charge I had a bullet in my left ankle and a shrapnel blast in my right hip and was rendered unfit for further action and lay out on the field until the morning of July 11th when I was picked up by some boys of 14th Battalion and carried to a dressing station.

The Germans threw back the second attack too, but the Welsh

reformed again and being reinforced by, I think, the South Wales Borderers or Royal Welsh Fusiliers, they went on and captured the wood and held it.

It was found later that the liquid fire shells just burned the trees. The Germans were safe down in bunkers 30 or more feet below ground and only came up when the attack was on. Their snipers were posted in look out boxes and gave the alarm when action was pending, and they were so carefully placed that they took some finding and they caused a terrible havoc to our forces.

I cannot vouch for it, but it was thought that the confusion with the 16th Battalion was due to an order to retire, thought to be given from a German officer by loud hailer or some other source.

Considering the fact that our battalion has witnessed the decimation of the 16th Welsh in their abortive attack on Friday July 7th, I must say that the morale of our men was really good. We had saved up two days' rum rations ready for the morning of July 10th and before 4.00 am all the platoon sergeants had a jar of rum from which we gave each man who wanted it a splash of rum in their mugs or Dixie can as they filed past. It was surprising to see the effect of this, as they drank it. Some were gasping as the stuff burned their throats.

I know that when I took a swig of it I thought I would never get my breath back. It was neat rum – thick stuff – not what one gets in the bottle today. Anyway, no doubt that added to the tension of the event, increasing the courage necessary to face the attack. The descent down the embankment was quite orderly and we took up our position on what was a sunken road at the front of the chalk cliff, as it is referred to on the maps, and waited for the order to go.

We attacked on a two-company frontage, 'A' and 'B' companies 13th Welsh leading, followed by 'C' and 'D'. I was in 'A' Company, No. 5 Platoon. Sergeants Common and Condon were in charge of No. 1 Platoon on our right, myself and Sergeant Barber in charge of No. 2 Platoon. We were loaded up with four Mills bombs each in our pockets and four bandoliers of ammunition across our shoulders, which was quite heavy, and which made the approach to the wood quite a physical task.

As the barrage started we moved off in quite an orderly fashion and followed the barrage at some distance. The tension and noise cannot be described, what with the traction of shells through the air and the noise of explosions all around us, it was almost impossible to give verbal orders and we had to rely on hand signals for directing any move.

I noticed on our way across the open field to the wood that there were a number of bodies laying around – a results of the previous efforts to attack the wood. Quite a lot of them were Scots troops.

We did not notice any barbed wire, at least not at the point where my section were in. What did surprise us was the number of the enemy there, as we had assumed they would have been blasted out of their forward positions, but not so. They were down in the safety of concrete bunkers until the alarm was given for them to come out at us.

Men were falling in all directions due to the intense machine gun fire coming against us. How we got to the wood I do not know, but we got there and entered it for a short distance before the Germans came at us – head on – and there was quite a lot of action before we were forced to retreat back into the field again where we got into shell holes or any other form of cover we could get. The Germans followed us to the edge of the wood and when our lines were able to open fire on them they quickly returned to the protection of the tree stumps – all that was left of what were trees.

Our 'C' and 'D' companies had now come forward to us in the shell holes and following a further artillery barrage we launched the second attack against the wood and unfortunately in that push forward I was wounded and took no further part in the action.

Anyway, after some time our troops were driven out again and retired back to the shell holes. At that point I was really frightened for the first time as I was between the two lines and saw the Germans coming towards me. Fortunately, they again retired to the wood.

After some considerable time, or so it seemed to me, our line moved forward again and from what I know they were successful in holding the enemy and with further reinforcements managed to push on to the other end of the wood and hold it.

I managed to pull myself into a shell hole and was there until well into the morning of Tuesday July 11th, when I was picked up and taken to a first aid post under the shelter of the chalk cliff.

During my lay up in the shell hole – in which there was a dead

German – the only person I saw was Captain H. R. Chapman of our Company, who stopped and gave me a drink of diluted rum and water, which tasted good.

I no doubt passed out a couple of times but I saw no one else until I was found by four men of the Signals Section of the 14th Welsh.

It was an experience I would not like to go through again. We were amateur soldiers, volunteers in war and we were led by officers driven from civilian life – our Company Commander was a bank manager from Swansea (Major Bond). Our other officers were colliery managers or owners, brewery owners, surveyors etc. who had guts enough to lead us into action against a trained Prussian force, and I consider what we did was wonderful.

The whole Somme offensive is described as a failure, when counting the loss of lives against the amount of land captured, but a move had to be made out of the stalemate of trench warfare, and in order to bring the war to an end.

What the Welsh Division did – in my mind – was not a failure. It was certainly a sacrifice, but was something towards an end and I am proud of being one of the Welsh Division.'[46]

Private J. Jenkins of the 14th Welsh told his family what had happened when he went into Mametz Wood. He was hit by a bullet in the arm and compared it to being kicked by a mule. But he kept advancing until a shell burst nearby and he was hit in the back of one leg by shrapnel, which also peppered his back. Using his rifle as a crutch he made his way back out of the wood and to the casualty clearing station. Years later his son would remove pieces of shrapnel from his back, digging out the thorn-sized pieces with a needle.

Corporal Geoffrey H. Crick served with 'D' Company of the 14th Welsh:

After the trench duties at Givenchy, Laventie, Festubert etc. we went to the Somme. We entered Mametz Wood on the 10th July 1916. A few Germans came out to meet us and more or less surrendered. In fact if we had known it was nearly deserted. The wood itself, well, the dugouts were of very good stuff and so deep down and full of everything. It seems that they were to stay there forever. It was taken by the 16th Welsh or the 11th S.W.B. I'm afraid I have no knowledge of that. All I know is when we came out of the wood we were paraded by some big noise, a General, I forget his name [Brigadier-General Marden]. He spoke to us and thanked us etc. Then we were off again somewhere. Alas, up to the Ypres Salient, a worse place than ever. I still get nightmares thinking about it.[47]

In a second account he wrote:

I thought that the wood was taken by the 16th Welsh because when we went into it, there were still Germans about. About the actual attack on the wood. I can remember spreading out across the field in front of the wood. I was close to my company officer, Lieutenant Arnold Wilson, in case he wanted any message sent I suppose. There was no barbed wire or trenches. When we got close to the wood some of the Germans came out. Lieutenant Wilson had his revolver pointing at them, but they more or less were surrendering. Into the wood itself. Well we were running around paths leading into big and gigantic dugouts. Coming across a few Germans here and there. Altogether I can't remember what happened but to this day I cannot even remember how we came out. All I can remember is being on parade in front of General Marden, and me in front of the parade fixing and unfixing bayonets, the usual feature on 'big noise' parades. It's a wonder I didn't poke my bayonet through my trouser pocket.[48]

Later in the war Crick was a guard at the 56th Prisoner of War Camp at Rouen in France where he was given a silver cigarette case engraved with the Welsh Regiment badge and 'Mametz Wood (Somme) 1916' on it – the work of a German prisoner.

By 18 July the wounded were reaching the hospitals in Britain and newspaper reporters were able to conduct interviews with some of these. A report in *The Western Mail* on this day gave more information on the conduct of the battle:

CLEARED THE WOOD – WELSHMEN'S BIG HAUL OF PRISONERS

Wounded heroes who are now reaching the home hospitals continue to pay warm tribute to the glorious part which the gallant Welsh regiments are playing in the 'Great Push'. The most-sought-for hero at one of the sectional hospitals of the 3rd Western General Hospital on Monday was a Bargoed man who has been wounded in the face.

'The big advance' he said, 'had been in progress some days when we were moved up to assist in clearing a certain wood. So our battalion and another from Wales were assigned the task of testing the strength of the enemy in the neighbourhood. We were held up about 200 yards in front of the wood by devastating shell and machine gun fire. Heavy stuff was flying all around us, but once we got into the wood we made a desperate fight for it. It was a bigger job than we had bargained for and the reinforcements came up just in the nick of time to save our positions. I never saw such an eager lot of chaps as ours once the order to advance was given. It seemed a 'washout' at the start, with the terrible fire which faced us, but our captain manoeuvred his men with skilfulness. I am glad to say that our division finally cleared the wood.

'The Welsh boys fought like very demons through a wood which was well-nigh impregnable, and dotted here and there with cleverly concealed guns. If it had been a fair square fight it would have been all right, but the enemy was in the wood and we were outside, and our task was to drive them out. Once in the wood it was a case of everyone for himself, as it resolved itself into tree to tree fighting as the enemy were bent upon holding the wood at all costs. The whole of the Welsh boys, however, fought with great bravery and proved themselves to be splendid fighters.'

URGED ON BY WOUNDED COLONEL

A member of the Welsh Regiment, whose home is at Aberdare, said that it was a Welsh brigade which saved the position.

'Our battalion' he said, 'was moved up quietly as reinforcements. We had not proceeded 20 to 30 yards when our colonel got hit, but in spite of his injury he stuck to his post, urging his men to the attack. Directly my squad got into the wood we came across 20 to 30 Germans. Our wounded colonel urged us on with the remark "Get at them, Welsh; they have no heart." No sooner said than we were on top of them with our bayonets, but the Boches held their hands up in token of surrender. We sent them back in charge of a couple of men, but as soon as we got the other side of a tree, bombs were thrown at us from behind. I saw one of our corporals killed by a shell. I was making my way back to get my hand dressed after a gunshot wound when a shell burst near me, and in the confusion which followed I found myself back again in the wood. German dead were lying all about the place as evidence of the good executive work which the Welsh boys had done in their mad rush.

'I cannot say what happened after I got back to the dressing-station, but later in the day an officer in the Royal Garrison Artillery patted me on the back and said, "Bravo, Welsh; you have won possession of the wood at last. I have just had the news down by 'phone." I might add that during the whole of this time we were in the wood there was terrible firing going on.

'I never saw a cooler lot of men under fire than the Welsh boys, and in this connection our own commanding officer set a fine example, for after being wounded he continued to give us encouraging advice. In clearing the wood we took hundreds of prisoners.'

TEUTONIC TREACHERY

A Senghenydd soldier, in hospital at Newport, asserted that he and his comrades of the Welsh Regiment had more than once seen Germans holding up one hand and shouting 'Mercy', but with the other hand manipulating a machine gun. 'I have seen them do that at 50 or 60 yards range,' he said. 'Yes, and I have seen some of them bringing up machine guns on ambulances,' interrupted a comrade.

Private J. Evans of the Royal Welsh Fusiliers, whose home is at 35 Glynrhondda Street, Treorchy, said, 'I saw a German officer as we came along throw open his tunic to show us he had no weapons, and at the same time he put up his arms and shouted, "Mercy, Kamerade." I thought he was all right, but as some of our men passed a little way off he pulled a revolver from somewhere and shot at a man's head. The man was wounded but he was able to rush at that German officer and put his bayonet through him. I saw one German prisoner in our uniform. He must have taken it off one of our prisoners or a dead man.

Several times we saw the Germans killing German prisoners with machine guns.'

LUXURIES
Second Lieutenant Harold Vanderplank, a Newport teacher, who has been wounded, wrote home to say that when the British troops entered the German officers' dug-outs in the attack on Mametz Wood, they found pianos, sofas, easy chairs and plenty of food and wine.[49]

The *South Wales Evening Post* of 7 September 1916 carried the following story:

A Brynamman soldier, now in civilian life, has an enthralling incident to relate of the time when they won Mametz Wood in 1916. On reaching the wood, after the memorable charge across the open, during which so many of our gallant lads were laid for ever low, there were innumerable hand-to-hand battles fought with Huns, who were striving to retain their hold. Somebody from a Rhondda Battalion on the left was heard to enquire of his sergeant, 'What shall I do with this one?' 'Damned gun!' was the reply, 'he didn't shout soon enough. Give him six inches' ('Rho 'wech modfadd iddo fa!').

The next thing the Welshman saw was the figure of a burly German soldier running for his life, with a slightly-built lad of eighteen (he had 'cheated' his age on enlisting) in full chase. When the pursuer and his quarry reached a light clearing amongst the trees, the burly German noticed the slight build of his adversary, and turned around to finish him there and then. But the little Welsh lad gallantly stood his ground and for a few exciting seconds there followed a fierce series of thrusts and parries with two bayonets. There was one lucky 'jab' and the German lay on the ground squealing 'Kamerad! Kamerad!' 'What shall I do, Sergeant?' exclaimed the lad as he planted his foot in triumph on his adversary's chest. 'Let the devil go back,' was the reply, 'for he showed some guts.' And the German is now 'somewhere in England'.[50]

Accounts by men of the 115th Brigade

Brigadier-General H.J. Evans later wrote an account of the battle.

> There was no definite information as to the strength of the enemy in that portion of the wood but that the edge was held but not in great strength. I decided to reconnoitre to the edge of Caterpillar Wood whence I thought I should obtain a close view of the ground over which the attack was to be made and thought GSO was accompanying me. However when I got into the wood I found he had not followed.

Instead Evans was accompanied by the officer who was commanding Caterpillar Wood. Evans noted: 'From the position I attained I noticed that troops could form up for attack if not pushed too far up the hill towards Bazentin-le-Grand Wood... That a considerable drop had to be negotiated early in the attack.' He also noted that the ground offered no protection from enfilading fire from Bazentin-le-Grand Wood and from Mametz Wood itself. When orders arrived from Division '... they differed so materially that I had to hold them up. The Divisional orders were so voluminous that they required very carefully going through and I had to make many alterations in those drafted by Brigade.' They left Evans 'aghast'.

He was also critical of the underperformance of the artillery. 'The artillery had not previously registered on the positions on which fire was directed and observation was very difficult. Consequently their fire was ineffective and did not attain the desired results.' He criticises the dispositions saying they were all 'cut and dried' and that the reconnaissance 'was simply made to satisfy them and that I was a mere figure head.' He claims that this was the first he knew that the attack was to be made on a two-battalion frontage. All his plans had been made on the basis of a one-battalion frontage.

Evans felt that if another consultation had been held to discuss this change then 'communication would have been made more effective. The artillery would have been more effective and the attack would probably have been successful.' Evans debates whether he should have rung up Divisional Headquarters and given his ideas, but states he had already:

> ... undergone great physical exertions and the battle had already been begun by the artillery and I gave credit to Divisional Headquarters knowing more of the situation than I did. I considered therefore that any protest on my part at that late hour would have been ill-timed and an intimation of lack of nerve... But looking at it after the event I cannot be held blameless in the conduct of the attack on the following points.
>
> I should have impressed most strongly on C.O.s when I saw them in the Nullah the absolute necessity of going straight for the wood at all costs. Had more determination been shown by them at the outset it is possible that the edge of the wood might have been gained, though with heavy casualties.
>
> I should have followed my inclination and have gone down to Caterpillar Wood when I could get no information. I should then have obtained a better grasp of the situation and my personal order that a direct advance was to be made that it was not an occasion for attack... would have had more weight than such an order given through the Staff Captain.
>
> Again I should at a later stage have gone down with 10th S.W.B. I should then have been there sufficiently early to draft definite suggestions for a further attack in the event of success not being gained with the 10th S.W.B.
>
> When I reached Caterpillar Wood the situation was such that I was still convinced that to have then prosecuted the attack would have only entailed very heavy losses and failure... my message to Divisional H.Q. gave an inadequate account of the situation and I did not make clear what was in my mind that with a modification of the artillery programme, replenishing the trench mortars and thoroughly reorganising units and explaining in detail on the ground, I should be prepared to again attack in two or three hours. (I did not however in my message want to create gloom and despondency by a too gloomy report and my physical exhaustion was such that probably my brain was not capable of expressing clearly and definitely what had been my ideas under normal

conditions and the message itself was dictated under difficult conditions.)

The failure of the smoke barrage undoubtedly affected inexperienced leaders, but it seems to me that the attack should have been launched before the expiration of the artillery bombardment.

It was a case also in which the first... becoming failed, each succeeding attempt became more difficult, the enemy was more fully prepared, elated by their first success and our men correspondingly disheartened.

The congestion in the trenches was so great and the going across country so heavy that I did not reach the Nullah until 4.00pm. I found much disorganisation, many casualties amongst officers, and the men somewhat shaken. I at once got together the C.O.s and issued orders for an advance on the wood at all costs as soon as they had reorganised their battalions, putting the two freshest battalions in the front line.

Evans then calculated that the earliest this next attack could take place was at 5.20 p.m. The artillery barrage had been arranged from 4.30 p.m. to 5 p.m., as an attack was required at 5 p.m. This was evidently not possible.

At this time the effect of the artillery fire would have worn off and the advance would have been exposed to very heavy machine gun and rifle fire both from front and flanks. The men were much shaken and it seemed to me that under the then conditions any attack would entail very heavy casualties and success would be very problematical. It appeared to me that the artillery fire on the edge of the wood wanted better direction and that heavier fire was required in the direction of Bazentin-le-Grand Wood from which direction the flank machine gun fire seemed to be coming.

The defences at the edge of the wood he could see though his field glasses were intact; too much artillery fire was falling in the wood itself.

He concluded:

The prime cause of the failure of the Brigade to attain its objective was in my opinion the haste with which the scheme had been carried out. It was a deliberate attack which required careful preparation and personal reconnaissance of the whole area by me with my commanding officers. This it was physically impossible to do and the position chosen for my brigade was one which I had not chosen.[51]

Emlyn Davies enlisted in the 17th Royal Welsh Fusiliers in July 1915. He later wrote:

The enemy had retired to strongly held defences in Mametz Wood, two square miles in area, and to Caterpillar Wood, smaller but equally defended, leading to the formidable defences of Bazentin. Each rose on higher ground, the upward slopes lengthened to 700 yards. Between the woods a wide meadow with similar contours intervened. The assembly position lay in a narrow valley [Death Valley]. The margins of both woods were packed with a massive barrier of machine guns supported by heavy artillery fire, equaling in intensity our own massed batteries. Preliminary bombardment seemed to set the wood on fire, smoke pouring forth in quantity and density almost obscuring all vision. As the other two of our Brigades urged forward to the charge, there went forth the flower

of Wales' young manhood. The suicidal attacks failed, though twice more repeated. Mown down like corn, there they lay prone and motionless, remindful of a mass of Moslem pilgrims making their obeisance to Mohammed. But these Welsh pilgrims would not rise again until the Day of Judgment. In their faith they had looked through death.[52]

Private Emlyn Davies

Davies was in doubt where the fault for failure of this attack on the first day lay:

> Rather than attack on the whole front allotted to the Division, why not first attempt the reduction of the defences in the smaller Caterpillar Wood.'[53] [He possibly meant one of the other copses held by the Germans. This would have reduced the fire from three sides to just one.]
>
> At nightfall the following day, the 14th R.W.F. charged up the slope, bombing and bayonetting the defenders, thus occupying the wood.[54]

He wrote of the 10 July: 'The assault was... preceded by bombardment on the margins of Mametz Wood, the sound of its deafening progress exceeding any previous demonstration. Smoke and flame emerging from the burning undergrowth produced swirls of blackness almost obscuring vision of the target of greenery. Better still, on this occasion, the massed collection of machine guns were masked and destroyed.'[55]

Davies advanced '... via a good deep German communication trench, more or less free from mud but strewn with ghastly remnants of former travellers; severed gory heads, hands, feet and longer limbs lay about in awful abundance.'[56]

He says in his battalion five Jones brothers served and four died on the same day. Also a father and son on the same day.

> The order was given to go over. In a long single file in the nearby Queen's Nullah, a smooth grassy declivity wherein on one knee, rifle butts firmly held at an angle of forty-five degrees, we were ready. Just then a heavy shell burst on the Nullah's rim and I felt a heavy blow on my right shoulder, my rifle shuddering out of my hand. Stunned, I thought the blow came from a shell fragment; it turned out to be a heavy lump of earth.[57]

He entered the wood.

> Gory scenes met our gaze. Mangled corpses in khaki and field-grey; dismembered bodies, severed heads and limbs; lumps of

torn flesh half way up tree trunks; a Welsh Fusilier reclining on a mound, a red trickle oozing from his bayonetted throat; a South Wales Borderer and a German locked in their deadliest embraces – they had simultaneously bayonetted each other. A German gunner with jaws blown off lay against his machine gun, hand still on its trigger.[58]

Davies pays tribute to strength of the German resistance.

After forcing them back, in the face of murderous storms of machine gun fire, the enemy made a determined stand within the wood, repelling the continuing pressure of the attacking forces. A counter-attack was being built up which eventually materialised in force with the violent accompaniment of shell and machine gun.

The arrival of a monster block-buster scattered us, each seeking shelter in nearby shell holes. Two of us made for the same shell hole, I in front by no more than a foot, my head just downward of the rim, when a second giant exploded, stunning both of us. I had begun my slide into the hole, remaining there a few minutes. Rising to return I saw my companion lying motionless. No wounds were visible. The sole indication of injury was a tiny trickle of red in one ear. He didn't move. Concussion had killed him.[59]

Davies offers an explanation as to why the men retreated:

Added to the pounding German barrage was now that of our own, falling short on our own men. Presently numbers of our men were seen trampling to the rear, crowding the wide track. A co-signaller, R. T. Evans, one of their number, called out to me – 'Come on Double Dot. Retire.' Picking up my telephone, I rose out of my shell hole. Standing nearby was an officer pointing his revolver at his own men. He dared not fire. Was this to end in tragedy; to lose all this hard won ground involving terrific losses? The silent officer remained silent. Suddenly the loud shout of a sergeant rang out in the wood: 'STICK IT WELSH!' To a man they stuck it, halted, turned round. Their lines were reformed as to three lines of a square whence would come the expected attack. The order had been 'Retire two hundred yards.' The order in passing along the lines was reduced to 'Retire'. They retired, but tending to crowd into the ride, some confusion arose. There was no sign whatsoever of panic. Cool as cucumbers, and little else, were in their stomachs.[60]

He describes vividly the final capture of the wood:

Our barrage crept slowly forward in full fury, the riflemen followed. Battered, bludgeoned, frustrated and angry, they burst forward with unsurpassed ferocity and determination. In severe hand to hand encounters they savagely flayed the bewildered enemy at bayonet point. Ne pointe de quartier. No prisoners taken. Thus was Mametz Wood finally and completely emptied by the 38th Welsh Division.[61]

Davies tells of the loss of one more man, even as the victory was won:

After Gerry's last fling their dead and wounded remained. Darkness falling fast, a cry of Kapilen! Kapilen! Kaplien! was heard again and again from a short distance away. Sergeant Powell, Signalmaster and Boy Scoutmaster with two young sons in the Army, was a quiet and efficient fellow. He heard the cries. I see him now, crawling through the undergrowth in the direction of the voice. He was an excellent First Aider. The cry eventually ceased. Sergeant Powell was not seen again. Unlike the priest on the road to Jericho, he did not pass by on the other side.[62]

Sergeant John Henry Powell, 42, and his wife lived at Connah's Quay in north Wales. His body was later recovered from Mametz Wood and he was buried in Morlancourt British Cemetery Number One.

The death and destruction was not yet over for Davies though, for after they had been relieved the battalion made its way back. As they did so:

... a heavy shell burst through the trees landing a few yards away. Screams of agony assaulted our ears, emitted by men whose limbs had been torn asunder. Prostrate forms lay about stripped of all their clothing. With a last glance at this carpet of whiteness in the summer darkness, with five others I started out on our return to the Happy Valley.[6]

Short of equipment and various miscellaneous items lost in the battle, we were ordered to scan the ground along the ridge with the object of replacement. So there we were in the shell-pocked arena, under fire, searching the prostrate forms for such necessities as small kit, water bottles, towels, socks, mess tins, forks, knives, spoons. We neither enjoyed, not unduly prolonged, the nauseating role of battlefield scavengers.[64]

Private G.C. Longworth of the 17th Battalion of the Royal Welsh Fusiliers was captured in Mametz Wood on 10 July.

On the 8th of July [he is a day out in these dates] the 16th Battalion failed to take the wood. We were in Happy Valley on the morning of the 8th [7th] when the 16th went over. From the valley there was a rise of about 200 yards. On this ridge the enemy played their machine gun bullets, mowing down wave after wave of the 16th. Their colonel was a casualty when our colonel took command and stopped the attack.

At the time they estimated their casualties at about 600. Two [three] days later the 13th and 14th Battalions took the wood. The 17th reinforced them. I was taken prisoner on the 10th in the wood.

The undergrowth was very thick. Our own shells were falling short, according to the theory of future planning, timing where the infantry would be at a certain time. The barrage would be extended as we advanced.

It did not turn out as they expected. Our own shells falling short brought down huge trees, causing greater obstruction, plus the undergrowth, killing our own men. Telecommunications being cut and no way of getting a message miles back to stop this ridiculous onslaught.

I was sent out as a scout before the main body. As we advanced the main body soon caught up with us. German snipers up in the trees, just sniping them off. When we got to about the centre of the wood there was a broken road running diagonally from one corner to the other. I took up a position on a bank rising on the left centre of the wood.

When things got a bit quieter Brigadier Price-Davies came along and said to us, 'How do you feel, men?' We answered, 'All right, thank you.' He then said, 'Pass it down the line that the whole line will advance to forty paces from the exterior of the wood at 4 o'clock.'

How far that message got I don't know. The advance was made by word of command – 'Advance.'

When we got to the estimated distance I took up position in a shell hole, evading machine gun fire. Then we saw Germans passing some distance to the left of us, and thought our lads would deal with that situation. Then later, we saw the enemy pass on the right. Then eventually they counter-attacked. I fired but my rifle became overheated and jammed. I ran for it but the wrong way. We were surrounded. That was my Waterloo.

There did not seem to be any Prussian Guards or any exceptionally big men there. In fact, they seemed a very mediocre lot. Their losses were very heavy, dead piled high. They hadn't time or men to bury them.[65]

George Longworth survived his captivity and was demobilised in March 1919.

Often one hears stories of men's lives being saved by Service Testaments (or the like) in breast pockets absorbing the force of a bullet. Private Hezekiah Thomas Jenkins, 17th Royal Welsh Fusiliers, of Neath, was not so fortunate. Aged 20, his Active Service Testament was shredded by the force of a bullet, possibly fired from close range, or a piece of shrapnel and he was killed inside the wood on 10 July. Although his Testament was recovered, his grave could not be identified later and he is remembered on the Thiepval Memorial.

A number of famous authors served with the Royal Welsh Fusiliers and left memoirs of their service during the Great War: Robert Graves, Siegfried Sassoon, Robert Jones, Llewelyn Wyn Griffith, Francis Philip Woodruff (also known as Frank Richards), J.C. Dunn and Ellis Humphrey Evans (also known as Hedd Wyn). Not all of these were present during or after the fighting at Mametz Wood, but several were and left behind vivid accounts of their experiences.

Robert Graves served with the Royal Welsh Fusiliers but did not take part in the fighting at Mametz Wood. However, his battalion moved into the area during the third week of July.

The next two days we spent in bivouacs outside Mametz Wood. We were in fighting kit and felt cold at night, so I went into the wood to find German overcoats to use as blankets. It was full of dead Prussian Guards Reserve, big men, and dead Royal Welch and South Wales Borderers of the New Army battalions, little men. Not a single tree in the wood remained unbroken. I collected my overcoats, and came away as quickly as I could, climbing through the wreckage of green branches. Going and coming, by the only possible route, I passed by the bloated and stinking corpse of a German with his back propped against a tree. He had a green face, spectacles, close-shaven hair; black blood was dripping from the nose and beard. I came across two other unforgettable corpses: a man of the South Wales Borderers and one of the Lehr Regiment had succeeded in bayonetting each other simultaneously. A survivor of the fighting told me later that he had seen a young soldier of the Fourteenth Royal Welch bayonetting a German in parade-ground style, automatically exclaiming: 'In, out, on guard!'[66]

Graves later famously converted this prose image to his poem 'A Dead Boche':

With clothes and face a sodden green,
Big-bellied, spectacled, crop-haired,
Dribbling black blood from nose and beard.

A close friend of Graves, Siegfried Sassoon was in the vicinity of Mametz Wood before and after the assault on the wood. Graves appears as the character David Cromlech in Sassoon's book *Memoirs of an Infantry Officer* in which Sassoon describes Mametz Wood as 'a menacing wall of gloom.' [67]

Sassoon witnessed the arrival of one of the battalions sent to take over the lines outside Mametz Wood:

In the evening we were relieved. The incoming battalion numbered more than double our own strength (we were less than 400) and they were unseasoned New Army troops. Our little trench under the trees was inundated by a jostling company of exclamatory Welshmen. Kinjack would have called them a panicky rabble. They were mostly undersized men, and as I watched them arriving at the first stage of their battle experience I had a sense of their victimization. A little platoon officer was settling his men down with a valiant show of self-assurance. For the sake of appearances orders of some kind had to be given, though in reality there was nothing to do except sit down and hope it wouldn't rain. He spoke sharply to some of them, and I felt that they were like a lot of children.[68]

Sassoon also commented on the suitability of these men for the task that lay ahead:

Visualizing that forlorn crowd of khaki figures under the twilight of the trees, I can believe that I saw then, for the first time, how blindly war destroys its victims. The sun had gone down on my own reckless brandishings, and I understood the doomed condition of these half trained civilians who had been sent up to attack the wood... Two days later the Welsh Division, of which they were a unit, was involved in massacre and confusion. Our own occupation of Quadrangle Trench was only a prelude to that pandemonium which converted the green thickets of Mametz Wood to a desolation of skeleton trees and blackening bodies.[69]

He heard reports of the fighting in the days that followed which reached him as wild rumours. 'If there had been a disastrous muddle, with troops stampeding under machine gun fire, it was twelve miles away and no business of ours...'[70]

David Jones served with the 15th Battalion of the Royal Welsh Fusiliers and wrote his epic poem *In Parenthesis* which described his experiences in Mametz Wood. Particularly moving is his account of tending to a wounded comrade:

But it's no good you can't do it with these toy spades, you want axes, heavy iron for tough anchoring roots, tendoned deep down.

When someone brought up the Jerry picks it was better, and you did manage to make some impression. And the next one to you, where he bends to delve gets it in the idle body. Private Ball is not instructed, and how could you stay so fast a tide, it would be difficult with him screaming whenever you move him ever so little, let alone try with jack-knife to cut clear the hampering cloth.

The First Field Dressing is futile as frantic seaman's shift bunged to stoved bulwark, so soon the darkling flood percolates and he dies in your arms.

And get back to that digging can't yer –
this ain't a bloody Wake
for these dead, who soon will have their dead
for burial clods heaped over.[71]

In 1969 Jones wrote in a letter:

Zero hour was 4.15am for the infantry to go forward. A heavy artillery fire began at 3.30am concentrating on the south-west corner of the wood, and the 16th Battalion R.W.F. were the first wave and suffered very heavy casualties, including their C.O. and were, I understand, twice repulsed by machine guns and other German fire. It was then our turn, and together with the depleted ranks of the 16th we advanced to the edge of the wood and then into it. We, or anyway I, as far as I can remember, had little or no information of the previous assault, but in retrospect it was because of that assault that we found in the first German trench at the edge of the wood little but dead or dying Germans (at least in the few traverses I saw).[72]

In a letter of 7 April 1971 he wrote:

I was astounded that one only of 'B' Company's officers was killed or put out of action in the assault on Mametz Wood – I thought that most of them were wounded if not killed. As recorded in 'In Parenthesis' one could not find an officer one knew once one had penetrated the wood – it was such a mix-up of units and the ratio of officer casualties was reckoned to be much higher than that of the ranks – naturally for a number of obvious reasons and in the Somme battle they still wore distinctive uniform which made them an easy target for the enemy.

As we worked our way into the deeper parts of the wood there was a mix-up not only of sections, platoons and companies but of battalions also – hence the difficulty of getting exact orders – even if one found an officer, he would be desperately trying to find men of his own platoon or company and could do little more than tell one to press on. No one seemed to be exactly informed beyond the general idea of clearing the wood of the enemy who just then seemed to still occupy it in unexpected patches.

We moved forward again into still darker mists of the wood and the confusion was no less (so it seemed to me) than before. I very nearly shot some British officer – mistaking him for a German.[73]

Jones could hear the noise of the German machine guns 'through the heavy German shell-burst and the roar of our own gunfire and the piteous cries of our own wounded.'[74]

Llewelyn Wyn Griffith also served with the 15th Royal Welsh Fusiliers and wrote his memoirs in the 1920s. He was quite clear in his account of the disagreement over the orders for the 7 July: 'Look at it now – it's a forest. What damage can our guns do to that place? If you had a good dug-out near the edge of that wood, and a machine gun, how many men would you allow to cross that slope leading up to the Wood? You'd mow them down as soon as they stood up.'[75]

He described the effect of the German fire on the two battalions of 115th Brigade:

There was a dug-out in the bank, with scores of stretchers down on the ground in front, each stretcher occupied by a fellow creature, maimed and in pain... Wounded men were crawling back from the ridge, men were crawling forward with ammunition. No attack could succeed over such ground as this, swept from front and side by machine guns at short range.[76]

He related a conversation he had with Evans: 'This is sheer lunacy. I've tried all day to stop it. We could creep up to the edge of the Wood by night and rush it in the morning, but they won't listen to me... It breaks my heart to see all this.'[77]

Describing the scene inside the wood, he wrote:

I reached a cross-roads in the Wood where four lanes broadened into a confused patch of destruction. Fallen trees, shell holes, a hurriedly dug trench beginning and ending in an uncertain manner, abandoned rifles, broken branches with their sagging leaves, an unopened box of ammunition, sandbags half-filled with bombs, a derelict machine gun propping up the head of an immobile figure in uniform, with a belt of ammunition drooping from the breech into a pile of red-stained earth – this is the livery of War.[78]

When the British artillery shells began to drop short, Griffith was ordered to send out three runners with messages to stop firing. One of these, unknown to him at the time, was his brother Watcyn who delivered his message but was killed on the return journey. His body was never found.

Lieutenant-Colonel C.D. Harvey was attached to the 10th Battalion of the South Wales Borderers and left a diary of his experiences:

Wednesday 5 July: Had a bath, had orders to be ready to move up to the Front near Mametz. Left billets at 1.30pm. Arrived in bivouac behind fighting line about 7.30pm, near Mametz.

Thursday 6 July: Battalion in bivouac all day. Left bivouac at 8pm for the attack. Spent the night waiting 600 yards in rear.

Friday 7 July: 16th Welsh started the attack at 8.30am, supported by the 11th S.W.B. At 1pm we came up to support the attack on east side of Mametz Wood. At 1.30pm Lt-Col Wilkinson was killed whilst observing the Hun position. The Battalion withdrew at 11pm. I took over the Battalion on that date.

On Saturday, 8 July, and Sunday, 9 July, the battalion was in bivouacs.

Monday 10 July: Battalion stood to at 3am and stood down directly after. Had orders at 11am to proceed to Pommiers Redoubt and stayed there for about 1 hour. Water and wire fatigues were found amounting to about 100 men. 100 men of 'A' Company went to Caterpillar Wood and 2 machine guns. At 1pm received orders to go and attack southeast edge of Mametz Wood. We attacked it by bombing and going around the enemy's flank and suffered a fair number of casualties. 2nd Lt.s. Everton and Taylor were killed. The Battalion took up a position in a trench in the wood for the night. Snipers were very active.

Tuesday 11 July: Battalion took their portion of the wood by 10am. 114th Brigade relieved 115th Brigade. We consolidated our portion of the wood. In the afternoon 2 Companies went in support of 11th S.W.B. and 2 Companies held their ground. The Brigade attacked the northern portion of the wood. At night we held the same portion of the line as on previous night. The shelling was terrific, the wood and vicinity being peppered with 5.9".

Wednesday 12 July: Battalion was relieved at 4am by the 10th West Yorks. They returned to bivouac and remained there all day. Officers wounded; 2/Lts Williams, Parry, Captain Galsworthy (at duty), Major Howell (at duty), 2/Lt Davies 'C' Company, 2/Lt Kilburn, 2/Lt Younger, Lt Gill, 2/Lt Davenport.[79]

Ted Gill had left school at ten and became a miner at 15. He attended Oxford on a scholarship provided by the South Wales Miners Federation and by 1914 was a Labour councillor. Initially opposed to the war, he enlisted in January 1915 and

was commissioned as a second lieutenant. He was awarded the Military Cross for bringing in a wounded corporal under enemy fire. At Mametz Wood he was shot through the face and spent weeks in hospital recovering before being discharged with the rank of captain.

Lieutenant Edward Gill

Private George Millership was a stretcher-bearer with the 10th Battalion South Wales Borderers. He left an account of his time at Mametz Wood:

Our job was to keep with the men, to give first aid to the wounded, send the walking wounded back to the ambulance men, and, when possible, carry the badly wounded back. It was common talk amongst our boys that some of the casualties in the 16th Welsh were caused by our own artillery. I don't recollect hearing that the 11th S.W.B. suffered in that way.

The advanced casualty clearing posts were manned by the Royal Army Medical Corps. Each regiment had its own post and causalities were cleared as quickly as possible. The slightly wounded would be returned to their own regiment later and these could spread talk amongst their battalion.

I left for France underage. When the Somme battle started on 1st July the talk was that the 38th Division would be mobile, i.e. ready to go in any sector which had successfully broken through the German line. No advance was made where the 10th Battalion was (Beaumont Hamel?) so we did not take part.

Later we foot slogged along roads congested in both direction with ambulances, waggons carrying non stretcher casualties and other military equipment. We must have been well back. There was no artillery fire.

When we arrived at the Mametz area we did not occupy any trenches. We were positioned behind a battery of 9.2 howitzers which were firing over a ridge away in the distance. I distinctly remember this because from our position behind the guns shells could be seen, like tennis balls, until they reached their highest trajectory (I did not think this possible till then). Some time afterwards I recall walking in artillery formation towards the front positions. I am not quite certain but I think we walked through the village of Mametz or rather what was left of it. Further forward the men adopted single files. I don't know the date or how far we walked.

There was no enemy artillery fire but the Germans had only recently held that ground. We were walking along the edge of a thicket, I thought, when I saw a badly wounded German, alive and conscious. So this indicated that we were following up an attack made by our troops. Our men still had their rifles slung, which suggested that the Germans were on the retreat.

263

I will never forget that some part of the time towards nightfall he blasted us with his artillery. The noise was terrific. Thinking it over now it suggests to me that the forward troops, whoever they were, had dislodged jerry and had him retreating – that would account for the lack of enemy fire on we who were in support. Then when jerry was settled in new positions he blasted away to prevent supplies etc. getting up.

I didn't see or hear of any panic amongst our troops. Personally, I had the wind up to my neck. Treating other men helps to keep your mind off yourself a bit. I don't remember hearing any criticism of the behaviour of the troops. Most of the talk of course would take place in the estaminet and canteens, and I being a tea totaller wouldn't know much about it. For the same reason I lost all talk of war when I got back home. I was happy to forget it.[80]

George Millership served two periods in France. He later served with the 2nd Battalion of the South Wales Borderers and was in the Battle of Cambrai in November 1917. He was wounded in 1918.

Lieutenant Henry Apps of the 11th Battalion South Wales Borderers recorded the events of those bloody days in a pocket diary:

Thursday 6 July. Moved off at 8pm. I was in charge of Signallers. Very slow going. Shells dropping just over the battalion. The Guns are awful.

Friday 7 July. Arrival at our destination at 2am. I got the men into shell holes. The enemy started shelling us with gas shells. We attacked at 8. All went well till we reached the ridge and then machine guns opened on us and snipers picked off officers. Hamer the Adjutant killed. I took over his job. 'B' Coy lost all their officers. I paraded the Coy after the battle. 16 men, 3 Sergeants. Battalion withdrew at 9. The road out was awful.

Saturday 8 July. Arrived at bivouac at 5am. Absolutely wet through and muddied up. Fell down to sleep just where I arrived. But could not. Somebody covered me up. Held a roll call of my platoon. 8 killed, 12 wounded, 2 missing.

Sunday 9 July. Called up at 5.30am to go into action again. My nerves are all over the place for want of sleep. I reported sick to the Doctor and tried to sleep. It is useless.

Monday 10 July. The bombardment is awful. The wood was gained and a large number of prisoners taken.

Tuesday 11 July. Took over 20 Prisoners of War and sent them to the Provost Marshal except the last six which I placed under a strong guard in the bivouac. Things are going badly in the battle for the wood. We hear that Brigade Staff has been knocked out. Lt Fletcher killed and Heppel wounded.

Wednesday 12 July. The battalion began to straggle in about 2pm. I had some hot tea ready for the men. They have had a very rough time. The Colonel is absolutely done and had to be led to bed.[81]

Private William Henry Smith (21601) of the 11th South Wales Borderers also left behind a diary telling the story of the days leading up to the attack:

July 6th Left Fricourt for Caterpillar Wood for attack on Mametse [*sic*] Wood.

July 7th 8.30am. Started the attack. 9.30am. Wounded by explosive bullet in head. Crawled back at 11am. Arrived at Minden Post Field Ambulance 3.30pm.

July 8th Arrived 36 Casualty Clearing Station. Left 36 C.C.S. Arrived Queensland Divisional Hospital.[82]

Smith survived the war and returned to his home in Nantyglo.

Drummer Luther E. Morley served with the 11th South Wales Borderers. He wrote of his experiences:

My duties were carrying small ammunition slung over my shoulder so I was out in the open all the time. The artillery was shelling that wood day and night for a week. The losses were terrible. We had to plug our ears or else we would have been deaf.

We were laying them out on ground sheets, soldiers of all ranks, some were dying, some were dead. I lost some of the pals that I loved to respect. Sergeant Ivor Rees was with me all the time, that was before he won the Victoria Cross.[83]

Luther Morley later served with the Royal Army Ordnance Corps and was demobilised in 1919.

Major Fred Smith of the 16th Welsh wrote in a letter to a police colleague on 26 July 1916:

> We have passed through a very eventful period the last five weeks, and were in the heavy fighting of the 7th, 10th, 11th and 12th of July. Our men acquitted themselves well, but many have fallen. I could say much more which would interest you, but the censor must be obeyed. We have lost eighteen out of our old officers, but modern shell and machine gun fire is such that the toll of the attackers must be great. My chaps took a machine gun from the big wood. I have it still on our wagons. Those infernal things are the most to be dreaded of all the modern engines of war, and take the greatest toll when resolutely fought.[84]

John Collins of 13 Treharne Road, Barry, served with the 16th Battalion and wrote later of his experiences with the battalion:

> After training we spent one year and six months in the French trenches. We were gassed with Lachrymal Gas [mustard gas]. Our eyes would stream. We had celluloid goggles. We never had bread in the trenches only biscuits. We would put the biscuits in the dish with water. Soup, soup, soup day after day. There were no cooks. The kitchen was pulled by mules, ovens were dropped in the wagons until they were worn out. The officers were alright, they had their own cook. We sometimes used to steal eggs when billeted in France because we were half starved.
>
> French women had to run their farms when the husband and sons were

Private John Collins

conscripted. A French soldier could get cheap red wine because they only earned 1 franc a day. We earned 5 francs a day. Some went to my mum and some was kept for after the war. I used the tuck which I kept in my kit bag, corn beef, biscuits, tin with a bit of tea, and showering kit. The biscuits went blue with the paint from the tin. The water was undrinkable. We had a mascot, a goat. The goat would go for you. Being Corporal of the goats was not a bad job.

The runner was found drunk by our Sergeant, he knew where the service rum was kept (small spoonful each morning), he opened a tin and was unconscious when found. 'Private Collins, want a job as a Captain's runner.' 'Aye, I'd love it.'

We spent 4 days in the trenches and we were lucky if we spent 4 days out. We had to memorise the village layouts because we only came out of the trenches at night. There were only flares. On the Somme there was a farmhouse nearby where an old lady sold champagne for 5fr a bottle, we bought it. The best bath I ever had was in a village in France. The river running over us, we all undressed, it made the women laugh. We knew the Royal Army Medical Corps as 'Rob All My Comrades'.

In France, at Mametz Wood, I was wounded in my elbow. We had taken a trench. My Captain sent me with a message over to the Woods. I delivered the message, never got back. I went into a big shell hole. It was dark when I got out. They bandaged my arm and I had to find my own way back. A horse stepped on my toe. 'Good thing it was an Army boot.' Soon found my way down to Boulogne and off to England.[85]

Private William B. Joshua, 'A' Company, 16th Welsh wrote:

Marching from Armentières for nearly a week to the Somme area, 25 or 30 kilometres a day, we arrived footsore and weary. The air was heavy with gas, and we had to wear goggles as it affected our eyes severely. We were paraded for a speech by Colonel Smith who told us we had been selected to attack the wood. It had been shelled for the past three days, with everything, and it was thought that there was nothing there, and we were to walk over; but whatever we met we were to go on and not stop for friend or brother.

Next morning we assembled in Happy Valley, having a meal of

267

boiled bacon and bread, being advised to save some of it for the next meal, also the rum ration which I and a few others did not take. Our two sergeants, Harris and Thomas, ordered me to empty my water bottle and filled it with rum, saying they would see me all right. I knew they would as I often had extra food from them, being noted for my hearty appetite.

We were issued with two extra bandoliers of ammunition and a spade. I being a Lewis machine gunner had two canvas buckets with loaded magazines in each. Number 4 platoon 'A' Company led the attack, our Lewis Gun was on the left flank to prevent them being cut off.

We advanced about 50 yards when the German machine guns opened up. Sergeant Harris shouted out, 'They are yards high!' and it appeared so, then going down a gentle slope to the wood the enemy got range with deadly effect.

One of my gun team gave me the signal to take a casualty's place in the team, and as I struggled on I felt like a severe electric shock to my thigh and I was down looking for my leg, thinking I had lost it. Another platoon came along and rested for a breather, leaving about 10 casualties behind including a sergeant from the Cycle Corps of which a number had joined us to bring us up to full strength. Each wave passing me left, its quota of dead behind.

Our company runner came along and asked me where Captain Herdman was, as the order was to retire. I replied he was somewhere ahead.

A large number of our planes were flying low. Now the German and our guns started up, also to add to the horror rain started to fall heavily, making the churned up ground into clinging mud. I dumped my equipment and started to crawl back, hugging the ground. Some stretcher-bearers found me and took me to a large shell hole (they were members of the Tylorstown Silver band who had enlisted en block in our early recruiting days).

Back at Happy Valley was our Medical Officer dealing with the wounded, one almost naked shivering in the rain with five separate bullet wounds in his back and buttocks. After treatment the M.O. said anyone who was able should try to move farther back as ambulances could not arrive until nightfall.

An old school pal of mine, with a head wound, and I decided to try and slowly make it as some of our shells seemed to be falling short, making us think Gerry would counter-attack.

We arrived at Battalion H.Q. and were then transported to the nearest field hospital.

My pal later became unconscious, remained so for weeks. My two sergeants, Harris and Thomas, were killed, also my closest pals, G. Leyshon, Reg Davies. We three had each other's addresses to inform our relatives in case of being a casualty. Two brothers Tregaskis died. They were always first on parade when we formed in Porthcawl, made corporals the same day, officers the same day, and died together.

It always puzzled me why we were sent over in broad daylight when we could have made the attack just before dawn.[86]

William B. Joshua won the Military Medal and was awarded the Médaille d'honneur. He was demobilised in 1919.

Signaller W. Harold Bampfield of Number 9 Platoon, 'C' Company, 16th Welsh recalled in a letter in 1974:

We were all waiting under the bank for zero hour to attack when a cousin of mine from 'D' Company came to see me. 'I don't think many of us will come back from this attack, but you will,' he said. He was killed. We were right in front of the wood. We went over the top at 8.30 am.

I saw our platoon officer Lieutenant Otto Jones get wounded. We also lost our Captain J. Williams. He was killed, and also a lot of our own boys. After the battle was over what was left of us went back and had the roll call.

We thought now we were going back for a rest. Instead of that we had a general inspection, made us up and sent us back to the wood.

While we was in the wood one German came out of the brushwood. I couldn't understand why he didn't shoot me. He put up his hands and said, 'Don't shoot, Taff.' I said to him, 'You speak English.' He said, 'And Welsh.' He asked me what part of Wales I was from. I told him from the Rhymney Valley, working underground in Bargoed. He said, 'You must have seen me. I was working on top of the gantry, shoving the trams. They used to call me "Long Tom". Just before the war broke out they recalled me to Germany to fight for the Fatherland.' I handed him over where there was some more prisoners gathered in the wood. I often wonder did he get back to Germany because they were shelling pretty heavy.[87]

Harold Bampfield joined the Army Reserve in 1919.
Ronald Nathaniel Morgan, 16th Welsh wrote:

Friday July 7th 1916. A moon with drizzle threatening. We had laid the night previous in Happy Valley, which was sheltered by a gentle eastern incline. Breakfast was fat bacon and char. Just wondered why a pre-dawn over the top had not been the idea.

Close extended order, went up and forward. About 250 yards from the wood Gerry opened up. We could not see him. Incessant flashes and drum-drum-drum indicated his whereabouts and alertment. The machine gun fire was devastating.

Len Harris (he had been our platoon officer before becoming adjutant) was urging a final rush when his waistline flared with spikey blue flashes. Shouts of 'Get down!' A gallant effort was brought to an end by enfiladed machine gun Gerry areas. We just waited. Hundreds lay on the ground, many forever. Mother Earth was never so comforting. A red staining of grass. Many were groaning.

Hours later a crawling back, some dragging wounded men. Called to an old school chum and Park Hotel fellow workmate, 'I'll be back.' Never did. He looked at me and through me and the silly goof said 'Mother'.

Ran message to Brigade H.Q. Spent Saturday and Sunday there. Very early Monday dawn ordered to report as runner between Gwent and Swansea battalions. Believe message carried was a wood outflanking idea. Went into the fringes of the wood. There were one or two incidents I never mention.

Coming back was aware of earth and branches. Shelling all around. Then nothing. I was concussed.[88]

Ronald Morgan was discharged in January 1919.
Private George Link left an account of his time at Mametz Wood with the Cardiff City Battalion:

July 7th. We were set an impossible task to take Mametz Wood. We didn't get within 100 yards of it before we lost two thirds of the

Battalion. Major Angus, who was in command, gave orders for the retreat, but if anyone tried to retreat he was sniped. I lay out in front among the dead, not daring to move until it got dark.

Lt. Tregaskis was killed by me and word was passed to his brother, who was in charge of another platoon to our right. He crawled to see his brother and he was shot through the head. Sergeant Watkins went to see if he could do anything. He met the same fate. Then a Lance Corporal moved to the same spot and he fell, one on top of the other. That made me pretend to be dead until dark. When I got back and reported who was dead, I was told that I had been among those listed as dead.

We were then relieved by the 10th S.W.B. and we returned to Happy Valley.

July 10th. There was another attack on the wood from the Fricourt side which was successful. That night we were sent to reinforce the troops in the wood. We again lost a fair number of men in doing so, including our Captain and Adjutant Jones.

We again were relieved and sent to Mailly-Maillet sector to help bury the dead.[89]

Corporal William Olsen was interviewed in 1986 about his time with the Cardiff City Battalion. He still suffered from nightmares.

It was the wood. Mametz Wood. We'd been there three days and we were exhausted. I fell asleep. When I woke up I found that my pillow was a dead German.

It was terrible. They were killing us. I went forward with men I knew well and they just disappeared. I never got wounded, although a lot of the boys with me were finished. A lot of them... I don't know what happened but I never saw them again.

Standing in the trench on the duckboards. There's a whirring noise and whump... down comes a shell right between me and my mate. A dud.

I remember Germans coming across, hands behind their necks, surrendering. We'd take their watches but we wouldn't hurt them. Not like those Ghurkhas... they were hard. Slice their ears off, they would. It they killed a German, off came the ear and they'd hang it on their belt.

I remember our Colonel Gaskell. He used to say to us, 'Now

keep your heads below the parapet, boys, keep 'em down.' He was a tall man, with long thin legs, we called him 'legs Eleven'. Well he kept telling us this but one day he forgot and stood up and... bang. A sniper had got him.

I was going to get married but I went to France. I came home once between 1914 and 1919 but by the end she'd given up waiting. She's married someone else and had children.[90]

Private Albert Evans of the same battalion wrote after the battle:

It seemed quiet as we advanced up a slope towards the wood after the noise of the bombardment. The boys were steady, each taking courage from one another and the encouragement of our young officers. We crested the ridge and moved down the forward slope towards the thick wood and then suddenly all hell broke loose as machine guns opened up on us from the front and from the flank. We stood no chance and the boys were everywhere falling, but we kept moving forward.

Suddenly I felt a blow to my ankle, just as if I had been hit by a hammer, and I went down. I lay still for a while, as it was impossible to move due to the weight of the German fire. Then came shellfire and the rain, and the ground became muddy. I lay there till dark and then crawled into a shell hole where a man of the Gwent battalion lay with a bad wound in his stomach. He told me he was a married man with two children and we comforted each other, but he was in terrible pain as there is nothing worse than a gut wound.

The night seemed endless and the cries of the wounded were terrible – some swore and others called for their mothers. One sang softly in Welsh and I recognised the words as part of the 23rd Psalm, but after a while he went silent. My Gwent pal was obviously dying and I did my best to comfort him. I stuck my rifle up to draw attention but it was immediately shot at.

We lay there all of 36 hours before the stretcher-bearers came. I told them to take my mate, as he was a married man. He told them, 'I am done for. Take the boy as he will make it.' They lifted me onto the stretcher and carried me back to the forward first aid post. I never saw my Gwent mate again. I cannot remember his name but his face will live with me forever.[91]

Private William Davies also served with the 16th Welsh:

We could not make any headway as we were in the open with no
cover, so we hugged the ground until it became dark, when I was
relieved. We went back in on the Sunday night and while forming
up to renew the attack on the Monday morning we were very
heavily shelled. I was wounded in the leg, thigh and arm just as the
attack started.[92]

He remembered little of the time he lay there under fire, as
he was barely conscious, but he could recall the sorrow he felt
at watching his comrades fall under the hail of German fire.

While he was there a cousin who had been brought up with
him, and whom he regarded as a brother, located him, and did
what he could to make him comfortable. Then he moved on
into the wood and was never seen or heard from again.

William carried reminders of the battle with him long after
the war – in the 1980s he had 11 pieces of shrapnel removed
from his leg.

An unknown private of the 16th Welsh gave the following
account to his daughter:

Our Headquarters were in Suicide Valley. We marched up the hill
and down to Happy Valley just before 6.00am, which was supposed
to be zero hour. Then everything was cancelled till 8.00am and
cancelled again till 9.00am. By this time the tension, and the
language, were dreadful.

Minor accidents started to occur, possibly due to the great
tension. One man leaned on his rifle and shot himself in the armpit
– the safety catch was off! Apart from these incidents everything
was very quiet. There was no shelling and no rifle firing. In fact, it
was a lovely sunny morning.

Then it was time to stand to and it was 'over the top'. At once
everything opened up – machine guns on top of the huge trees
mowed many down; they just went on sweeping across the whole
front. We had only gained about two yards when we were given
orders to lay flat.

'C' Company ran through but were mown down. They too were

told to lay flat. Orders came to creep back to Happy Valley. (Only 40 left in the Platoon out of 250 men.)

Orders came to line up again and we went over the top again after 15 minutes but were swept down again. We were once more ordered to lay flat and were not able to move till darkness fell. We were told to make own way back to Headquarters (Suicide Valley).

10th July. 'D' Company was too weak in numbers to hold line so we acted as ammunition carriers to the others of the City Battalion.

Those in charge said the wood was clear (aeroplanes had been over) so they advanced in daylight. A couple of yards into the wood and all hell broke loose. There had been no British artillery fire, no German artillery fire, until the 10th July.

Eventually, we were told by the officers in charge to take cover wherever we could and to get back as best we could after dark. I and another man went down some steps in the wood and found ourselves, we thought, in a deserted underground hospital. We fell asleep and awoke some hours later to find two German soldiers staring at us. We wondered why we hadn't been killed but instead the Germans were anxious to surrender and were duly taken prisoner.'[93]

On 15 July 1916, *The Western Mail* carried an account from a Private from Merthyr Tydfil titled 'Huns Outflanked: Thrilling Charge by Welsh Borderers':

The really lively time was when the Germans had a try at taking back the ground we had won in Mametz Wood. We were ready for them, and we fairly pumped the lead into them as they came forward out of the darkness, shouting for their Kaiser, and stabbing and thrusting like madmen. Whole lines went down like ninepins, and at some places corpses were piled high enough to make a breastwork, under the protection of which survivors were able to rest and reform their line.

It was from behind one of these human breastworks that the final assault was made. Directly they sprang up we opened fire again. I never saw such beautiful work. We smashed them to bits with our first volley, and what was left of them bolted like frightened rabbits. All unknown to them other troops of ours had been working round both flanks, and just when the Huns had settled down nice and comfortable in their quarters behind their dead mates, our flanking parties got on to them. They fairly skipped with fright at the first volley, but before they could clear out our boys were into them with the bayonet. There was some dandy work, I can tell you, and many a Hun was sent packing.

That finished them for the night, but next morning the arrival of fresh troops put new life into them, and they made another attack, which was led up to by a furious bombardment. We reserved our fire until the attacking masses were close up. Then we let them have round and round of rapid. It paralysed and pulverised them. They didn't know what to fire, and cut their lines to ribbons again and again. Quickly they were redressed by the countless reserves that were being rushed up, and like madmen they swept into our trenches. We flung them out headlong in quick time, but they came back again and again, and the slaughter was absolutely sickening. In front of our position for as far as the eye could reach, the ground was littered with dead and wounded. The flying Huns after their last repulse had to pick their way back over the dead bodies of their comrades, and scores of them were shot down to keep their mates company.[94]

One survivor who had an unusual tale to tell was Private Gwilym Jones from Kenfig Hill. Gwilym entered the wood with the 19th Welsh but during his pioneering duties he became cut off from his fellow soldiers and found himself behind the

German line. He took cover in a poultry hut and stayed there for the next three days until the Germans retreated and he was able to make his way back. He was just 18 and so should not have been serving abroad at all.

Private Gwilym Jones

Accounts by the men of The Royal Field Artillery

John Daniels served with 10th Brigade of the Royal Field Artillery, which was attached to the 38th Welsh Division. He took part in the attack on 10 July as a signaller.

He recalled the order being given to the infantry to fix bayonets and they advanced down the chalk cliff. He advanced with the second wave after signalling to the gun batteries from the top of the cliff. John carried a telephone and semaphore flags, a revolver and his rations. The ground had been cut up badly by artillery fire and was full of shell holes. Royal Flying Corps planes flew overhead. The artillery fire meant that the men around him were optimistic about the attack, expecting it to be easy work.

He noticed that the barbed wire had been smashed in places, but in other places it was still intact. Before the advance the men had blamed local French people for providing information to the enemy regarding transport movement. However, he said, it was discovered that the Germans had a secret weapon, which consisted of copper pipes driven into the ground about 150 yards apart. These pipes were wired together with a receiver, and through these they were intercepting the British telephone conversations.

There was a German trench on the outside edge of the wood, pillboxes with machine guns, but no barbed wire on the edge. Dead Germans lay all around.

When he got into the wood itself he could see only stumps in the semi darkness. All was terrible confusion, with no general policy followed, but there were no signs of panic.

John was later awarded the Military Medal for his conduct that day, trying to keep up communications between the infantry and the guns. He recalled sending messages back to the guns to fire on places where the German machine guns were concentrated.

Gunner C.B. Thomas served with the 113th Siege Battery of the Royal Garrison Artillery:

I was on the 6-inch howitzers right behind the 16th Welsh and 11th South Wales Borderers. I well remember how we kept up the barrage for several days and we were told they were going over the top at 8.30am so we had to keep on firing all through the night, and what a dreadful massacre that was.

One thing that sticks out in my mind was the number of German snipers hanging dead up in the trees (what was left of the trees). I don't think I shall ever forget that sight.

As for our own Battery we suffered very heavy casualties during that time, and the majority of our dead are buried in a little place called Carnoy Valley. We were the old Territorial Army and most of our lads came from Cardiff, Barry and Penarth, and sometimes in the summer months, when we take a trip to Penarth, I always go through the names of the boys who are on the war memorial.[95]

Accounts by the men of the Field Ambulance Brigades

George Henry Jickells enlisted in Barry on 1 December 1914 as one of a St John Field Ambulance Brigade that was being formed for the new 'Welsh Army'.

He arrived on the Somme on 1 July 1916.

The sight of that day I shall never forget, as at this place Puchevillers there was a big Casualty Clearing Station and the wounded were coming to the above place in hundreds, in fact for hours along the road leading to the C.C.S. you could see nothing else but ambulance cars, motor lorries etc. conveying wounded to the above place.

Our Officer Commanding sent nearly all we stretcher-bearers up to the C.C.S. to help unload the ambulance cars etc. It was a pitiful sight to see the hundreds of wounded lying out in the boiling sun and the majority of them as helpless as babes. The above could not be helped as all the Divs. etc. were working like slaves dressing wounds, operating etc., and without that all the wards etc. at the C.C.S. were full up. Amongst the wounded at the above were a few Boches and they were always treated well.

On the morning of 8 July [he is a day out with these recollections] our small party of stretcher-bearers left the Citadel, marched to Carnoy, a distance of about two and a half miles across country. Also all our stretcher-bearers left headquarters

Men of the 130th (St John) Field Ambulance

at Morlancourt and rode in motor lorries to Carnoy, a distance
of seven miles. At the above place all we stretcher-bearers joined
together and stood to, a little, while awaiting orders.

Well, after a bit of fussing with our Advanced Dressing Station
we were marched down towards the Mametz Wood, a distance of
nearly four miles from Carnoy. I must say that at the later place
Carnoy, a temporary hospital had been fixed up and the 129th
were working same between the above and the Mametz Wood, a
distance of two miles.

We had what we called the A.D.S. and from the aid post we
brought all the wounded down to the A.D.S. The A.D.S. we called
Triangle Post and the hospital at Carnoy we called Minden Post.
I will now give the chief particulars of the fighting by our Div. for
the above wood.

It was 8am on the morning of the 8 July [see note above re
dates] that the first attack on the Mametz Wood was made by the
16th Welsh (Cardiff City) and the 10th South Wales Borderers.
The above was a complete failure and the slaughter of the above
battalions was terrible. It was as they were going over the brow of
the hill towards the wood, a distance of about fifty yards, that they
were cut up so much with Fritz's machine guns etc.

Well it was on the following day that all we stretcher-bearers went back to our respective headquarters at Morlancourt and the A.D.S. at the Citadel, Fricourt. After a little rest all we stretcher-bearers again left the above headquarters and marched down towards the wood for the second attack.

This second attack came off on the morning of the 11 July at 6am. The above attack proved successful. I must say that this second attack was taken part in with all the battalions in the Div. and same attacked the wood under our artillery fire. This took Fritz on the surprise and this broke the back of Fritz for a start.

Well at this second attack the wood was fought for and also successfully taken, but by Jove the cost in the sacrifice of lives was too awful for words. The above days that we were in the attack we were carrying wounded from the wood to the Triangle and from there to the hospital at Carnoy as fast as we could. Very little food we had, and sleep was out of the question altogether.

It was on the 12 July that our division was relieved from the Somme fighting and we of our Field Ambulance were taken back to our headquarters at Morlancourt in motor lorries, absolutely dead beat. I must not forget to say that our division worked equally hard as we did down at the wood and at the other posts I have before mentioned.

I am sorry to say that we lost two of our boys killed just near the wood, Lance Corporal West and Private Houston. The former was killed by one of our premature shells and the latter by a sniper. Also we had three wounded, Privates H. Williams and Lui Jones, and Lance Corporal Rees, although by Jove we were lucky in not losing nearly all the lot, as to term it, up there it was like Hell let loose. Our divisional artillery did good work down the Somme. I fancy I can hear the guns now firing on the wood.[96]

Private George Groves wrote in his diary:

Division went into action in Big Push July 7th at Mametz. Had the job of taking the wood. Had a hell of a time while we were there, about 4 hours sleep in 5 days, short of food, living on biscuits and bully. One day our field ambulance dealt with 1700 patients. Poor old Bill West and Houston killed. Was talking to Houston when he was sniped. Our Division took the woods at a heavy cost.[97]

Men from the 129th and 131st Field Ambulances arrived
and at 6 a.m. worked to retrieve the casualties who had lain out
on the open ground all night. As the first group left their trench
to move forward, Private William Houston from Bolton was
shot through the left eye. He was taken back to the Regimental
Aid Post of the 16th Welsh and his wound dressed. An attempt
was made to evacuate him along the trench but he died on the
journey. He was buried in a shell hole alongside the trench. At
this time a very severe bombardment was taking place and the
men of the 130th had to dress a large number of casualties who
were hit in the trench they were in.

Neither West nor Houston's graves were able to be located
later and they are both commemorated on the Thiepval
Memorial to the missing.

When the attack on the wood resumed on 10 July, the scale
of the casualties threatened to overwhelm the Regimental Aid
Posts. A request was sent for additional stretcher-bearers and
31 men who had spent all night dressing wounds volunteered
to go forward. Men from the 77th Sanitary Section also
volunteered to serve as stretcher-bearers, as did men from the
Army Service Corps.

Captain Ffoulkes of this brigade wrote later of his
experiences:

130th Field Ambulance
38th Division British Expeditionary Force France
July 18th 1916
Annwyl deulu bach,
    Dyma gyfle o'r diwedd i ddanfon gair bach a dweud ychydig o
hanes yr ymladd.
    [Dear Little Family,
    Here's a chance at last to have a quick word with you to tell you
a little about the fighting.]
    I have wanted to write so often but it has been out of the
question during the last fortnight or so. Had there been a time, I
had no writing material as all our transport with kits were unable

to come to the front area. We have had a trying time and thankful as I am to have come through it untouched, I would not have missed it for anything – it has been a wonderful experience. You have all read of the great fighting that is going on and probably feel as we do that our superiority over the enemy is gradually beginning to tell. We are still a great distance from our goal, and great sacrifices will still have to be made – but we believe that it will bring us to success and a satisfactory termination of this tedious war.

I cannot tell you much of my experiences until I see you – whenever that may be. Some of it I wish to forget and part of it is still rather vague to me. We got into action on July 7 in a place whose name is probably well known to you. Mewn coedwig fach wyddoch – a sill gyntaf yr un enw â'r Cymraeg am 'mother'.

[In a small forest, you know – the first syllable of the Welsh word for 'mother'.]

Our Advanced Dressing Station was about 2½ miles behind it, so our stretcher-bearers had a long distance to carry. I took them up in the morning to a slight hollow about 300 yards from the wood, where the Regimental Aid Posts – with battalion doctors were stationed. We had to evacuate wounded over the open under shrapnel and machine gun fire which was most trying.

Our men worked splendidly, without a stop until the night of July 8 and we only had 10 casualties amongst the stretcher-bearers – 2 killed and 8 wounded which considering the dangerous ground was wonderful. That night I took them out to rest and we again went up on the evening of the 9th. We were at it with very little sleep and food until the evening of 12th Wednesday. I hope I may never again have to ask men to work so terribly hard in such desperate surroundings without food or rest. At times it seemed hopeless even to get out of it with a whole skin. German shrapnel and machine gun fire was killing wounded all round us, but we did get out, with the exception of our casualties, without being very much the worse for it. Some of our men were badly shaken from shell concussion but they were recovering after rest.

The first two days I was with medical officers of the Cardiff City and one of the Gwent battalions. Both suffered heavy losses. The former especially. Many of my friends are either killed or wounded but I had the satisfaction of dressing some of them and doing all I could to make them comfortable. Medical Officers are also among causalities. Poor Dr Raymond Jones was killed – a bullet through his lung which killed him almost immediately. Dr Lawrence, a battalion MO was killed by shrapnel. Drs David and Walsh were wounded. The former through the shoulder, the latter shot through the wrist. Most of us who were in the front line had so many narrow escapes, but we all feel proud to have been there and to have been able to attend to a great number of wounded – Germans as well as ours.

I cannot but admire the German wounded for the splendid way in which they bore their pain and some of them had dreadful wounds but there was no complaint and in very many cases, expressions of gratitude. One German officer whom I dressed gave me his helmet which I hope to bring home with me when the time comes.

We are still in the front area, a little to the south of where acute fighting is taking place. At present the division is doing ordinary trench warfare which is blissful rest after what it has gone through. We are manning two advanced dressing stations, but I have not yet seen them. I am having absolute rest at present as I am supposed to have had a strenuous time. Later I hope to take charge of one of them and enjoy life in the same peaceful old way as we used to when trench fighting in Flanders!

Thank you all very much for your letters – yours and Gwen's have been very helpful during the last few days. Gwen told me the sad news that her cousin – the son of Mrs Jones, Penmaenmawr, has died of wounds received in action. Poor boy, it is such a tragedy and such a trial for his mother who simply adored him. Fortunately for us, we have no time to brood over these sad losses which are so many nowadays, but the anxiety must be very great at home where there is such long waiting and where people cannot possibly realise the circumstances under which battles are fought. Gwen tells me her cousin is buried in a little town not very far from here. If I have an opportunity, I shall go to see his grave – she asked me to do that and let them know.

I will write again as soon as I have an opportunity. Please don't worry about me – I am none the worse for wear – little thinner perhaps but they are feeding me up like a fighting cock and I shall soon be enormously fat! So be prepared when I come home on leave. Whenever that may be. I look forward to it very much and long to see you all, but that happy time is sure to come with a little patient waiting.

Cariad mawr iawn atoch oll deulu annwyl – a chofiwch ysgrifennu eto.

Oddiwrth Meredydd

[Much love to all my dear family – and remember to write again soon,

From Meredydd]

Send this letter to Annie and Ada as soon as you can they will also be anxious to have news of me.[98]

C Section of the 130th (St John) Field Ambulance

A letter from an unnamed fellow officer in September of that year stated: 'It was sad about poor Ned Lawrence. I was with him here for some time and in the trenches. Poor Jones who was at my last Dressing Station was also killed and David was wounded. I had a very narrow shave when my dug out was blown half away whilst my servant and I were asleep in it!'[99]

The wounded were evacuated to the Main Dressing Station at Thièvres, or the two associated Advanced Dressing Stations – which were steel dug-out shelters – and other posts, which between them could care for up to 630 sick and wounded men. Baths were also available through which 100 men per hour could be bathed. This was essential in order to remove the hair and body lice, the scratching from which resulted in skin conditions such as ulcers, impetigo, scabies, boils and myalgia. At Thièvres the 130th Field Ambulance converted a barn into a scabies hospital. Infected lice also caused 'trench fever', a condition that began with sharp pains in the shins followed by a high fever. While the men bathed, their uniforms were disinfected with Creosol and fumigated. Clean shirts and underwear were issued but within hours the men were usually lousy once more.

Accounts by the men who were Prisoners of War

Private Thomas Morris of the Welsh Regiment was captured at Mametz Wood and arrived home in Port Talbot in July 1918 after 18 months in captivity in Germany. He had been reported killed at the time and his family went into mourning, holding a memorial service. He was in fact wounded before being taken prisoner and had experienced great suffering, his wound being untreated for a week. He survived on the parcels received from home.

Another man taken prisoner at Mametz Wood was Private Stanley Watkins of the 14th Welsh. He arrived home in Swansea in December 1918 and complained of ill treatment, bad food, kicks and curses. He said that without the parcels he received from home he doubted whether he would have survived the previous two years. He had worked in different parts of Germany, working with wood and iron.

Charles Watkins was born in Hereford and when the war started he was working as a collier at Abercynon. On 23 March 1915 he enlisted in the 13th Welsh, claiming he was 19 years old; he was only 17.

He was listed as missing on 10 July but on 10 August he was reported to be a prisoner of war. Watkins spent the rest of the war in a German camp and returned to Great Britain on 3 December 1918 – almost three years to the day after he had first landed in France.

In February 1919 Charles Watkins was discharged from the Army at the Military Hospital Barracks in Cardiff. At the discharge medical he complained of knee pain and declared 'I am suffering from rheumatism due to the conditions under which I lived in Germany'.[100]

A Welsh newspaper reported the experiences of a soldier captured by the Germans at Mametz Wood:

We were taken to Cambrai and from there, travelling in a railway van (60 in each van), with the doors shut for three days, to Dülmen Camp in Westphalia. In the first few months we were treated outrageously, and suffered many indignities. We were forced to be inoculated five times and vaccinated once in the first three weeks. The food was of a very poor quality and exceedingly small in quantity. The only solid food we had was the daily ration of bread – one slice half-an-inch thick.

We were forced to work every day, when we were unable to stand on our feet almost through weakness. It was a common occurrence for us to go and look into swill tubs and refuse heaps etc., for anything we could find, and considered ourselves lucky if we got some potato peelings, which we ate with relish.

In November 1916 I was included in a working party sent to Russian Poland to work, and arriving at our destination after a train journey of four days, were sent out immediately to work. As soon as it was light enough to see in the morning, we started to work, and worked until it was too dark to work any longer, with half-an-hour's break midday.

We were put in a barn to sleep on some straw. We were given no blankets and the cold was unbearable. Owing to ill nourishment and weakness, we were infested with vermin.

After six weeks of this treatment we were sent back to Dülmen. Our parcels from England were coming through by this time and things improved a little. The Germans would never try to make us comfortable but they would go a long way out of their way to make us uncomfortable.

I was shifted from Dülmen to the camp at Sennelager, where, after a little time, I was appointed the bandmaster of the British concerts; and in this position was given many privileges.

I was an eyewitness of many murderous assaults and atrocities committed on our men by German sentries. Early in 1917 I witnessed the arrival of a party of British prisoners who had been made to work behind the firing line for two or three months. They were in a terrible and emaciated condition. They looked like mere bags of bones, and they died at the rate of six and seven per day. Very few of them pulled through. All our thanks are due to our own Government for supplying us with food. We could not possibly live on the German rations. They are a barbarous set of people and after being in their hands for two and a half years, I need hardly say how much I appreciate the fact that I am home again.[101]

General Sir Douglas Haig wrote in his diary on Tuesday, 4 July:

I visited Sir H. Rawlinson soon after noon. I impressed on him importance of getting Trônes Wood to cover right flank, and Mametz Wood and Contalmaison to cover left flank of attack against the Longueval front.[102]

7 July: After lunch I visited H.Q. Fourth Army and saw General Rawlinson. I directed him to get Mametz Wood and push on towards Pozières.[103]

8 July: Sir H. Rawlinson stated that his plan was now to pierce the Enemy's second line near Bazentin-le-Grand. I pointed out the necessity for having possession of Mametz Wood before making any attempt of that kind. The moment for taking the Enemy by surprise here had passed, and the fighting in Mametz Wood showed that the Enemy's 'morale' was still good. I therefore gave

Rawlinson an order to consolidate his right flank strongly in the south end of Trônes Wood, and to capture Mametz Wood and Contalmaison before making any attempt to pierce the Enemy's second line. This was later confirmed in writing.[104]

9 July: We then visited H.Q. XV Corps at Heilly and saw General Horne. He was very disappointed with the work of the 17th Division (Pilcher) and 38th Welsh Division (Philipps). Both these officers have been removed. In the case of the latter division, although the wood had been most adequately bombarded, the division never entered the wood, and in the whole division the total casualties for the 24 hours are under 150! A few bold men entered the wood and found little opposition. Deserters also stated Enemy was greatly demoralized and had very few troops on the ground.[105]

10 July: Two brigades of 38th Division (Welsh) had succeeded in entering Mametz Wood, and 2 battalions were pushing on and clearing it. After lunch I visited Querrieu and saw Rawlinson and his Chief of Staff. [Rawlinson's Chief of Staff was Major-General Bernard Montgomery.] As regards the first day of the bombardment, I said Mametz Wood and Contalmaison must be in our hands to secure our left flank, while Trônes Wood must be held on our right. At present the enemy is in Trônes Wood, but we'll recapture the whole of it tonight. Progress in Mametz Wood is satisfactory; and we should capture Contalmaison this afternoon.[106]

Haig was incorrect. More bloody fighting would be necessary on subsequent days to capture Mametz Wood.

More than two years after the battle for Mametz Wood had ended, an article appeared in *The Cambria* newspaper:

The Fight at Mametz Wood – A Full Narrative of Welsh Gallantry by a Soldier of the 38th Royal Welsh Fusiliers
   The full narrative of the fight in 1916 when the 38th (Welsh) Division took Mametz Wood has never been related. Below we print from the pen of a soldier who took part, a vivid story of the great battle the first, we hope, of a series in which the epic story will be related in all its phases.
   In the darkness of the early hours of December 1st 1915, the first battalions of the 38th Division marched out of Winchester.

Nine days later they received their introduction to trench warfare at Laventie and Neuve Chapelle with the Guards' Division, with whom a year and a half afterwards they fought side by side on Pilkem Ridge. On 5th January 1916 the Welsh Division first held a sector of the line on their own at Richebourg. For the next few months their history was in connection with places, since become famous, from Frauguiseart to the Brick – fields at Givenchy-la-Bassée.

Training

The 38th Division for a long time was not split up, and its constitution was the same when at last, on the night of June 10th, it was withdrawn from the Laventie line, as when exactly six months earlier it first saw the trenches, or when it did divisional training on the Hampshire Downs.

Then followed days of marching south through pleasant country and colliery districts, through the regions of divisional rest they had not seen before, each day leaving the line farther behind until they arrived in the St Pol area, where the serious training for the Somme was to begin.

Divisional training came to an end and St Pol was left behind during a night of marching in the rain now towards the line, past miles of ammunition and supply wagons, marches that ended sometimes in villages that had never seen English troops before. Each night brought the constant distant roar of the guns nearer, and occasionally individuals would get into touch with troops who were waiting close up for the day of the attack.

July 1st 1916

July 1st was a glorious sunny day. The 38th were behind the 8th Army Corps, and about nine o'clock they saw the first string of ambulances laden with dust-covered men of the 4th and 29 Divisions of Gallipoli fame – Ulstermen, Newfoundland, South Wales Borderers and Monmouths, while all day walking cases and prisoners arrived at the clearing station and cages. From the wounded they heard tales of disaster – of Gommecourt, Beaumont Hamel, and apparently impregnable Thiepval.

Soon they were night marching south again, past streams of wagons moving up and ambulances coming down and all night long the sky was a constant flicker of shrapnel, with here and there the steady stream of a Verey light, until the early hours of July 4th they arrived through at Treux. Treux had 'gone dry'. Madame was very sorry, but everything had been consumed by preceding divisions, and all road transport was monopolised by the Army. The rain eased off, and that evening, a train left with troops going back laden with souvenirs of the fight. The atmosphere was one of victory. The Germans had been driven out of Fricourt, Mametz and Montauban, and the powerful enemy trench system in that quarter was ours. It was there that the 38th were to play their part, when in the morning the flying column came to an end and they moved up to go into action.

The 38th relieved the 7th Division on famous ground. Driven out of their frontline, the enemy had put up a still resistance in Danzig Alley and Pommiers Redoubt before being forced into Mametz Wood. In one corner of the famous communication trench a machine gunner had made a stand, and taken a heavy toll of the attackers as they advanced up the slope from the village below. On the far side the ground was covered with the bodies of Germans killed in their flight, and the trench was littered with ammunition and rifles. The 2nd Royal Irish had held a trench in the wood but had been forced to retire and when the 38th Division arrived the 1st Royal Welch Fusiliers were holding White Trench with a sunken road between them and the wood.

Mametz Wood, Danzig Alley and White Trench were dug in the chalk. Pommiers Redoubt and Fritz Trench in sticky clay, and during the days that followed, heavy rains made these trenches anything but pleasant. Here the Welsh waited for five days, and from Danzig Alley on the Friday [July 7th] witnessed the attempts to take Quadrangle Support and Contalmaison, whilst in front of Mametz Wood was being enacted, in the rain and mud, a tragedy which was to be felt all over the eastern end of South Wales.

In conjunction with attacks on their right and left, two battalions of the 115th Brigade – the 16th (Cardiff City) Battalion, Welsh Raiment and 10th (Gwent) Battalion, South Wales Borderers – made a frontal attack on Mametz Wood. They advanced out of the sunken road on to the strip of ground in front of the wood until they suddenly came under a devastating fire from the German trench, where the machine gunners and riflemen had the rise of the ground and the screen of the shrubs in their favour. The attacking battalions were at last forced to stop. Unable to advance, and unwilling to retire, they lay down in the open and took what cover they could in the sodden ground, many using their steel helmets as a shield. There they stayed, being sniped at from the trench and the tops of trees, until the attack was abandoned.

That evening a brigade of another division made an unavailing attack on the wood.

Still it rained, and the dull atmosphere of Mametz Wood, which had already cost dearly, assumed a more sinister aspect. It was known to be the largest and thickest wood in the Somme district, and it had defied repeated attacks. By day its black bulk seemed to offer an impenetrable front, whilst by night, lit up with shrapnel and H.E., it seemed impossible that anyone could live there.

On Saturday the weather improved, and on Sunday part of the division withdrew to the hollow for a rest. The sun was warm and the ground dried rapidly. Everything was favourable for an attack, when that evening an order was sent round drawing attention to the deeds of other Welsh battalions in the battle, and stating that in the morning it would be left to the 38th Division to decide whether the name of the Welsh Division was to live in history. It has figured on more than one glorious field since then, but this was the blooding of the Welsh Division.

The Attack Starts

Shortly after midnight, the troops for the front line of the attack began to pass down to White Trench. Then the barrage dropped on Mametz Wood. The bombardment had been continuously heavy, but now it was terrifying in its intensity. Soon the Germans were searching for our guns and raking the trenches down, which the supports had to pass. The din was deafening. The Germans were to be driven out of the wood that day. If they had to be burned out, and waiting alongside a special brigade of Royal Engineers who were shaking the earth and lighting up the form of the wood with the terrific explosions of their aerial torpedoes, was a French brigade ready to turn on the enemy their own fiendish flammenwerfer. This, however, the success of the first assault rendered unnecessary.

The attack was from the south, with the 114th (Welsh) Brigade on the right, and the 113th (Royal Welsh Fusiliers) Brigade under Brigadier-General (Now Major-General) Pryce Davies [sic], V.C., D.S.O., on the left, the battalion for the first line being the 13th

(2nd Rhondda) Battalion, Welsh Regiment on the right, the 14th (Swansea) Battalion Welsh Regiment in the centre, and the 16th Battalion Royal Welsh Fusiliers on the left. It was a dismal morning, and the light was still dull when the line went over.

The 16th Royal Welsh Fusiliers were in position in the sunken road about 3.00 am and whiled away the trying hour before the attack with banter and snatches of song. Their colonel had come in to lead the attack. A regular cavalry officer, who had been a prominent figure in polo circles in days of peace. Colonel Carden was a striking figure known throughout the whole brigade. Immaculately dressed, cane in hand, his appearance had now a reassuring influence. Someone had struck up 'Aberystwyth' as the moment of going over drew near. When the singing had finished Colonel Carden called for silence, and addressing the men he was about to lead into the wood that had the grave of many, he said, 'Boys, make your peace with God! [The words are taken from a letter written soon after the action.] We are going to take that position, and some of us won't come back but we are going to take it. This,' tying his handkerchief to his stick, 'will show you where I am.' Then with a few instructions as to a slight change of direction, he waved his stick and said, 'Come on.' He was hit almost immediately, but refusing assistance he rose and, encouraging his men, made another dash at the trench before he was hit a second time and fell dead.

Local Battalions

In spite of the fierce bombardment the enemy had not left their trench just inside the wood, and the 16th now without their colonel and several officers ,were practically held when they were caught up in the waves of the 14th (Caernarvon and Anglesey) Battalion, Royal Welsh Fusiliers and the 15th (London Welsh) Battalion. Royal Welsh Fusiliers and the whole lot, breaking through a hail of bullets and bombs in which it seemed impossible for men to live, fell on the Germans with their bayonets. The defenders had no intention of giving up the wood. About an hour before the attack they had been reinforced by a division who had been sent there to a quiet sector for a rest from the Verdun front, and had brought with them their brand new kit, which were now trampled underfoot in a furious bomb and bayonet struggle. The Lewis gunners, advancing with their guns, had received close attention from the snipers, but one gunner, who had been firing from the shoulder all the way, now stood on the parapet pumping bullets into any who attempted to get away into the wood.

Everywhere the enemy had clung to his front line, but the Swansea Battalion in the centre went through without a check, one officer taking a machine gun single-handed. The 2nd Rhonddas entered the wood, but had to be reinforced by the 15th (Carmarthen) Battalion, Welch Regiment and soon the 10th (1st Rhonddas) Battalion, Welsh were in the fight.

In the Wood

Every alternate tree in Mametz Wood appeared to be blown up, and yet it was an impenetrable tangle of standing trees, prostrate trees, roots and branches and dense undergrowth as high as a man's head. To keep a sense of direction was impossible. The odds were all on the defenders who could be expected to know what paths there were, but the Welsh followed them everywhere. They bombed the trenches that ran round each side of the wood until the Germans had to break for the open, where they were shot down by the machine gun in White Trench and Caterpillar Trench or try to find a way through the undergrowth, where our men followed over the bodies of British troops who had been killed in the first occupation, and unburied Germans. Sometimes they had to struggle through the clinging branches with rifle and bayonet about their heads until their chance came, and against an extra stiff thicket, a solitary corpse or wounded man would tell a tale of single combat. The wood rang with the noise of rifle and bomb, the shouts of men and Captain Haggard's slogan, 'Stick it Welsh!' Snipers posted amongst the branches caught many a pursuer, and one Swansea battalion man limping back said he had been blown out of a trench by a small hand-mine. The movement of the troops amongst the trees set up a cloud of acrid dust, deposited on the leaves through the explosion of shells that made some believe they were being gassed. Men following each new enemy they started and the shouts of their comrades found themselves fighting on battalion fronts far from their own, until at last the drive across the wood was reached where, with a short open space in front, the line righted itself.

The advance now showed signs of being held up by the fire from Wood Support Trench, and an arm of the wood that went off to the left. At 6.30 the 13th Royal Welsh Fusiliers were moved up, and they cleared the trench, but persistent sniping and fire was kept up from the wood, and the enemy attempted a counter-attack which reached the hastily formed line. A halt was called at this point, and the battalions which had become mixed in the first rush were reformed.

The Afternoon

In the afternoon the advance was resumed and a body of Germans between 80 and 100 strong – the garrison that had caused the trouble to the left flank – laid down their arms to the 13th Royal Welsh Fusiliers. That afternoon the wood was cleared on the left beyond the railway, and our men reached the fields on the far side but, owing to the German resistance on the right, they had once more to withdraw into the wood.

Meanwhile, below the wood a diminishing army of stretcher-bearers was performing wonderful feats of endurance and gallantry in an attempt to deal with an every growing crowd of wounded. Over the ridge which is surmounted by White Trench they went time after time, choosing this route, which offered no cover from the barrage, as being the shortest route to Queen's Nullah, where the aid posts were placed. About three o'clock a shell dropped right into Queen's Nullah and destroyed the 13th Royal Welsh Fusiliers' aid post, killing the battalion doctor and killing or wounding six of the bearers. The bravery with which bearer parties carried out the tremendous task of searching for and evacuating the wounded from Mametz Wood – a task which called for nerve and stamina beyond the usual without the excitement of the fighter, was beyond praise.

The Germans had begun to shell the captured portion of the wood, and to the other sounds of battle was added the tearing, splitting noise of fallen timber, and big trees crashed to earth amongst the advancing troops.

The Division had already captured the strongest defences, a large howitzer which lay near the central drive, about three hundred prisoners and a number of machine guns, but an old chateau on the right was causing trouble, and the enemy was bringing a heavy fire to bear from a trench on a ridge beyond. Night fell, and the morning saw very little change in the position. The wood was practically all captured, but they couldn't get out on the farther side.

After more shelling the 115th Brigade were put into the attack, and they made some progress, but did not clear the place, and every hour spent in it meant casualty upon casualty. Every time a platoon reformed there was a tale of death and wounds to tell, added to which was the trial of moving in a place where one could see no distance ahead and the prospect of a second night, such as the first, to be spent in a wood already drenched with Welsh blood.

The Second Day

The Germans replied to our fire on the second afternoon with the heaviest barrage they put down so far. The battalions resting around the Central Drive were heavily battered and one shell put out of action the colonel of the 13th Royal Welsh Fusiliers [Lieutenant-Colonel O.S. Flower] who died of his wounds the next day, the second-in-command, the adjutant and a couple of runners. To add to the effect of the enemy's fire, some of our own light shells would now and then catch the top of a high tree and explode prematurely. A telegram later indicated that Flower had died from the effects of a bayonet wound.

The experiences of two men of different brigades will give some idea of what the fighting was like.

One bomber of the 115th Brigade, wounded in the arm during a dugout fight in the advance on the second day, made off for what he thought was his rear, when he suddenly found himself confronted by a dressing station and a man with a red cross brassard on his arm, but the dug-out was a German one, and the man a member of the German Medical Corps – not our own R.A.M.C. He then knew that he had been making rapid strides into German territory far ahead of our own front line. The German motioned him down five steps and dressed his wounds. There he sat amongst German wounded speculating as to the nationality of the hospital he would eventually reach, when he heard the shout of our men advancing and pacing beyond the dressing-station.

Another man of the Carmarthen Battalion was lying helpless with a shattered leg when an enemy patrol came up to him, but, seeing he would be a rather awkward prisoner to remove, passed on. A little later a Welsh patrol came by, and he told them of the first one, which they set out to find. They must have missed it, for the Germans again passed him, making for their own line. Whilst he was lying there a figure crept up and, levelling a rifle, ordered him to hold up his hands. He was getting used to being captured by this time, and opened his eyes as well as he could but a German, seeing his helpless condition, was overjoyed, and throwing away his rifle, explained in broken English that he wished to be taken prisoner.

He proceeded to prove his amicable intentions by dressing his helpless captor's wound, and giving him cigarettes, settled down to await the return of the Welsh patrol who removed captor and captive.

Relieved

That night the attack was resumed, but the 38th Division had suffered so heavily that towards midnight a relieving division was sent in, and what was left of the Welsh Division withdrew. To those in the action the losses, of course, appeared far heavier than they really were, but they must have amounted to at least one out of every three men who entered on the morning of July 10th and the following day.

The Welsh Division has since captured Mametz Wood a second time, but the wood of July 10th 1916 is no more, and the present stretch of shattered tree stumps gives no idea of what the first struggle cost the young manhood of Wales.[107]

The remains of No. 10 Platoon 15th Welsh Regiment

CHAPTER 10

The German Perspective

EACH BATTLE IS seen primarily from the viewpoint of the victor, and descriptions of the fighting for Mametz Wood sometimes neglect the German accounts, with an over-reliance on the British perspective without seeing the battle from the German side.

By July 1916 the German Army was a formidable fighting force at the height of its powers. The failure of the Schlieffen Plan in 1914 had limited its future ambitions, focusing from that time onwards on a primarily defensive war, holding the high ground and restricting itself to only limited attacking moves, but it had formidable quantities of manpower: there were 2.85 million German soldiers on the Western Front and a further 1.7 million on the Eastern Front.

As previously noted, on 3 July Mametz Wood was devoid of Germans. However, as XV Corps delayed its movement forward, so units of the German Army began to occupy the wood. Units of the 3rd Guard Division and the 28th Reserve Division now held the sector, while Mametz Wood was held by a battalion of the Lehr Infantry Regiment of the Prussian Guard, with a further battalion in and around Flatiron Copse. The western side of the wood was held by the 163rd Regiment of the 28th Reserve Division.

The German 3rd Guard Division had relieved the 28th Reserve Division soon after the mauling it had received during the first phase of the Battle of the Somme. On the night of 7 July the 3rd Guard Division was itself relieved by the 183rd

Infantry Division, comprising the 122nd Reserve Infantry Regiment, the 183rd Infantry Regiment and 184th Infantry Regiment. While the 184th Infantry Regiment was sent to assist the division engaged in the defence of Trônes Wood, the 183rd took over the line between Ovillers and Contalmaison, and the 122nd Reserve Infantry Regiment the area between Contalmaison and the south-western corner of Mametz Wood. The Lehr Regiment, part of the 3rd Guard Division, was not relieved; they occupied Flatiron Copse and the southern edge of the wood.

Reserve *Leutnant* Ballheimer observed the opportunity missed by the British to capture and hold the wood on 3 July:

> About 9.00am we saw dense lines of British infantry move through Mametz Wood. As far as possible we engaged them with machine gun fire, but it was not possible to bring down fire from our position over part of the hollow. Soon the British had disappeared into the wood and over the hill to our left rear. This was followed by a dense mass of British soldiers emerging from the left hand corner of the wood, who pressed down on our left flank.'[1]

This attack was beaten off and the wood left for the Germans to occupy later.

In the German official history of the Battle of the Somme, *Somme-Nord*, the historian wrote of the battle:

> 7 July – At about 10 am, a severe English attack against the positions between Contalmaison and Mametz Woods, as well as against its southeastern edge began. 9 West Riding Battalion and 12 Manchester Battalion (52 Brigade) attacked 2./ Lehr-Infantrie-Regiment, 12., 9. and 11./163 while 16 Welsh and 10 South Borderers Battalion (114 and 115 Brigade, 38 Division) attacked 10./163 and II./Lehr-Infantrie-Regiment. These strong English forces emerged mainly through the Schrapnellmulde in order to attack 11./163 from behind. *Leutnant* of the Reserve Boss took the left wing platoon and rushed forward; he bombarded the English who advanced in a single phalanx formation and subsequently

297

retreated suffering substantial losses due to their confusion by the surprise attack.[2]

10 July – At 5.30 am, the enemy began to attack Mametz Woods. 16 Royal Welsh Fusiliers Battalion (113 Brigade, 38 Division) advanced to the west of the big North-South forest aisle while 14 and 13 Welsh Battalions (114 Brigade, 38 Division) approached to the east of it. 5. and 6./ Lehr-Infantrie-Regiment were overrun at the southern and south-eastern front of the woods despite their brave resistance. Since then, all contact with 5./ Lehr-Infantrie-Regiment, whose commander had fallen into enemy hands, was lost. Some men of 6./Lehr-Infantrie-Regiment had been able to retreat through the dense woods. 16 Welsh Battalion, who had been deployed against the left wing of III./R122 to the west of the big forest aisle, suffered considerable losses, even before they had reached the woods. Also, their commander [Colonel Carden] was killed in action.[3]

Meanwhile, 8./Lehr-Infantrie-Regiment had succeeded during their counter-attack to employ a machine gun against the south-eastern edge of Mametz Woods which resulted in heavy losses for the advancing 13 Welsh Battalion and the death of their

Soldiers of the Lehr Infantry Regiment

commander [Colonel Flower]. In the meantime, the English had pulled in another Welsh Battalion for reinforcement. Their commander [Colonel Rickets] was killed during their advance.[4]

This further attack, which started at 5pm and was carried out over 300 metres, was unsuccessful. In the morning, the English had advanced with 17 Royal Welsh Fusiliers Battalion (113 Brigade) and 10 South Wales Borderers Battalion (115 Brigade) through Mametz Woods. These fresh forces launched yet another attack in the afternoon.[5]

11 July – At 7pm, III./Lehr-Infantrie-Regiment which was positioned at the east side of the woods was attacked by 11 South Wales Borderers Battalion (115 Brigade). They penetrated a part of 9. Company's position. Their insignificant success, however, was paid for with severe losses.'[6]

The *Official History of the Lehr Infantry Regiment* describes the fighting for Mametz Wood thus:

On 7 July, the enemy artillery increased fire until it became a barrage and in the evening, their artillery tried to penetrate the 5./L.I.R. (Lehr-Infanterie-Regiment) and parts of the I.R. 122. They did not succeed.

West of Mametz Woods, the English Infantry tried to advance towards the Bavarian I.R. 16. Here, too, they did not manage to gain a foothold. The platoon Setzermann of the Machine Gun Company Ludwig was able to counter these attempts of attack from their position at the South-West edge of Mametz Woods with great success and supported the Bavarian I.R. 16 effectively in their defence.

However, what sacrifices were made to obtain this defence! *Leutnant* R. Posse of the II./L.I.R. was wounded, the *Unteroffiziere* Josesofski, Marbur, v. Schmeling, Tacke and 22 fusiliers of the Guards fell, 134 wounded, 7 missing.

On 8 July, 7.30 am, the Machine Gun Company Ludwig relieved its two platoons in the Mametz Woods and replaced them with the platoons Böcker and Behrend, which had been held back in the II. Position, without any losses. It had been raining the whole night again.

Nothing of importance on 8 July. Thus, the II./L.I.R. could

reflect on the events of the day. *Feldwebelleutnant* Lehmann, the *Unteroffiziere* Kallis, Manns and 6 men had fallen, 42 wounded, 2 missing.

Nothing of importance happened for the II./L.I.R. on 9 July either. However, the enemy devastated the trenches with its Artillery fire once more, destroyed two machine guns in the Mametz Woods with a direct hit, wounded Gunners Graf and Grone and Private Klingenstein, killed Gunner Fischer who had all rushed forward with replacement guns from the II. Position; due to the collapse of the defensive power on the left wing, it was necessary to remove the 8./L.I.R. from covering the flanks and put them in with the 7./ L.I.R.

When the victims of the II./L.I.R. were counted in the evening of 9 July, 12 brave soldiers had fallen, 50 were wounded, 5 missing. Even the officers were decimated. The *Leutenants* of the Regiments Hendewerk, Bölke, Ferfer were wounded.

The III./L.I.R. had suffered tremendously due to the enemy artillery during the days of 8 and 9 July. The artillery raged through the trenches and back terrain, clearly wanting to destroy all life after their unfavourable experience in Mametz Woods, before their infantry set out for another attack. However, there were definite signs that decisive enemy attacks were imminent. We saw infantry movement in various places, saw entrenchments on the hills west of Montauban, observed constantly circling aircraft above us, saw travelling artillery and vehicle convoys and we had the impression that powerful forces gathered in the Granat and Artillerieschlucht.

How many great targets they made for our artillery! But we were powerless due to our reduced arms and ammunition and had to make do by using curtain fire to keep the enemy attack at bay.

On 8 and 9 July, the casualties for the III./L.I.R. were *Unteroffizier* Könnicke and 8 Fusiliers of the Guards who fell, 67 wounded and 1 missing. The Machine Gun Company also had 1 dead, many wounded or buried alive.

The night of 9 and 10 July passed with uninterrupted artillery fire for the II. and III./L.I.R.. None of us who looked death in the eye every second of the day, enraged about our defencelessness in the face of the enemy artillery which had been raging day and night, thought we would ever come out of this battle alive.

Soldiers returning from leave rejoined their troops on a daily basis in order to protect their threatened fatherland together with their comrades. Maybe they would die within minutes of returning to the Front. Maybe they went missing and nobody knew where they were. If they were still alive after a few days, they considered that a gift from heaven which no one expected anymore.

Yet, worse was still to come. A final conclusion had yet to be made. None of the soldiers who had survived up until now were to fail. The fatherland, their own honour and the honour of their regiment, their battalion, their company, their platoon, their troop, their every machine gun demanded it.

Shortly after, Battalion Commander Hauptmann v. Schauroth suffered a shrapnel injury above his left eye. He stumbled against the trench wall. His eye swelled up in no time. A messenger from the battalion headquarters stepped forward, dressed his forehead and eye, calmly and carefully as if there was no enemy around. When the Commander said: 'Stop dressing my wound now, go back to the others or you might fall into the enemy's hands,' he said calmly as if it goes without saying: 'If the Commander has to die here, so can I!'[7]

Guards Officer

Gefreiter Erich Berndt served with the 8th Company of the Lehr Infantry Regiment (3rd Guard Division). He wrote later:

The next afternoon [6 July] the company commander, *Leutnant* der Reserve Hawlitschka, called together the orderlies (including myself), saying he would lead us to Mametz Wood that evening so we could orient ourselves to the occupied position. I carelessly neglected to bring along my gas mask. By chance, enemy fliers were absent and artillery activity remained within its usual boundaries. Yet it required a great deal of exertion to proceed forward through the badly battered communication trench. A short distance from the wood we abandoned the trench at a place where a Bavarian from the 16th Regiment had breathed his last.

Whether it was coincidence or the enemy saw us moving about, a blanket of explosions suddenly spread over the area. A musty smell accompanying the impacts indicated gas shells were falling, and so commenced a rush to get out of there. [At 5.30pm on 6 July the eastern edge of Mametz Wood was bombarded with gas shells by French guns.] Diagonally we hurried through the wood, and more than once had to seek refuge behind colossal tree trunks to escape flying chunks of muddy dirt. My physical resistance had deteriorated. Lacking willpower, I wanted to settle down on the ground. Knowing, however, that gas is heavier than air brought me to my feet again. In my flight I had already lost my field cap in the undergrowth, but that mattered little. Luckily I escaped from the danger zone and soon reached the company.

During the night the shelling in the wood increased dramatically, destroying a dugout to our right. In addition to other comrades, my good friend *Garde-Fusilier* Friedrich Bierkamp met his end there. *Offizierstellvertreter* Jablonsky was buried for a short time. Extricated whole in body but disturbed in spirit, he was killed several days later.

Early in the morning of 7 July we were moved to frontline positions at the wood's southeast edge. Our losses increased. An immense shell burst near the company commander's dugout. Among the dead was the *Leutnant's* batman. Those comrades in holes and craters out front had nothing to laugh about, for it seemed Tommy had exhausted all his small-calibre shells and now substituted his heavies. Only now and then in this hell did smiles appear on the mud-smeared faces of my fellow *Garde-Fusiliers*.

And that was when the English sent over 'empty crates'. Many of the shells were duds.

The telephone functioned only occasionally; when it did not the poor telephonists were out trying to patch the line. So we had to use runners. This duty was anything but easy. The wood's tree trunks, most with foliage still attached, lay like enormous broken matchsticks all over the ground, thoroughly confusing one's orientation.

Next to hunger, thirst tormented us the most. There was no drinking water in Mametz Wood. In desperation, most resorted to scooping what lay in the bottom of craters. In order to filter out the worst of the dirt and filth we used our handkerchiefs, which were better than nothing. I was more fortunate than my comrades. At night, while they remained squatting in their holes, my duties took me several times to battalion headquarters, where I could briefly refresh myself. Coming and going it was always the same:

Officers and soldier of the Guards

here, two stretcher-bearers struggling with a heavy load; there, a few lightly wounded men, or perhaps a ration party, trudging back. And always the new, 'uneducated' replacements moving to the front. In squid-size groups, lying scattered on the ground to 'escape' the shells, they were led forward by corporals.

The English had 'lubricated' the wood with shells, so that in the blink of an eye the surrounding ground had been transformed. I was so tired I fell asleep standing against a tree.

The sun had already climbed high in the sky when *Leutnant* Hawlitschka and I left Mametz Wood, heading for the rear. We dashed from crater to crater in order to avoid the English artillery. At one point we stopped to rest. Did it matter if the *Leutnant* and *Gefreiter* drank from the same canteen? Probably not, for we were comrades.'[8]

He thus escaped the carnage at Mametz Wood. Erich Berndt was awarded the Iron Cross 2nd Class later that day for bravery on 5 June 1916 in hand-to-hand fighting with the French. He was then made an orderly to *Leutnant* Hawlitschka.

Unteroffizier Gottfried Kreibohm of the 10th Company of the Lehr Infantry Regiment wrote a diary detailing his experiences at Mametz Wood:

10 July 1916: After being relieved in the morning we returned to the dugout in the wood. The artillery fire there was absolutely frantic. Nearly every shell landed in the trench. Some men were buried alive while others were blown into the air. *Unteroffiziere* Wahlen's squad had dug the deepest hole into the side of the trench for protection. It was too deep, for two shells landed directly on top of them and six men were entombed inside. We immediately began tearing away at the earth and could hear someone shouting, but our rescue efforts did not save everyone. Wahlen, Wolnick and Weber had suffocated.

Apparently a counter-attack was made, for part of the 3rd Platoon under Dittrich was hurried forward. The rest of the company remained in its dugouts and holes, and endured more of Tommy's shell fire. That evening Dittrich returned with only half of those he started with.

11 July 1916: At 4 am, I left with three men and took up residence

in the field of craters between the company's forward trench and Mametz Wood. We immediately set to work deepening our holes, digging for two hours. Around eight o'clock the English began to systematically strafe the company sector with heavy-calibre shells. Geysers of earth a hundred feet high shot from the ground. With my field glasses I could see past Mametz Wood all the way to the village of Mametz. The entire area was swarming with the activity of English troops, wagons and ambulances moving forward, and prisoners going to the rear. It was a shame we did not have contact with our artillery. We sat watching this panorama until midday. No relief came. The shell fire increased in our vicinity and every fifteen minutes we had to shovel clods of earth from our holes. Pieces of equipment were sent flying out of the Company's trench, while the barbed-wire stakes tumbled crazily in the air. The ground rumbled and heaved with each explosion. Suddenly, a noise like a roaring freight train rushed down upon me, and I instinctively covered my head with my hands. I waited one, two, five agonizing seconds – for the explosion. When nothing happened I opened my eyes and saw, to my immense relief, a large shell half buried in the earth, only one and a half metres away from me. It was a dud. Thus we waited in our holes for ten hours – the most fearful ten hours I had ever experienced in my life.

Sometime after 5pm I changed position in the crater, lying back with my right hand over my knee. I had just got comfortable when a shell blew up not far behind my hole. I suddenly felt a stabbing pain in my hand, which spurted warm blood. A two-inch long splinter had cut through the back of my hand. Luckily, it was not a larger piece or else my entire hand would have been sliced off.

Around 8.30pm Tommy's shelling lessened. I decided it was useless to stay, so with a shout to my men we ran as fast as we could towards the rear. Several nearby shell bursts hurried us along until we found the trench, or what was left of it. There was no one about. We moved down further, eventually reaching a dugout that was blown in by a direct hit. Dead, mangled bodies were strewn and piled everywhere.[9]

An unnamed German *leutnant* described what happened to him and his men on the 10 July:

The ground behind our trench was being continually shelled, but about midnight the fire ceased and we decided to rush for it. The plan worked successfully, and although a number of men were wounded by shells and stray bullets, we succeeded in reaching the barbed wire in front of our second line position at 1.30am. Here we were greeted by a machine gun which suddenly opened from the trench, but throwing ourselves on the ground and shouting we soon convinced the gunner of his error and luckily with no cost to ourselves.[10]

After the battalions of the 38th Division entered the wood early on the morning of 10 July, the 5th Company Lehr Infantry Regiment became trapped between the 16th Royal Welsh Fusiliers who were attacking along Strip Trench and the 14th Welsh in the centre. Some of the Germans left their positions and surrendered at the foot of the cliff, while others continued fighting until they were overrun. *Leutnant* D.R. Pfeiffer extricated his men of the 7th and 8th companies from the encirclement and led them back to their trenches at the northern edge of The Hammerhead and thence to Flatiron

Lehr Infantry Regiment field kitchen

Copse, where they linked up with the 3rd Battalion of the Lehr Regiment.

A machine gun company who were sited at the south-eastern corner of the wood withdrew back to their second line, leaving two guns behind but taking three with them. They used these to hold back the attacking Welsh troop, moving from one shell hole to another until they reached their comrades.

In the centre of the wood the remnants of 6th Company withdrew to the positions held by elements of the 16th Bavarian Infantry Regiment where they held their positions until they too were forced back later that day.

The 3rd Battalion Lehr Infantry Regiment in Flatiron Copse had suffered heavy losses during the British artillery bombardment. They were surprised though that no British infantry attack followed this up, so the regimental commander, *Oberst-leutnant* Kumme, urged Major von Kriegsheim, the battalion commander, to reinforce the 2nd Lehr Infantry Regiment in Mametz Wood. Von Kreigsheim concurred and sent one platoon each from the 9th, 10th and 12th companies, plus one from the 5th Company of the 184th Infantry Regiment to assist the defenders in the wood.

Led by *Leutnant* Kummetz, this force entered the eastern edge of the wood and reinforced the troops in The Hammerhead. Later von Kreigsheim was forced to send another platoon into the wood but he did this reluctantly as he still believed the British would order a flanking attack east of Mametz Wood and he did not want to weaken his second line unnecessarily.

The official history of the 163rd Regiment stated:

> The trenches filled with water and mud so that working and moving around was made very difficult. The shelters turned into water holes and thus, lost their purpose of protection; some of them collapsed altogether.
>
> A battle fought during a dark and rainy night with the use of so much ammunition and material is probably the most difficult task ever demanded of human nerves. On a bright day, the moment of weakness is easily overcome. The soldier sees his comrades, he

sees his leader, the weak can feel uplifted by the strong. During the night, everyone is on their own as, at night, every event has a profound effect on a human being; the approaching enemy suddenly appears in front of him, he does not see him coming, the enemy seems to be stronger that he actually is, he feels alone, his comrade and his leader seem out of reach.

Military physician Dr. Schlitt in Contalmaison and assistant physician Dockhorn in Mametz Wood have tended to innumerable wounds during days and days of tireless medical work, thus keeping alive many comrades. The work of the orderlies was above and beyond praise. During heavy fire they gave first aid to the wounded, they searched tirelessly for the wounded and carried them back through horrendous fire; there was no sleep, no rest for them. Despite hunger, thirst and fatigue they continued their difficult task.[11]

By 9 July the 3rd Battalion of the 122nd Reserve Infantry Regiment held positions to the west of Mametz Wood, with its battalion headquarters located within the wood itself. The 8th Company of the 2nd Battalion, which had been in reserve in the German second-line defences behind Contalmaison, was sent into the wood as support for the 3rd Battalion but was soon to lose half of its strength when it was ordered to reinforce the 1st Battalion at Contalmaison.

The 2nd Battalion of the Lehr Regiment was in the southern part of Mametz Wood, while its 1st Battalion was in the trenches at Flatiron Copse. The 3rd Battalion was in reserve at Bazentin-le-Petit.

A post-war German history stated:

Over 400 prisoners of five different regiments had been captured [on 10 July], the defenders being reduced to 140 men of the II./ Lehr Regiment, II./184th, and engineers. The various German headquarters had no clear knowledge of the situation: the 183rd Division felt sure that the British had reached the northern edge of the wood which the 3rd Guard Division thought was still in German possession. The 183rd Division, having no reserve left, begged for reinforcements to retake the wood, but only one battalion was available, and that not until next morning. The only reinforcements received on the 10th were a company of the 77th Reserve [2nd Guard Reserve Division], 120 recruits and two machine guns.[12]

In the official history of the 122nd Reserve Infantry Regiment, *Leutnant* Kostlin wrote an account of his time at Mametz Wood:

Through the Curtain Fire
In the afternoon of 9 July, I received the order to advance to Mametz Wood with 6. Company and two machine guns in order to strengthen III. Battalion. I was told to bring as many drinks, food, hand grenades and flares as possible. Two men of III. Battalion, who were to lead us to their position, were ordered to meet us at 11.30pm by the field kitchens in Martinpuich.

As dusk fell, I left R-Position along with my company in order to first go back to our field kitchen and then to the ammunition depot in Martinpuich. I used that opportunity to leave all knapsacks at the field kitchens in order to relieve us of any unnecessary ballast. I had a combat pack made (only tent, mess tin and emergency rations) as we had enough to carry with all the ammunition, the hand grenades and the food. Our breakfast was abruptly interrupted by a sudden shell shower quite close to us in the middle of the village road. That frightened our horses to an extent that they immediately galloped away taking our kitchen with them. After we caught them again, they only reluctantly stayed. I gave the order to prepare to leave at about 1am on 10 July. After eliminating some footsore soldiers, I divided the company into three platoons. Then we advanced. My Bézard compass rendered me an extraordinary service finding the way in the pitch-black night. For I could not and did not want to rely on the guides provided for me by III. Battalion.

Leutnant Schmid, who had also advanced to III. Battalion with 5. Company during the night before, had informed me via his batman, whom he had sent back to the company, that I should possibly not choose to move through Mametz Wood if I had to go to the Front, as he had suffered heavy losses caused by the curtain fire. Hence, I had decided to advance through the Shrapnellmulde located between Mametz Wood and Contalmaison, so to avoid the woods entirely.

On our advance, I had everyone move in a line, but I noticed fairly quickly that the line was too long and continuously broke down during our march through many trenches between Martinpuich and the Southwestern corner of Bazentin, and we lost too much time. So I gave the order to form a group convoy which allowed us to move more easily.

There were no noteworthy incidents to report up until Bazentin where we crossed R-Position once again. Shortly after, before we crossed the Bazentin – Contalmaison road, the first shrapnel sped by which immediately cost us lives. First, my batman Häberle, who had been walking closely behind me, was slightly wounded on his hand, while a number of my company's men were lying on the ground, some severely wounded, amongst which was Sergeant Koppisch. The stretcher-bearers had their hands full. The rest of us who had not been wounded had to move on so we would not be surprised by daylight.

It was a difficult task; much shrapnel hit close to us, and almost every time, we counted some wounded. We noticed that the area between the front trenches and the second (R) position was constantly sprayed by enemy artillery, and we had to get through this curtain of fire, which was particularly heavy in the woods to the left of us, if we wanted to get to the Front.

When we were close to the front position, according to our guides from the III. Battalion, I gave the order to stop, take cover as best we could and sent the two guides forth to the III. Battalion to inquire where our company should be deployed to. After a long 20 minutes, they returned with the message that we were in the right place, right behind 10., 11. and 12. Company. I immediately had everyone fall in again when something completely unexpected happened. We heard the rat-tat-tat of a machine gun originating from the elevated area a few hundred metres to the right of us, and the bullets whistled low above our heads. Everyone scattered away; there was utter confusion. I ordered: 'Forward, march! Into the trench in front of us!' But the trench was a fair distance away, maybe 300 metres. I ran ahead and thought that the entire company had heard my order and had followed me. Whether part of my men didn't hear my last order among the confusion or the noise of the machine gun fire, or whether they might have thought we were standing in front of an enemy trench, in short, the result of that surprise was that only me, *Leutnant* Koch and about 30 men of 6. Company instead of about 50, minus the wounded, reached III. Battalion's trench. Of course, some time had passed until I came to this sorry conclusion, and although I immediately sent back one of my best men, Dengler, who had volunteered for the task, to get the missing men and mainly the two machine guns, the plan failed. But at least, I was reassured by Dengler's report that my men had not ended up in the machine gun fire as he had not been able to find anyone in the area in question, not even any wounded or fallen.

As I found out later, the men had retreated to the 2. Position at dawn after they had lost contact with us, not knowing where to go. Some of the men were forced to stay in some grenade holes in the area between us and the 2. Position for the entire day and were only able to return to the 2. Position in the evening.

Bypassed

Leutnant Irion, who greeted me upon my arrival in the trench, informed me that during the night the English had broken through to the right from us, i.e. on the hill at the eastern edge of Contalmaison and that there must be a pocket of English troops with one machine gun located on the hill behind our right wing. That was, of course, true as this machine gun had shot at us when we tried to advance to our current position and had blown apart my entire company. It was a pity that we had not been informed about that earlier, a bit further back, about where we had stopped last. From that position we could have launched a comprehensive surprise attack and crushed that pocket. But now it was too late and not possible anymore because of the dawning day, especially now that we were in our position here at the Front.

From 4am onward, we had no longer been able to establish contact with the Battalion Commander, Major v. Zeppelin, whose battle station was approximately 600 metres from us at the southern edge of Mametz Wood, as the adjacent valley was covered with blanket fire by the enemy. The latest order for the Battalion had been that we were to act on our own without awaiting further orders. For that very same reason, we were not able to find out how the other companies had fared, namely 5., 8. and 9. Company located in the positions to the left of us above the valley over at the southern and eastern edge of Mametz Wood.

With that information about our situation in mind, I, as the senior officer, took command of the rest of the remaining four companies, which consisted of only 6 officers and about 160 men. Our trench followed the slope between Contalmaison and Mametz Wood in a southeasterly direction towards the southern corner of the wood. It dropped off quite considerably to the north and east and ran parallel to and about 200 metres to the north of the road Contalmaison – Mametz. The terrain in front of us rose considerably towards the above-mentioned road in a southwesterly direction, towards the enemy, while to the southeast of us we had an unobstructed view of the hills of Mametz and Montauban. So, for the main part, we were lying at a slope away from the enemy and thus were quite protected from artillery fire. However, our shooting range was considerably reduced towards the south and southwest.

On the hill near Contalmaison, the advantage we had over the artillery fire had gone. Our position there had been completely leveled, causing 10. and 12. Company severe losses. The trench there was still under constant fire, which was the reason for only a few necessary guards being posted there. Furthermore, we were offered protection by three or four dugouts which were relatively well built and covered with about 7 metres of soil. During battle breaks, those few and far between safe shelters were often densely occupied, especially the steps. Among us were also a few involuntary occupants – a few wounded prisoners whom we had pulled inside from our rampart as they were quite helpless. In return, they filled the air with a fragrance, the memory of which still stings my nose today.

During the morning the English carried out hourly hand grenade attacks on our trench. These originated from a siege-trench to our left where they had been able to sneak up on us to about 20 metres, completely safe from our fire. Their siege-trench was continuously being replenished from behind, as noticed by our guards from the steel helmets popping up at the front of their trench.

Then it was time to call the trench crew up on the rampart to defend our position as shortly after, while we were still hearing our guards' warning calls: 'They are coming, they are coming!', they emerged from their siege-trench brandishing their weapons. We duly welcomed them with well-executed rapid fire, which was downright cataclysmic due to the short distance. Most of them fell immediately. A few who had managed to come close to our rampart collapsed there after being hit by our hand grenades. The rest rushed back to their trench suffering further losses.

By midday, a considerable amount of dead and wounded English soldiers had piled up at the head of the siege-trench. Unfortunately, we had also lost a number of our brave men during our defence, mainly through an enfilade coming from behind us to the right, probably from the English pocket mentioned above firing from the elevation at Contalmaison. Soon *Leutnant* Koch was severely wounded by a shot in the back. Although our men recognised the danger caused by the enemy enfilade, they often, in the heat of the battle, came up too high over the parapet, which caused a number of fatalities.

At this point, I would like to mention the outstandingly brave actions of one man of III. Battalion whose name can no longer be determined. He was one of our keenest and best throwers of hand grenades. Every time an enemy attack had been fended off, he rushed out from our trench and pursued the few remaining retreating enemy soldiers all the way to their siege-trench and threw a few well-aimed hand grenades down onto their heads. Time and time again, he returned from these daring forays without injury until, at midday, he died the death of a hero outside the enemy trench.

I would also like to mention the brave actions of the bugler Albert Florus of 6. Company. He had suffered a very painful wound in his lower arm during the march to our position, but that did not stop him. Irrespective of his pain, he took over the medical service in our trench and gave first aid to our numerous wounded men by expertly applying bandages. This was especially valuable to us, as we did not have any stretcher-bearers left.

At about 9am in the direction of the village of Mametz, we witnessed quite an inexplicable spectacle in the distance. Coming from that village, which was not visible to us due to its low-lying location, several English marching columns appeared led by their mounted Company Commanders, crossed a bridged trench there and marched in an easterly direction up the hill towards Montauban, only to disappear over the ridge of the hill. We were utterly bewildered. Was that a dream or reality? We rubbed our eyes but it was what it was. It was true. 2500 - 3000 metres

from us English troops were marching in broad daylight. I had
never seen such cheek! Why did our artillery not shoot at them?
Unfortunately, we were not able to notify them as we had not
had any telephone contact back there for days. None of them
should have gotten away with that. Our artillery had not seen the
opportunity; we looked behind us to find out if we could see a
captive balloon somewhere but it was in vain; while on the English
side there was one balloon next to the other. It was too crazy.

For a while, we tried to help ourselves. I gave the order to open
fire but, as I thought, the effect was minimal at that distance,
and then we had to withdraw at the Front as our most dangerous
opponent attempted another approach. Ultimately, I consoled my
men and myself by saying that those men over there were none of
our concern. We could not wage a war with everyone.

At midday, we observed for the first time that we still had
manpower in our trenches situated to the left of us outside
Mametz Wood close to the Battalion's command post. We saw a
few men move toward us along the so-called 'White Trench' and
then they stopped for a while at a *Schulterwehr* [a shoulder-high
wall in front of a trench]. Judging by their behaviour, we assumed
that they had to be officers on some kind of reconnaissance. To
our astonishment, we soon watched them leave the trench one
by one and run, no, almost skip back to the woods chased by the
raging enemy machine gun fire. Using my binoculars I thought
I recognised *Oberleutnant* Seidel. What was all that supposed to
mean? From that point in time, we failed to see anybody else in
those positions. They were abandoned. I had the feeling that there
was something terribly wrong.

Maybe an hour later, one of my guards drew my attention to
the southwesterly corner of the wood which was situated about
400 metres behind us to the left; he thought that there was a man
standing by a stand-alone pine tree. I quickly aimed my binoculars
at him. Yes, what was that? A couple of times I put my binoculars
down. That was just not possible, an Englishman in yellow khaki
and steel helmet putting himself in full view? Yet, that's what it
was. There was an Englishman standing there, and there was
no way he was on his own. I was right. Soon I discovered close
by a second and a third one by the next tree. All of a sudden,
it became clear to me what must have happened earlier that
morning over there and at Montauban. The English must also

have broken through the area to the left of us without us noticing let alone preventing it. They must have penetrated the completely destroyed positions* at the southern edge of Mametz Wood during the morning, and the only thing we had seen had been the retreat of the last remainders of the companies who had been able to free themselves from the enemy after having been entirely overwhelmed by the superior enemy forces.**

[* Subsequent investigations revealed that *Leutnant* d. R. Schmid along with many brave N.C.O.s and troops had died heroes in the emplacements there.

** Major v. Zeppelin and *Oberleutnant* Seidel, along with a few men, had managed to return to the Second Position by passing through Mametz Wood but were, unfortunately, both killed by shell fire close to the regiment's command post at about midday.]

So now there was already an English patrol at the southwesterly corner of the wood. I immediately had some troops open fire on the corner of the woods in order to drive away the patrol, which was pointless really as Mametz Wood was already in English hands.

Our situation had become quite alarming: not only was the left flank threatened but the English had already bypassed us with the occupation of Mametz Wood which could only be a matter of a few hours now. That was the explanation for the mysterious convoys at Mametz and Montauban that morning, that was for sure. We knew we had a restless enemy in front of us who tried to wear us down through continuous attacks. We did not know how our I. Battalion fared to the right of us, as we had lost contact since the breakthrough earlier that night. We found out later that the English had already managed, at that time, to advance and push the remaining men of I. Battalion back through Contalmaison. However, we were well aware, even without exact information about the situation in Contalmaison, that the danger had closed in, that we might be cut off and taken prisoner.

But the surprises that day kept on coming. While we were still watching the suspicious edge of the wood through our binoculars, waves of riflemen appeared in a southeasterly direction to the left of us on the elevation in front of Mametz Wood; they moved directly towards the trenches of 9. Company outside the wood. We were able to attack their flank nicely, distance 600 metres. There was no need for me to give any orders, my men had seen that opportune target straight away, and our quick fire started promptly.

Every gun was employed, all officers were shooting, too; before long, our gun barrels were burning hot. None of the approaching English soldiers reached the trenches which, by then, were probably only occupied by our fallen comrades. As far as we were able to see through our binoculars, they all succumbed to our enfilade. Thus, the left flank protection of the enemy's main body of men, who had been advancing in the woods undetected by us, was finished and destroyed, but not the enemy's main body itself. We were about to find that out, as a short time later we were able to see through our binoculars several larger and smaller English patrols frequently emerging from the woods. My next and biggest worry was that they might launch an attack from there; if there was also an attack from the front at the same time, we would be lost.

While I was still pondering that scenario, the attack from behind, that I feared, had already been in preparation. Without us noticing, the English had positioned a strong patrol to launch an attack from behind us. They had positioned themselves by sneaking up one by one along the narrow gully which was surrounded by bushes and trees and swept past our left flank from the above-mentioned southwesterly corner of the wood. We only noticed them when the first wave of riflemen suddenly burst out of there from behind. Now our plans had to be thrown out, only quick action might avert the danger. I shouted to the troops close to me: 'Towards the back, the direction of the gully, sight 400, fire, aim and shoot calmly. Every shot must hit the target.' They only just managed to start firing. Only a few metres from our left flank, we saw the first wave lying in their own blood. But soon enough the second wave emerged from the gully. All our guns were aimed towards the back of us at the gully, and the second enemy wave found a bloody end as soon as they emerged from their hideout. Over and over again I was looking towards our front, worrying about our original enemy in the siege-trench. But luckily they did not engage in that battle, although that would have been very successful. Thus we were able to stave off the third and final wave emerging from the gully. We must have left a lasting impression over there in the wood, for there were no more attacks although we still had to be on the lookout for more, of course.

Even our old, more immediate enemy at the Front attacked less and less frequently, probably due to the many impressive lessons we taught them when their ineffective attacks were constantly warded off. Later in the afternoon, they left us in peace altogether.

Our numerous and great defensive successes should have put us in a certain uplifting victorious mood, if it had not been for the desperation of our overall situation which would fill us with deep concern for the next few hours. How long would we be able to withstand all that, surrounded from all sides and subject to surprise attacks? Added to that was the fact that none of the messengers and runners we sent back had returned so far, meaning we had not had any contact with anyone since our departure from there. The men were also exhausted due to the constant battles; they drank the yellow dirty rainwater from the shell holes, as they were so painfully thirsty. We were quickly running out of ammunition and hand grenades. We gathered together what was left in the trench, the dugouts, and from the dead and the wounded.

It also started to dawn on us that the fact that the enemy, who had been quite active up to a certain point in time, had all of a sudden left us alone could only mean that they must have thought, in light of the whole situation, that it was no longer necessary to attack us as we would possibly soon fall into their hands without the need for fighting. In the light of those circumstances, we felt almost certain of our inevitable fate of death or captivity, when we heard intense infantry fire coming from the northern edge of Mametz Wood and from the R-Position. That reignited our hope that the English might have been thrown out of the wood by a counter-attack from our troops. However, almost immediately, there was intense English artillery fire with heavy shrapnel which rained down in mighty black-green clouds of smoke and tremendous noise north of Mametz Wood. Slowly the infantry fire died down again and along with that the quickly ignited hope of a change in our situation. Was that the end? Was there no longer a solution? Being the commanding officer of that small group of men who had been defending themselves so bravely up to now, I asked myself those very questions. And the feeling of responsibility for the fate of my men weighed twice as heavily on my shoulders.

After some deliberation with the remaining officers had not brought about any feasible results, I decided that, under the veil of darkness, all of my troops still fit for action, as well as our wounded, would try to make our way through to the R-Position unless we received news from behind and reinforcements during the night. At the break of dawn, I sent my best and bravest despatch runner, Dengler, to Contalmaison with my decision and an account of our situation. I waited in vain for his return or a reply. Dengler described in a subsequent report that during his passage to I. Battalion he had encountered a large number of dead English soldiers, lying around a machine gun, who had been killed by grenade fire. The pocket of Englishmen from that morning whose machine gun fire had fallen silent since midday had fallen victim to the blind zeal of their own batteries at that time. Dengler had delivered his message to the Commanding Officer of I. Battalion, *Hauptman* Baumann, so that the latter was able to adjust his actions accordingly. Dengler, however, was kept behind by the Commanding Officer.

In the evening we had the satisfaction of watching the crash of an English aircraft above Mametz Wood. The plane spun slowly, revolving around its own axis, crashing from a considerable height down onto the canopy of the trees where we lost sight of it.

The Breakthrough

At about 7pm an intense barrage onto our trench and curtain fire onto the area behind us resumed and lasted the entire night. We were rather worried about a potential surprise attack in the dark as we were without barbed wire and flares. For that reason, I remained at my post on top of the rampart for almost the entire time. Dusk seemed to last forever, darkness did not want to come; the barrage, however, continued mercilessly. That worked in our favour for we knew that as long as the fire continued, the enemy would not approach. Should it stop or move back, the attack would be sure to follow. For our plan to succeed we were not to allow an attack by the enemy, as an escape during a barrage was inconceivable. That was why I came up with the following plan, which was passed on to everyone in the troop by their N.C.O.s:

As soon as the barrage dies down, ceases or is moved back, all troops fit for action are to get ready immediately for a surprise hand grenade attack on the enemy siege-trench. After pushing back the presumably battle-ready enemy, everyone is to move back to R-Position, by climbing over our own trench and spreading themselves out as widely as possible. The edge of Mametz Wood serves as a guideline and should be left as far to the right as possible. All weaponry and what is left of our ammunition and hand grenades, as well as all wounded comrades are to be taken with us. In case we come across a potential new enemy line between our current trench and R-Position, we will break through it with all our force. R-Position must not be crossed, i.e. left behind.

Finally, at about 1am [11 July], I believed the firing to have abated. Now it was time to carry out the plan immediately. When everyone was ready, I threw a hand grenade in the direction of the enemy siege-trench as a sign to take action. The enemy responded immediately; it looked like they had been ready to attack, just like I thought. But they were unable to withstand our sudden and severe hand grenade attack which was carried out simultaneously along their entire line and they withdrew. Thus, we got our intended result. So we started to slowly move one by one and were able to sneak away undetected.

It was true that the intense curtain fire, which we had to march through, cost us a number of wounded men but we managed to lead out all men, 5 officers (*Leutnant* Schwenzer died of a stomach wound on the evening of 10 July) and about 120 men, as well as our numerous wounded, thus, escape certain captivity. We did not encounter any more resistance on our way back. At about 2.30 am we arrived at the barbed wire defences of R-Position where we were greeted by the sudden rat-tat-tat of our own machine gun. We were forced to throw ourselves to the ground right where we were. We quickly cleared up the mistake by shouting out who we were.[13]

On 9 July the 122nd Reserve Infantry Regiment lost 13 officers and 217 other ranks; on 10 July it lost 17 officers and 964 other ranks.

Oberstleutnant Bedall, commanding the 16th Regiment of the 10th Bavarian Division, was taken prisoner on 13 July and his diary was taken from him. In it he wrote:

In the course of 10 July there was very heavy fighting in Mametz Wood. No.1 Section of the Machine Gun Company suffered exceptionally great loss by a direct hit. Fifteen men and one platoon commander were killed and twelve wounded. July 11:

> During the day there was a very intense and methodical shelling of
> the regimental sector from nine a.m. till late in the evening by guns
> of very heavy calibre, but the sector held by the 3rd Battalion of
> the Lehr Regiment suffered no loss.[14]

Captain G.C. Wynne, a Great War veteran and historian, wrote in an article in the *Army Quarterly* in January 1925 that the Germans had found it difficult to build defences in Mametz Wood owing to the tall trees and the thick, almost impenetrable in parts, undergrowth that grew beneath. The British artillery bombardment, which preceded the 10 July attack, in particular, had smashed many of the trees, which made the wood even more impassable. The Germans had therefore restricted their efforts to machine guns in shelter pits along the ridges and in the small clearings, and had concentrated their efforts on the trench at the southern edge, with support lines in open ground running up both sides of the wood, in particular a line of trench around Flatiron Copse in the east.

The assault on the morning of 10 July was made against the 2nd Battalion Lehr Infantry Regiment at the southern end of the wood. The final bombardment was so effective that the attacking battalions were able to capture the trenches on the flanks of the wood before the Germans could properly reinforce them from their dugouts. Though the Germans were able to hold up the centre of the attack for some time, the flanking elements were able to enter the wood when the remnants of the 2nd Battalion either retired or surrendered.

The area of Wood Trench to the west of Mametz Wood still held by two companies of the 122nd Reserve Infantry Regiment were now outflanked by the British soldiers in the wood so they ran back under heavy fire to Wood Support Trench where they continued their resistance.

The panic amongst elements of the 38th Division that is often referred to at this stage is given an interesting rationale by Wynne. He writes that the 3rd Lehr Battalion at Flatiron Copse gave the Welsh regiments incessant trouble. 'As soon as the Welshmen had advanced up the wood beyond the level of their trench a number of men would run into the wood and fire into them from behind, causing a temporary panic and loss, and then would withdraw to their trench again.'[15]

Wynne also gives a voice to the German post-war historians' view of the battle for Mametz Wood and states that the Germans, while being at the peak of their efficiency, having many of their original regular officers and non-commissioned officers and soldiers who had undergone a winter of hard training, were nevertheless outnumbered by the British divisions set against them.

When one considers the attacks made on the wood from the west, approximately 36 British battalions were arrayed against nine German battalions. The British infantry are viewed by the immediate post-war German historians as determined and full of go, but lacking in intelligent tactical work and failed to make full use of the successes they had. However, the determining factor is seen as the strength of the British artillery, even more so than the weight of the attacking infantry battalions.

> The comparatively few German batteries available were quite incapable of dealing with the mass of British guns and howitzers arrayed against them and were consequently unable to give much assistance to their infantry in the defence. Further, the British artillery shot very accurately and picked up their targets quickly and well, their observation being undoubtedly much assisted by having command of the air.[16]

Of course, this was not the case once the British infantry entered the wood, and the casualties caused by the British artillery falling short were to be expected when clear information as to the position of the front line was not forthcoming. It would have been better for the artillery to have been ordered to fire on the German second line of defences, rather than trying to protect the men in the wood itself.

The historian of the 122nd Reserve Infantry Regiment maintains that his regiment had done all that could be expected of it, and that it was owing to the stubbornness with which it held its ground that the British had had to deploy such a mass of infantry, expend such a great number of lives, and waste such a vast quantity of ammunition and so much valuable time in order to capture an intermediary position held by a comparatively small force.

One of the German soldiers killed at Mametz Wood was Leonhard Schachtner who fell on 11 July. His death card translates as:

> In memory of the honoured eighth youth, Leonhard Schachtner, a farmer's son from Oberdingolfing. Private in the 16th Bavarian Infantry Regiment, 11th Company. He died a heroic death for his homeland on 11th July 1916 at the age of 20 years in Mametz Wood in the western theatre of war. The poem that follows says: 'You died far from your homeland and the ones who love you. To the ones who mourn you there remains a strong hope that dear God will unite us with you in Heaven.'

Jüngling Leonhard Schachtner † gefallen 11. Juli 1916.

Leonhard Schachtner

CHAPTER 11

How the Press Reported the Battle

THE OFFICIAL WAR Correspondent Philip Gibbs wrote an article published on 9 July in newspapers across Britain:

Mametz Wood was very quiet this afternoon. As neither side could see exactly the position of its troops underneath the heavy foliage – our men, who were fighting last night, hold a line about half-way through – the gunners were chary of shelling it severely. Now and again a burst of shrapnel smoke puffed against the dark background of the trees, and the shell slashed through the branches, but that was not often, and the wood seemed very peaceful. Looking at it one's imagination found it difficult to realize that perhaps there were men there who had dug themselves into the earth beneath the spreading roots, and that British and German patrols were feeling their way, perhaps, from one tree to another, through the glades, until they came into touch and exchanged some rifle shots before falling back to their own line. I could only guess at that, and could see nothing but the tight foliage, yellow in the sun and black in the shadows.[1]

Gibbs continues:

It was a good day for us, in prisoners, for about 500 have come down from Contalmaison, Mametz Wood, and the Trônes Wood as living proof of our advance in all those places. All the prisoners speak of the terror of our artillery-fire, and documents captured in their dug-outs tell the same tale in words which reveal the full horror of the bombardment. 'We are quite shut off from the rest of the world,' wrote a German soldier on the day before our great attack. 'Nothing comes to us; no letters. The English keep such a barrage on our approaches, it is terrible. To-morrow morning it will be seven days since this bombardment began; we cannot hold out much longer. Everything is shot to pieces.'[2]

On 10 July he wrote:

At 3 o'clock on Monday afternoon last our troops advanced to the capture of the wood – a wood whose gloom was brightened by the frightful flash of shells, whose tree-trunks were broken and splintered and slashed by sharp axes hurtling through the leaves, and about whose gnarled roots, in shell-holes and burrows, German soldiers crouched with their bombs and machine guns. A wood of terror. Yet not dismaying to those men of ours who went into its twilight. Our own guns were shelling it with a progressive barrage.

Our men were to pass forward in short, sharp rushes behind the barrage, but some of them in their eagerness went too fast and too far, and went through the very barrage itself until a signal warned a gunner officer sitting in an Observation Post behind, so that he suddenly seized a telephone and whispered some words into it, and made the guns 'lift' again.

Waves of bullets were streaming like water through the trees from German machine guns. Many of our men fell, and the others, checked a while, lay down in any holes they could find or dig. All through the night shells broke over them, and through the glades there came always that horrible chatter of machine guns.

It was a night to which men think back through a lifetime with a wonderment that it brought any dawn for them. But when dawn came their spirit was unbroken and they made a new attack, and went forward with

Philip Gibbs

324

bombs and bayonets to the encounter of other men. Not less brave, in truth and fairness to them. There was a fierce fight before the last of them surrendered, so that Mametz Wood was ours, for a while at least.[3]

Gibbs wrote of the battles for the woods on 12 July:

Mametz Wood, Bernafay Wood, and Trônes Wood are still dense thickets under heavy foliage hiding the enemy's troops and our own, but giving no protection from shell-fire. It is for these woodlands on high ground that our men have been fighting with the greatest gallantry and most stubborn endurance, suffering more than light losses, meeting heavy counter-attacks, gaining ground, losing it, retaking it, and thrusting forward again, with a really unconquerable spirit, because they know that these woods are the way to the second bastion of the German stronghold.[4]

The Press Association's Special Correspondent gave his view of events at Mametz Wood on 10 July which was also widely circulated, including in Welsh newspapers:

In the Field, France, July 10
This has been to me a day of many impressions of much spectacular incident, of traversing many miles of hot and dusty roads thronged with troops and blocked by guns and transport, and yet with all of little knowledge of what of actually happened in the progress of the offensive. So it is almost bound to be.

I lunched with a divisional commander who bears a distinguished name. He later accompanied me on to a high ridge, from which we commanded a panorama of the places that had become historic within the past few days. He indicated the tracery of chalky parapets with his walking stick, told me the dispositions of his troops, and then added that it was impossible for him or for any other general in this species of semi-subterranean warfare to say at any given moment just what the position really was.

Shelling of Mametz Wood
From a fine vantage spot I watched the heavy artillery bombardment directed upon Mametz Wood and Contalmaison.

325

The mottled sky was flecked with shrapnel puffs and fat black fountains of smoke incessantly spurted from the earth, heralded by preliminary winks of flames. I could distinguish, by my knowledge of where our positions ran, which were our shells and which those of the enemy, and it gladdened me to see in what preponderance the former were.

I furthermore knew that a British attack upon Contalmaison was being delivered, and I would even see the ant-like wavering fountains at times emerge into the sunlight, cover the space to the next chalk tracery, and vanish again. But as to how the day was going, who could pretend to say?

Dispatch Rider's Gallantry

My distinguished host had several anecdotes to relate of incidents of the battle. He told me of a very gallant man in the Northumberland Fusiliers who was charged with the mission of carrying an urgent dispatch. When within 200 yards of his destination, he was brought down by a bullet. Although he must have been suffering terribly, he managed to drag himself across the intervening ground, literally fall into a dug-out, put his hand upon his breast where the precious missive lay, feebly murmured 'it is here and fell back dead'.

Another tale was of a wounded lieutenant who lay in a shell crater throughout the long day, sniped at every time he stirred, who was in this way wounded a second time, but shambled back to his trench after dark with his revolver dangling from one hand and two German prisoners mutely obeying the pointed directions of the other.

Prisoners from Mametz Wood

On my way back from the Front I came upon a high-walled enclosure, bearing a deal board upon its portal with the inscription: 'Prisoners of War.' A very business-like sentry told me that there was a bunch of about 100 inside, most of them just brought in from Mametz Wood. Oh yes; I might go and look at them if I thought it worthwhile.

An intelligence officer courteously invited me to step into the barbed-wire kraal, within which the captive sat and lounged. They were a trench weary bunch, caked with clay, and in many cases bandaged about the head or hands. One of them was a huge

Prussian Guardsman, who, as I passed, grinned at me and said, 'Yah, what a life'.

A young soldier in the Manchester Regiment who was one of the sentries, and who took particular pride in announcing he was a Jew, because, as he explained, the Yiddish and Low German dialects had much in common, undertook to get me all the information I wanted. Through his fluent offices I learn: that the prisoners belonged to the 122nd Infantry Reserve Württemburgers (who scowled and became sibilant when I enquired what they thought of the Prussians) the 16th Infantry, and the 3rd Prussian Guards Division. They were all being issued biscuits, tins of bully beef, and cans of fresh water, and ate and drank ravenously.
Chat with the Captives

They all had the same story of not having received any rations for five days owing to the intensity of our barrage. Fighting, they declared, had reached the stage when it ceased to be war and was sheer murder. Our artillery was simply hellish. I told them we were only just beginning to fight, and they answered grimly, that it seemed so indeed. They all confessed their satisfaction at being out of the trenches alive and their agreeable surprise at receiving such treatment after what they had been told about British barbarity. One very intelligent man in gold-rimmed spectacles, and with a benign countenance, who spoke French very well, told me he was a baker in Metz; that he was 40 years of age, and had never before eaten such beautiful biscuits as he was now munching, that his country was in a very bad state and terribly weary of the war; that he had been upon the Russian front, which seemed a sort of nightmare to him and that he had long sighed to be captured'.[5]

In a second report he gave a report of the subsequent fighting:

HOW MAMETZ WOOD WAS WON – THRILLING STORY OF BRITISH BRAVERY
In the Field, France, July 12
Mametz Wood is an irregularly-hyphenated shaped wood covering about 200 acres of the gentle slope the ridge of which reaches the northern skyline at Bazentin-le-Petit, some half a mile beyond. It is a typical French bois, densely overgrown through two years' neglect of forestation. The great trees are not numerous, but

between these are crowded 20 foot high saplings, and the ground is covered with waste-high growth such as in peace time would harbour foxes and possibly a wild boar or two.

A single railway line runs through it, but – as though conscious of its incongruity – with a very minimum displacement of verdure. In one spot only, towards the western edge, does the dense green twilight give place to broad daylight, near where down to 3 or 4 days ago a large military store dump existed, now a charred clump from which thin jets of bluish smoke still raise.

Along the western skirt a grassy parapet marks the course of a trench some seasons old, burrowed at intervals into dug-outs. On the northern fringe an irregular line of smoke-grimed chalk shows where a quite recent cutting has been made.On the whole the incessant shell-fire to which the place has been subjected for the last twelve days has wrought less havoc than might have been anticipated.

AN IMPERISHABLE LANDMARK
True, many a white-jagged patch shows upon the trunks, many a branch dangles from its all but severed stump. Many a sapling rests slantwise athwart its supporting neighbour, but the place still remains a wood which more than can be said of Acid Drop Copse, for instance, which is reduced to a most complete, gaunt, and blackened desolation.

This same Mametz Wood, unheard of by the world all the while it lay well behind the German front line, has now become an imperishable landmark in the story of the great battle of Picardy. It has been the centre around which has waged some of the bitterest fighting of the struggle.

Thus far it was regarded as such a difficult position to tackle that I am not betraying any secret now when I say that the original plans did not contemplate any direct attack upon it at all. A process of working around and getting across the communications, when the defenders would be soon forced to yield, was intended. Developments, however, served to demonstrate that the principal difficulty to these squeezing tactics was the resistance which came from the green stronghold itself, and so the scheme of attack was modified accordingly.

ONLY TWO ENEMY BATTERIES IN ACTION

Upon the progress of the early fighting which led up to the drive through Mametz Wood I have proposed to touch very briefly. During the night of July 2–3 the pinching tactics against Fricourt succeeded completely, and our troops pushed on right through the village, finding no Germans left in the deep and spacious dug-outs, but capturing a great quantity of stores and material and enemy machine guns. Rose Cottage and the Chateaux gave a good deal of trouble and it was only after the artillery had been turned on to these places that they were stormed and taken.

Incidentally, our men are unanimous in their tribute to the remarkable sighting of the German machine guns – a testimony which is the real token of good soldiers. The havoc wrought by our artillery was evidently extraordinary. It seems that all but two batteries ceased to fire upon the troops working towards the Mametz Wood during the time to which I am referring.

On July 3–4 the position was that our double advance around and beyond Fricourt had joined up and straightened their line through Bottom Wood and Shelter Wood into the valley toward Montauban, establishing good positions at various vantage points and securing a big haul of prisoners. During the 5th Birch Tree and Shelter Alley were occupied after bombing fights. In the small hours of 6th, our positions having been steadily advanced by means of saps, we got the Quadrangle Trench.

During the next 3 days progress was slow and somewhat òf the give and take order, but as a net result we established ourselves in Marlborough and Caterpillar Woods and posted machine guns at a strong tactical point covering the north-eastern exit of Mametz Wood, in addition to successfully fighting our way into Pearl Alley, Quadrangle Trench, and Quadrangle Alley.

I am giving all these names not because they are very likely to convey much to the average reader, but because there is really no other means of conveying the main idea of the progress of our troops towards Mametz Wood.

At midnight on July 9 we took Wood Trench, which appears to have been the last success attempted in this particular region prior to the launching of the organised attack upon the wood itself which resulted in our securing all but a very narrow fringe of the northern portion of it.

THE FIRST COUNTER-ATTACK

At 2.20 on Monday afternoon last, the Germans began a counter-attack against our position south-west of the wood. They had apparently increased their artillery, for the bombardment was very heavy, the great trench-mortar crumps literally shaking the earth by their explosions. Our own gunners developed a hot response, and although the enemy infantry temporarily drove our men from the western corner of the wood, they did not succeed in maintaining a footing here owing to a bombing attack which cleared them out.

About 3.00 in the afternoon, under cover of an intense barrage, four British battalions advanced from the south-west to try and establish possession of the Mametz Wood. One battalion deployed eastwards, another pushed on straight up the centre of the rise, and the other two inclined westwards, where the stiffest opposition was anticipated. Many German corpses were encountered during the advance, which was bound to be slow on account of the obstructive character of the growth and fallen trees.

A great deal of desultory rifle fire was experienced, and machine guns began to rattle from several strong points amid the foliage, whilst the shells of the enemy artillery crashed incessantly betwixt the trees.

PASSED THROUGH THEIR OWN CURTAIN

The British barrage had been timed to begin lifting slowly, so as to progressively sweep the ground ahead of the advance, but whether owing to a miscalculation, or whether in spite of the obstacles to which I have referred the attacking infantry proceeded more rapidly than the lengthening of the fire, the fact remains that so keen was the enthusiasm of the men that they actually passed through and beyond the curtain of shells, not without casualties. With great promptitude the gunners were signalled to and lifted the range on to the second line of German trenches.

The opposition grew stronger as the assaulting battalions neared the northern edge of the wood, and at one time the advance was not only held up by sweeping squalls of bullets, but had to withdraw some three hundred yards. Here a reorganisation was effected prior to going on with the attack, and meanwhile our batteries concentrated intensely upon the spot whence this strong resistance proceeded. But the bombardment had failed to search out the masked machine guns.

The second attempt to advance promised no greater measure of success beyond the recent holding-up point than the first, and dusk found the men lined along the railway, extending thence eastwards across the wood about two-thirds the distance through it.

In the early daylight the attack was renewed. Literally laden with bombs, the gallant troops plodded forward again in defiance of the machine gun fire, which, doubtless owing to the effects of our sustained artillery work, showed a tendency to slacken.

A partly-made German trench running within the northern corner of the wood was reached and occupied, a pioneer battalion rendering an invaluable service by improving the shelter and wiring. At the north-east apex of the wood a flank party was able to penetrate into the open and establish itself under the protective machine gun emplacement to which I have previously referred, supported by a cyclist machine section.

Thus was Mametz Wood won to its furthermost confines, and at the time of writing our tenure of this important tactical position is stoutly maintained.

MOST VALIANT REGIMENTS

For military reasons I am at present precluded from giving the names of the most valiant regiments which achieved this notable victory, but the veil will not remain long drawn over their famous titles. They sent to the rear a long and clay-caked procession of prisoners from the 77th Prussian Infantry, and left three heavy guns and a great howitzer standing until the hostile-fire had slackened sufficiently to enable teams to be brought up to remove them.

I have since heard that relief troops passing through these same guns the following day have also claimed them as captured, and I suspect a few pleasantries will be exchanged upon the subject.

The taking of Mametz Wood brings our troops at this point within about 300 yards of the first trench of the second German line.

BOCHE-PACKED DUG-OUTS

Meanwhile, whilst the struggle I have described was in progress, a fierce conflict had been proceeding for the possession of

Contalmaison, for without Contalmaison in our hands Mametz Wood must have proved costly to hold. Indeed, the ruined village had already been found a perfect honeycomb of Boche-packed dug-outs, the inmates of which lay hidden until our men had entered the apparently deserted place and then poured out, dragging machine guns and bags of bombs in their wake.

During the first attack, which began on the afternoon of the 8th and extended over the small hours of the 9th, so heavy was the concentrated fire of hostile artillery and machine guns that only detachments succeeded in fighting their way into the place. Recognising that to endeavour to stay would merely be to court annihilation, they collected 60 prisoners and returned with these to report upon the position.

The second, and successful, attack was launched simultaneously with the assault on Mametz Wood on Monday afternoon last. Under cover of a terribly and wonderfully effective progressive barrage by our guns, our men advanced into the village, meeting with comparatively little opposition. Here they found the remains of a German battalion and a German company, and some sharp bayonet work ensued, but the struggle was too uneven to be long sustained. The enemy fled to the shelter of his dugouts, whence ultimately 120 prisoners were gathered.[6]

A reporter gave testimony to the after-effects of the battle as the fighting moved on to clear the other woods in the vicinity:

Prisoners continue to protest that the war has degenerated in to sheer murder on our part owing to the incredible violence of our artillery bombardment. This might well form a text to adorn every munition works in the United Kingdom.

The outstanding features of the fighting since Friday last [the first day of the attack on Mametz Wood] have been the extraordinary fierceness of the combats for the woods. In a dank undergrowth lie British and German soldiers locked together by the interchange of bayonets through their bodies. Everywhere dark brown patches testify to the prodigality with which bombs were flung, whilst the place is ragged and torn and ghastly with shell wreckage.[7]

Poems were written to commemorate the action at Mametz Wood and one appeared in *The Aberdare Leader* on 23 September 1916:

'Twas a glorious July morning,
And one I shall never forget,
When with but a few hours' warning
We were told the Wood for to get.
That night we slept in the open,
Our thoughts went to those at home,
To others, fathers, and brothers,
And all loved ones far over the foam.
At daybreak that beautiful morning
Our troops advanced to the fray,
Just as the light was dawning,
The light of another day.
We charged the Wood like madmen,
My God! What a charge we made.
The observers who watched behind us
Says 'twas better than being on parade.
There were many brave men from the Mount,
With never a thought of fear,
It never seemed to cross their minds
That for them the end was near.
There are many names I could mention,
But one I shall always revere,
And that's brave Captain Lawrence,
The tried old Fusilier.
You have heard of the deeds of others,
Deeds that have never been hid,
But why so very little
Of what the Welsh Division did?
Driver W. H. Davies, Mountain Ash[8]

A story with a macabre ending was printed on 8 July 1918:

Thrilling story of duel with bayonets.
This incident related by an officer recently home from France has a special interest to Welshmen. It occurred in Mametz Wood where

the Welsh Regiment won undying fame. The wood had been taken and occupied by the Welsh, but there were evidences by occasional sniping that in some of the recesses of the wood there still lurked some of the enemy. Consequently, it was decided to scour the wood thoroughly, the searching parties working in sections. Every bush, tree, boulder, and crevice was scrutinised, and the members of one of the parties working up towards a sharp slope were surprised by seeing a stalwart German heading furiously towards them with fixed bayonet. He knew it was all up with him, but he was resolved to die fighting. He rushed towards the party with the ferocity of a madman, but, being so greatly outnumbered, he could have become an easy victim.

But the fighting instinct of the Welshman and his spirit of fairplay, even against such a barbarous foe, prompted one of the Welshmen to shout out, 'Cwareu teg, boys. [Fairplay, boys.] He's only one. Give him a chance. Let me have a go at him.' And the little Welshman, from the neighbourhood of Pontypridd, engaged him single-handed. He was one of the crack bayonet-fighters of his regiment. He evaded the first mad onslaught of the Hun, and then for what appeared to the others to be an hour's time they fought, while the rest of the party formed a ring of interested spectators around he combatants. Every thrust, every parry, and every dodge known in bayonet fighting was introduced into the combat by both opponents. At last the Welshman gained the ascendancy and caught the Hun full in the throat. The great sigh of relief which emanated from each one of the spellbound onlookers was an indication of their tense, pent-up feelings. 'Never did I feel prouder of being a Welshman,' said the officer who related this incident, 'than when I witnessed this fine exhibition of fairplay by my countrymen, and never did I feel such a sense of relief than when I saw Taffy standing victoriously over his fallen foe.'[9]

While the story of 'Hedd Wyn' posthumously winning the Chair at the 1917 National Eisteddfod is well known, what is almost forgotten is that at the following year's Eisteddfod in Porthcawl the winning Chair prize poem, written by the Reverend Arthur George, was entitled 'The Welsh at Mametz Wood'.

The summer morn dismissed the stars, and in its light we stood,
With Mametz village in the rear – in front was Mametz Wood.
We watched the silver mists disperse, we saw the poplars rise
Like marshalled sentinels to guard the sylvan paradise,
Where laughing Innocence and Love once heard the pipes of Peace,
And garlands wove in fairy glades fanned by the playful breeze.
These fleeting visions vanished when the foemen's shrieking shell
Forewarned us that our footsteps trod the borderland of Hell.
Then nature seemed in herb and flow'r, in tree, in light and air,
Resentful that the bestial Hun should foul a scene so fair.
The Prussian Python's lustful eyes with all its reptile brood,
Glared at us from the waving fringe and aisles of Mametz Wood.
But like the Sainted Knight of old who slew the dragon, we
Were strong in valiant faith and dared the Teuton devilry.
Our souls aglow with Love of Right and steeled with Hate of Wrong
Could not be pierced by coward fear but were divinely strong.
One fierce constraining spirit in our Cymric ranks prevailed –
The spirit that makes light of death when Justice is assailed,
The spirit that defied the foe in our illustrious sires,
Who bore the flame of Liberty across our rugged shires.
The Cardiff men, the London Welsh, the men of Swansea town,
The Monmouth men, Carmarthen men, and men from dale and
    down,
In gallant comradeship were one, crusaders all were they,
The magnet of a holy cause had drawn them to the fray.
A righteous anger raged within our spirits as we stood
Expectant of the word to storm the foe in Mametz Wood.
Ill-timed, alas, that fateful word along our trenches sped,
The Cardiff men obedient charged towards the 'Hammer Head'.
But in the realms of death between No Man's Land they fell,
No bird could wing its passage through that storm of shot and
    shell.
We cursed the triumph of the foe, we cursed with every breath
The reckless word that blindly sent such gallant men to death.
We cursed our impotence to save the valiant dwindling few
That calmly faced the fiery hail that from the woodland flew.
In spite of hope forlorn they charged as only heroes could,
'Tis my belief their spirits fought the foe in Mametz Wood.
That woeful day went wailing down behind a dismal cloud,
The night in raven raiment came and spread a sable shroud

Across the world, and hid the stars, and in the dark we shed
The silent tears of sorrow for our Cardiff comrades dead.
'Tis he who for a comrade weeps will for a comrade die,
And tears are not inglorious in a gallant warrior's eye.

***

Another sunset came, and still we kept the foe at bay,
Whilst vengeance potent in our hearts prepared us for the fray.
The ninth day of July we saw sink in the purple west,
And in its wake our fancy flew to those we loved the best.
Our captive spirits beat their wings against their mortal bars,
And longed to seek the hills of Wales beneath the midnight stars.
Delirious dreams of anxious homes were ours as there we stood
With heavy eyelids startled by the Hell in Mametz Wood.
The frequent terrors of the hour could never make us blench
Nor still Devotion's holy voice along our battered trench.
And many a prayer and plaintive hymn, despite the murd'rous
    flight
Of Hunnish shells, soared heavenward o'er our parapets that night.
Then suddenly a bustling sound along our lines was heard,
It came towards us like the flight of some low flying bird.
It was the whispered order and no word was slurred or lost,
'At early dawn attack the wood, and win at any cost!'
Loud were our heart beats when we knew what meant the stern
    command,
No epic heroes ever had a mightier task in hand.
With every shell that sought our ranks our teeth were firmer set,
And with a will of steel we fixed the steely bayonet.
Though taught in youth to follow Peace and worship Christ – not
    Mars,
We were the tempered spearpoint in the greatest of all wars.
It is our faith that He who reigns supreme by righteous laws,
Inspires the warriors fighting for a great and righteous cause.
The visions of those waiting hours lit in our hearts a fire
Of holy wrath that seemed at one with Heaven's avenging ire.
We saw the plains of Belgium strewn with Belgium guiltless dead –
Her virgins raped, her temples fouled, her weeping children led
To bondage by her bestial foes, her cities desolate, –
And supplicating Heaven we cried: 'Save Wales from Belgium's
    fate.'
Then the expected tumult fell upon our wakeful ears,

Its echoes scared the distant dawn and shook the starry spheres.
Six hundred British guns sent forth their challenge to the Hun,
Their epic voices woke the world long 'ere the rising sun.
To us it was a fearful joy to hear their mighty pean,
And hear the loud avenging shells burst in the woodland green.
That clamorous hour thrilled our frames and held us by the throat,
When we beheld its sands run out, tense feelings cancelled
   thought.
'Advance!' our gallant leaders cried – then we to danger blind
Swept onward like the prairie fire fanned by a furious wind.
Mighty in faith and will were we – sons of our Spartan shires,
We sang of victory amidst the foeman's barrage fires.
The Gwentians and the London Welsh, our world-famed Fusiliers,
Morganwg men, Carmarthen men, in battle were compeers.
How Valour lived in No Man's Land no mortal tongue can tell,
Its dread dividing space appeared in hostile league with Hell.
We dared its flames and terrors but our souls were stabbed by
   pain,
When in the final rush, alas, we trampled on our slain.
Their spirits marched along with us, and in our ranks unseen
They fought against the grey-clad fiends within the woodland
   green.
We slew the gunners at their guns, and wished that we could slay
With one fell stroke the Frightfulness that rends mankind to-day.
The champions of the Tyrant's throne had not the will to face
The glitter of our vengeful steel, and courage of our race.
How oft Morganwg's miners laid with swift and mortal thrust,
The tow'ring guardian arrogance of Prussia in the dust.
We fought among the tortured trees, unconscious of the price
We paid for Right and Liberty in our great Sacrifice.
In its meridian glory shone true martial glory when
That woodland citadel was stormed and won by Cymru's men.
Bloodstained, dishevelled, battered, worn, we stood beneath the
   stars
Victorious o'er a cruel foe that worships Thor and Mars;
And in a vision of the night I saw a gleaming cross
Glide westward o'er the heaven's expanse, a symbol of our loss.
Methought I heard a voice proclaim, 'God crowns with sovereign
   good,
The sacrifice and triumph of the Welsh at Mametz Wood.'[10]

George's poem was described by the adjudicators as 'the kind of poetry for a subject like this, and the kind of poetry that will be read by the people.'[11]

In 1917 Volume 8 of *The Great War – The Standard History of the All-Europe Conflict* was published. It described Mametz Wood thus:

> The wood was a masterpiece of defensive strength. In the autumn of 1914 it had consisted of two hundred and twenty acres of finely cultivated saplings, which were being gradually thinned to produce good timber. The enemy allowed the wood to run wild for two years, until it became a tangled jungle of young trees and brambles, through which a man had to twist his body in order to get forward. In this impenetrable growth the enemy cut drives to facilitate the movement of his troops, built a light railway, concealed batteries of guns, most of which he afterwards removed, constructed machine gun redoubts, and thickened the southern end of the wood with lines of barbed wire.[12]

It went on to analyse the fighting that occurred there:

> There was three-quarters of a mile of broken woodland seamed with open drives, along which machine guns played, and full of caverns, gun-pits, and unexpected entanglements. The fighting was of a wild, rough-and-ready kind, for the clumps of unbroken thicket round which the men worked prevented close co-operation. It was a true soldiers' battle, and revealed both the virtue and defect of the new British levies. Their driving power, singly or in groups, was magnificent; to it the victory was due. But the leading men were at last carried away by the pure lust of battle. At the northern edge of the wood, when the entire position was practically conquered, the British artillery, working by the watch, were to maintain a heavy shell fire over the fugitive enemy. By this time the infantry had got well ahead of their time-table, and being more impatient than regular soldiers or veteran conscripts would have been in the same circumstances, the vehement young Britons advanced through their own shell curtain, in order to deal a quick and vital blow at the enemy.
>
> This was an example of courage in the wrong place. The head

of the British force was badly battered by its own guns, and then counter-attacked by the German reserves and compelled to fall back to the middle of the wood. In the night the Germans lashed the trees with a heavy bombardment, and then launched a strong counter-attack from the north-eastern and northern sides of the woodland. This counter-attack completely failed, owing to the fine musketry, machine guns, and bombing skill of the new British soldiers. In the morning of July 11th five Welsh battalions again advanced through the northern stretch of the broken tangle of trees. Most of the ground was won, but there was a strip of fifty yards on the northern edge which the Germans made impassable. In their line of works there they had trench-mortars as well as machine guns and rifles, and they checked every Welsh charge by means of big bombs and streams of bullets.

The Cymric troops retired from the zone of death, and for half an hour their artillery pounded the edge of the wood. Then another advance was attempted, but the bombardment had not put all the German machine guns out of action, and the newly-fallen timber made barricades against the attack. Nevertheless, the wasting Britons once more resumed their heroic work, and in a final effort of indomitable pluck they carried the enemy's lines in the afternoon. Among the spoils were four light or heavy guns, several trench-mortars, many machine guns, and some four thousand prisoners, all captured by one British army corps. The prisoners came from the 3rd Reserve Division of the Prussian Guard, the 16th Bavarian Regiment, and the 122nd Württemberg Regiment, with units from the 77th and 184th Regiments. These prisoners were exclusive of those taken at Contalmaison and beyond, and their numbers and diversity proved that the victorious army corps that captured Mametz Wood had at least beaten a German army corps and practically destroyed it. The British gunners engaged in the Mametz operations were also highly distinguished by their quickness and scientific precision. Prisoners by the thousand testified to the fury of their fire, and remarked that it was far worse than anything they had endured at Verdun, and Sir Henry Rawlinson especially congratulated the gunners for their work in Mametz Wood.[13]

This was further reinforced by a twelve-part series, *The Battle of the Somme*, which was also published in 1917. The conditions the attacking Welsh troops faced were described thus:

> So tight and twisted was the growth of trees and saplings, unthinned for two seasons, that to force a way through the stems and branches would have been a far from easy task, even had there been no opposition to encounter, whereas the Germans had spared no pains to increase the difficulties presented by Nature. They had stretched through the wood successive lines of barbed-wire nets; had cut paths and avenues for hidden machine guns to rake, and had installed several heavy batteries there. It was an ugly place to attack, and the wood itself had hitherto resisted all our efforts.[14]

When the attacking waves finally entered Mametz Wood on 10 July their progress was described in vivid terms:

> On through that terrible Mametz Wood, the gloom of which was brightened by the flash of the bursting shells, went our brave fellows. The stumps and fallen debris of smashed and splintered timber made a barrier almost as formidable as barbed wire, and the enemy's machine guns swished destruction through the wreckage. But still they pressed on, Welshman and Englishman vying with one another in their sublime indifference to the death which rained upon every yard. Once they had to draw back, while for half an hour the British artillery fiercely pounded the ground in front of them. Then forward they went again, and with bomb and bayonet forced their way onwards, killing the machine gunners, who fought their murderous weapons to the last, and carrying line after line of the hostile trenches, while the 'cleaners' who followed the fighting force dived down into the dug-outs and raked out the ambuscaders who lurked there; and before mid-day the greater part of the wood was in our possession.[15]

Even allowing for some inaccuracies in these accounts, and the jingoistic tone of the writing, it is worth remembering that, originally published as periodicals, these two series had a wide readership and their influence was considerable, thus positively influencing public opinion of the capture of Mametz Wood and the performance of the Welsh Division.

CHAPTER 12

The Medal Winners

A NUMBER OF the soldiers who fought at Mametz Wood over that terrible, bloody period had their courage recognised by the award of gallantry medals, but each man displayed his own level of courage and these snapshots are intended to give a flavour of the bravery exhibited by the men who were there.

The Distinguished Service Order

Lieutenant J. Edwardes of the 13th Welsh attacked and captured a German machine gun and was awarded the Distinguished Service Order.

The Distinguished Conduct Medal

John Henry Williams was born in Nantyglo in 1886 and started working at the Ebbw Vale Steel, Iron and Coal Company when he was 12 years old. In 1914 he gave up his job as a colliery blacksmith and enlisted in the 10th South Wales Borderers. He was promoted to Sergeant in January 1915. 'Jack', as he was known, was awarded the Distinguished Conduct Medal for his actions at Mametz Wood, and won the Military Medal the following year. Later in 1917 he was awarded a bar to his Military Medal, and at Villers-Outréaux in 1918, by now a Company Sergeant-Major, he won the Victoria Cross. Discharged from the Army in October 1918 after being severely wounded by shrapnel in the arm and leg, he was awarded all four medals by King George V in 1919. During the presentation the wound in his arm required medical attention, as it had not completely healed.

The citation for his D.C.M. for his conduct during the

fighting at Mametz Wood read: 'For conspicuous gallantry in action. He handled his men in the attack with great courage and skill. He has performed consistent good work throughout.'[1] Williams played a significant role in capturing enemy positions, prisoners and guns. He was also Mentioned in Dispatches.

Company Sergeant-Major Frank Thompson was awarded the Distinguished Conduct Medal for his actions at Mametz Wood while serving with the 14th Royal Welsh Fusiliers. His citation read: 'For conspicuous gallantry in action. He volunteered for and carried out in broad daylight, a dangerous reconnaissance of a wood and returned with valuable information. When his officers became casualties he displayed great courage and energy.'[2] Thompson was wounded during this action and in May 1918 he was transferred to the 3rd R.W.F. where he gained his commission.

In October 1916 the mayor of Swansea, Alderman T. Mercells, received a letter from Mrs Jarvis Jones, 28 St Helen's Road, Swansea, stating: 'I would like you to know that the pipe you gave to my husband, Sergeant Jarvis Jones at Winchester, before going to France was the means of saving his life in Mametz Wood. But for that he would not be alive today, with the hope of getting ten days' leave to receive the D.C.M. in England.'[3] The pipe was displayed in the window of the offices of the local newspaper and Mrs Jarvis Jones added: 'I look upon

it as my most valuable treasure, as you may guess.'[4] Presumably, it had saved his life by protecting him from a bullet or shrapnel whilst in his tunic pocket.

Acting Company Sergeant-Major Jarvis Jones was awarded the Distinguished Conduct Medal in November 1916 for 'conspicuous

Sergeant John Williams

gallantry in action. He carried out a valuable reconnaissance in daylight under heavy fire. Later, he showed great courage and determination in organising and superintending the work of his company. He had previously done fine work.'[5]

The Military Cross

Major A.P. Bowen, Shropshire Light Infantry, served as Brigade Major to the 114th Welsh Infantry Brigade during the attack on Mametz Wood and was awarded the Military Cross on 1 January 1917 for his actions.

Aubrey Percival Bowen, who completed his education at Corpus Christi, Oxford, was commissioned into the Shropshire Light Infantry in 1901 and joined the 1st Battalion in Poona in the same year. He subsequently served as Adjutant from 1908–11, and won in the latter year the Battalion's Subaltern's Cup for his victory on the Irish horse 'Topthorn'. By the outbreak of hostilities in August 1914, Bowen was serving as Adjutant of the 3rd (Special Reserve) Battalion, but he went to France as a Staff Captain in the following year and was appointed a Brigade Major to the 114th Welsh Infantry Brigade in 1916.

His commanding officer, Brigadier-General Marden sent him over to the scene of battle at 7.30 a.m. to re-organise the attack. Bowen reported back just over two hours later, confirming that the first objective had been taken and was

firmly held, and that the line was going to advance. Undoubtedly, too, he returned to Mametz Wood that afternoon, when his C.O. obtained permission to personally attend the Front and take immediate command. Bowen remained a regular soldier after the war and died in September 1953.

Major Aubrey Bowen

Second Lieutenant
Albert Green

Albert Green from Blackwood served in the 10th Welsh as a Second Lieutenant. He was severely wounded on 10 July and was awarded the Military Cross for his gallant conduct.

Lieutenant John Evans of the Carmarthen Pals was awarded the Military Cross after the battle was over. His citation read: 'For conspicuous gallantry during operations. He held on to a portion of a wood with great determination for several hours till relieved by another regiment.'[6]

Lieutenant J. Evans was awarded the Military Cross for his actions on 10 July. Shortly after 10.30 a.m. on 10 July the Germans counter-attacked the 15th Welsh and drove them back. Evans, however, held his position in The Hammerhead.

Lieutenant John McMurtrie of the Royal Engineers also won the Military Cross for his work at Mametz Wood. His engineers were to follow behind the main attack and consolidate and reinforce the captured enemy trenches, but because of the failure of the attack on 7 July they were unable to enter the wood until 10 July. His gallantry on this day led to his award.

In October of the same year he was shot in the arm and sent home to recover. He was killed on 26 July 1917 when a shell landed near a communication trench he was working on. By this time he had been promoted to the rank of Major.

Captain E. Evans, Medical Officer of the 11th Battalion South Wales Borderers, received the Military Cross for his gallantry and devotion to duty.

The Military Medal

Seventeen Military Medals were awarded to the Welsh Regiment alone: five to the 10th Battalion, five to the 15th Battalion, four to the 14th Battalion, two to the 19th Battalion and one to the 13th.

Sergeant Walter Howe of the 10th Welsh was awarded the Italian Bronze Medal in addition to his Military Medal for gallantry displayed when in charge of ration parties and acting as a guide from 10 to 14 July. He survived the war and rose to the rank of Company Sergeant-Major with the Leicestershire Regiment.

Sergeant W.J. Beavan was presented with the Military Medal for bravery at Mametz Wood in October 1916. A Swansea man, prior to being mobilised he worked at the Anglo-French Nickel Works. Aged 29, he had served with the Swansea Territorials for eight years and had been admitted to the Metropolitan War Hospital at Whitchurch in Cardiff.

Private Thomas James Dyer of the 14th Welsh was awarded the Military Medal for his conduct at Mametz Wood. Originally from Manselton in Swansea, he was 21 when he was killed in October 1916 and is buried in Essex Farm Cemetery. The circumstances of his death were relayed to his mother by his officer, Second Lieutenant T. Garvin:

> I am writing to you under very sad circumstances. Your son was killed on the morning of October 22nd. As you probably know he was my servant, and was in the act of preparing some meat when a high explosive shell dropped practically in the trench and killed him instantaneously. When I saw him a few seconds later he was dead. He can have suffered nothing at all. He was a good soldier and was always very brave and cheerful under trying circumstances.[7]

Private G.H. Stokes from Skewen was awarded the Military Medal for his conduct at Mametz Wood. He was 25 years of age and prior to enlisting had worked at the Bryncoch Colliery.

He had been a member of the Skewen Ambulance class and his proficiency in First Aid had enabled him to help many of his wounded comrades.

Corporal John Thomas Davies was awarded the Military Medal for his gallantry at Mametz Wood on 10 July. Serving with the 15th Welsh, his citation read that he 'was with Lt. Evans' party which was located in the south east corner of Mametz Wood on July 10th, 1916. By his courage and initiative in bombing the enemy, four counter-attacks were beaten off at this point and the enemy was prevented from regaining a footing in this part of the wood.'[8]

Lance Corporal J.R. Roberts of the 14th Royal Welsh Fusiliers was awarded the Military Medal for his bravery in holding a machine gun on his shoulder in Mametz Wood whilst it was being fired to keep back a German attack. He was killed on 24 February the following year and is buried in Bard Cottage Cemetery.

Private Hugh Jones, Royal Welsh Fusiliers, was awarded the Military Medal for conspicuous bravery in taking a machine gun single-handed, before being wounded on 10 July.

Private John Matthew Thomas was a pre-war collier who enlisted in November 1914, having served two years with the 2nd Welsh. He joined the 10th Welsh and won the Military Medal at Mametz Wood for bravery in the field. He later developed trench fever, which led to his discharge from the Army in August 1917 with tachycardia – a heart condition.

Quartermaster Sergeant H.V. Burnhill of the 15th Welsh also won the Military Medal at Mametz Wood. He greatly distinguished himself by his gallantry at a time when the German artillery fire was at its height. He rescued several men from no man's land and succeeded in bringing them back to the British lines. His local newspaper described it thus: 'H. V. Burnhill, 53, Old Castle Road, joined the 15th Welsh. In the fighting at Mametz Wood he rescued seven wounded comrades at the greatest risk of his life, and succeeded in bringing them back to the Welsh lines. Before the war he was employed at the Old Castle Works.'[9]

Private Robert William Jones fought with the South Wales Borderers at Mametz Wood. He won the Military Medal and was wounded. It is uncertain exactly what type of wound he received but the effect on his health got worse as the years went by. He had to stop work in 1928 but continued to serve in the family shop in Castle Street, Flint. The injury caused him to have blackouts and the local children knew him as 'Sleepy Bob'. In 1934 his condition got worse and he eventually became bed-ridden. He died in August 1938.

Private David Thomas of the 129th Field Ambulance was also awarded the Military Medal. He was 22 years of age and from Boverton near Llantwit Major, though he had been born at Parrog in Pembrokeshire. Educated at Llantwit Major Council School, prior to enlisting in January 1915 he was employed at the Aberthaw Cement Works. A fellow soldier wrote to the local newspaper:

> The work of the men of the R.A.M.C. in this fighting has been splendid. By their courage and devotion to their duties they have saved hundreds of our men. They all deserve honours, and I am glad to tell you young Dai Thomas (the Parrog), R.A.M.C. is recommended for the Military Medal, but do not publish this before it is confirmed.[10]

Corporal John Davies   Sergeant H.V. Burnhill   Private Robert Jones

347

Thomas himself wrote to his mother to confirm the award:

Dear Mother, You will be surprised to hear that I have been
awarded the Military Medal. A telegram came to-day to the Army
Corps Commander, so the A.P.M.S. of our Division pinned the
ribbon on me to-day. I do not know if I am coming home to receive
the medal or if it will be sent here. I would prefer to have it sent by
post, as I am sure I would collapse if I had to go through the same
ordeal as I had to when the colours were pinned on me.' [11]

According to the newspaper report, he was awarded the
medal for attending to the wounded and carrying them to
cover under heavy enemy fire.

His deed, as was the work of Lieutenant Raymond Jones
who was killed on 10 July, was immortalised in a poem that
appeared in print in October 1916:

Ring out the bells of old Llan Illtyd
To a hero of the Vale;
Let the notes waft o'er the valley
Till each ear has heard the tale.

'Neath the noble Red Cross banner
This Llantwit lad with others stood,
Till official word was given:
'Clear the wounded from the wood.'

Forward went these unarmed soldiers
To the dying and the dead;
Up the slopes of Happy Valley,
Where the bravest feared to tread.

While the foe no thought was taking
Of the Red Cross on our sleeves,
Shot and shell swept around our stretchers
As in autumn fall the leaves.

Have you heard the wounded crying,
Gazing through their eyes of pain?
'Give me water! Oh, for God's sake!'
Comes the cry again, again!

Lieutenant Jones, who led the bearers,
Strode coolly o'er the shell-swept plain,
Not with purpose of destruction,
But with balm to heal all pain.

Now the last long rest he's sleeping,
What greater love hath man than this?
What honour could replace our hero?
What pen describe the man we miss?

They say each man deserves a medal
For Mametz Wood, 'somewhere in France,'
But none more so than David Thomas,
Of the 129th Field Ambulance.

When the sword in sheath is hidden,
And pen defines the good and dross,
The world will sing a song recurring
Of the gallant, saving Cross.[12]

The Campaign Medals

Those men who served with the 38th (Welsh) Division and who saw active service before the end of 1915 were entitled to three medals: the 1914/15 Star, the British War Medal and the Victory Medal. Those who joined the Division after this time received the British War Medal and Victory Medal.

These medals were awarded for campaign service and while not being awarded for conspicuous gallantry, there is no doubt that many of the men who were awarded these medals had displayed courage in the field. Some of the men who were awarded these medals were:

Private Thomas Williams who was one of the original Carmarthenshire recruits into the 15th Battalion, Welsh Regiment – the Carmarthen Pals battalion. He survived some terrible battles: Mametz Wood, Pilckem Ridge, Langemark, the bombardments at Armentières prior to the German Lys Offensive, the abortive attack by the 15th Welsh on Aveluy Wood on 10 May 1918, and the great advance to victory, which included the famous crossing of the River Selle, and the

The First World War trio of campaign medals

clearing of the Forest of Mormal. Thomas was discharged on 4 April 1919, and returned home with the cadre of the Battalion to a reception at Carmarthen.

The same trio of medals was issued to Private John Fletcher, who was one of the original 300 Bolton and Farnworth enlistees into the 15th Welsh. John also survived the Great War and was discharged on 18 January 1919.

Private Gwilym Lewis was from Llangennech, near Llanelli, and was one of several enlistees from Llangennech into the 15th Welsh. He was discharged on 11 February 1919.

Private Morgan Bevan, a collier who resided at Heol Fawr in Nelson, enlisted in the 10th Welsh and suffered a gunshot wound to the hand on 10 July 1916 during the assault on

Mametz Wood. He subsequently served with the Labour Corps in Salonika.

Private David Price of the 10th South Wales Borders was a miner who enlisted in June 1915 at Blackwood, aged 28. He arrived in France in December 1915 after six months' training and fought at Mametz Wood. On 10 July he suffered a gunshot wound to his head and was evacuated for treatment. When he had recovered he was sent back to the Front and in August 1918 he was gassed. Recovering from this he was again sent back into action and on 9 October 1918 he was shot in the hand. He was demobilized to the Reserve in January 1919 and a year later he was admitted to Pen-y-Fal mental asylum in Abergavenny. It was recorded that he was 'Excitable, restless, exalted. Grandiose delusions.'[13] David died on 4 February 1923.

Other Awards and Artefacts

Lance Corporal Gwilym Ivor Rees was subsequently awarded the French Croix de Guerre for his actions at Mametz Wood. The citation read:

> On 10 and 11 July 1916, in daylight, he volunteered, with another man, and carried water, rations and dressings to a dugout which was isolated and under heavy shell fire, where between 40 and 50 wounded were collected and for 36 hours, with very short rests, this man carried wounded across the open. On 12 July, although wounded in both arms, he dressed under heavy shellfire in front of Caterpillar Wood, in the open, other men wounded by the same shell as himself, one of whom had both legs blown off at the knees. He efficiently dressed these men and remained with them until they could be moved to shelter.[14]

Private Major Phillips enlisted in the South Wales Borderers and was selected as batman for Lieutenant Raymond Barrington Parry. On 11 July he followed his officer into action. In the fighting inside the wood Parry was badly wounded. Phillips picked him up and carried him back

The cigarette case presented to Phillips by Parry

Private Phillips with two wound stripes after his actions at Mametz Wood

across the open ground under fire to a dressing station before returning to the wood.

Phillips did not receive any official recognition for this act of courage but as a token of his gratitude Parry presented him with an inscribed cigarette case.

Phillips, an ex-miner, was wounded at Mametz but returned to action and was killed on the first day on the Battle of Passchendaele on 31 July 1917. His body was never identified and he is remembered on the Menin Gate. For many years after the war Phillips' widow and young family received a basket of food every July as a token of gratitude from Parry.

A memorial plaque was awarded to the family of Albert Edward Boucher who was killed on 7 July while serving with the 16th Welsh (Cardiff City) Battalion. Albert was born in Cardiff in 1883, the third son of Thomas and Catherine Boucher of 172 Pearl Street, Roath, Cardiff. After leaving school he became a shop assistant but when war came he was one of many who felt compelled to do his bit and he enlisted in Cardiff on 10 November 1914 at the Labour Exchange, aged 31, joining the Army Service Corps. This act was not successful, though, as just over a week later, on 19 November, he was discharged as unfit for military service.

This was not the end of Albert's war as he reapplied to the Army and this time was successful in joining the Welsh Regiment. He was recorded as having blue eyes and fair hair, and standing just over five and half feet tall.

A memorial plaque was also struck in the name of Sergeant David Griffiths of the 17th Royal Welsh Fusiliers who was killed sometime between 10 and 12 July, aged 22. David was from Rhuallt in Flintshire and had enlisted in Llandudno in February 1915. He was reported missing during the fighting on 10 July but it was not until 12 July that his body was found. His personal effects were sent home to his mother and he now lies buried in London Cemetery and Extension, Longueval.

This brass cigarette lighter belonged to Edward (Ted) Morris who served in the 10th Welsh at Mametz Wood and survived, but later suffered from the effects of a gas attack.

The damage to his lungs lasted the rest of his life and he was unable to return to his previous employment as a collier. A relative who gave this lighter to me wrote:

I thought of Ted as my uncle [the brother of an aunt by marriage] and regularly in the 1950/60s on Sunday mornings after church

Sergeant David Griffiths and his memorial plaque

I would visit him 'for a chat'. He didn't go out of the house and relied on newspapers and the radio for his entertainment.

Sadly for me (I was between 10 and 16), he would never talk about the war – and that was all I wanted to hear about. All he would say was it was a terrible, terrible thing and he would never forget it, so I had to make do with the recent success/failure of the local/national rugby teams etc.

Despite his obvious difficulty in breathing, his coughing was like the last breaths of a tuberculosis victim, he still smoked 'roll-ups' made from pipe tobacco and would take this lighter from his waistcoat pocket to light his 'fag'.

He died in the late 1960s and at his funeral his brother Enoch slipped me the lighter – as something to remember Ted by. I've never smoked and there's no one left alive in my family with any connection with the late owner – so maybe someone else might cherish it.[15]

Ted Morris' lighter and a Welsh Regiment cap badge

CHAPTER 13

Conclusion

THE MEN WHO fought at Mametz Wood are now long gone, but their memories live on in the accounts they left behind. They had fought bravely and had taken the wood from an experienced, highly-trained enemy after days of bitter fighting. Yet even today the men of the 38th (Welsh) Division still do not gain the credit they are due for accomplishing such a momentous task.

One current historian writes that during the Battle of the Somme 'The 38th (Welsh) Division too had a low overall success rate (28.57 per cent) in 7 attacks, no doubt largely as a result of its unhappy initial experiences at Mametz Wood.'[1] The mud still sticks. The fact that the Division eventually took the wood appears to be ignored or understated by even the most distinguished of historians. Yet the facts of the battle evince their courage and skill in capturing Mametz Wood.

The attack on the 7 July was doomed to failure before it commenced. The route assigned to the battalions of 115th Brigade was the longest, most exposed and most poorly supported of all the attacks made by the Division. The lines of communication between Corps, Division and the Brigade were long, and led to confusion in orders. The failure of the smoke screen and the lack of control of the artillery bombardment left the attacking waves exposed to German fire, as well as shells falling from their own side. The plans that had been prepared were too hastily put together, given the short time between the arrival of the division in the area and the launching of the first attack. All these circumstances meant that the attacking

355

battalions were cruelly exposed to the German machine gun fire from their hidden positions.

Ivor Philipps' subsequent removal after the lack of success of the first day of the battle was bound up with the failure of 23rd Division on the same date. They had been charged with capturing the village of Contalmaison on 7 July and had initially succeeded, but lost it to an enemy counter-attack on the same afternoon and it was not retaken until 10 July. It was lost to the enemy in the German Spring Offensive in March 1918, and ironically recaptured by the 38th (Welsh) Division on the evening of 24 August.

The two events were linked by Haig as it was recorded he 'did not consider the withdrawal from Contalmaison on the 7th and the failure of the 38th Division to capture Mametz Wood were creditable performances.'[2] Haig required that the general advance continue, not allowing the Germans time to reinforce their defensive positions as they retreated, but trepidation had allowed the enemy to reinforce Mametz Wood before the attack

A soldier tending a grave near Mametz Wood

began. It has also been proposed that Haig lost control over events on 7 July as divisional commanders made their own plans for their own sectors in isolation, without considering the effect on the whole front.[3]

Haig had also been misinformed as to the scale of the casualties suffered on 7 July and of the effectiveness of the artillery bombardment. Had he known the true scale of the casualties suffered by the 38th (Welsh) Division, perhaps his opinion would have been different.

When 17th Division to the west of Mametz Wood failed to take Quadrangle Support trench on 8 July, and the small scale probing of the enemy defences by his Division failed to materialise, Philipps was removed, his fate being tied to misinformation and the failure of others. Yet on 10 July, the Welsh battalions entered the wood according to a plan that essentially belonged to Philipps. This time the artillery fire was far more effective and the ground less exposed to enemy fire. Nevertheless, raw courage was required by the soldiers who advanced to attack that morning.

The situation in the wood soon afterwards was confused, with units becoming intermingled – a natural consequence of fighting in such surroundings. But they drove the enemy back under horrendous conditions, in brutal close combat and with terrible loss of life. As darkness fell, men became understandably edgy and nervous but the positions were held. A further day's fighting was required before the Germans were forced to withdraw, which is testament to the stubbornness of the enemy defence of the wood.

Mametz Wood had been taken, at great cost, yet still there were few plaudits for their work. Price-Davies' ill-informed criticism of his own brigade, later withdrawn, harmed the reputation of the Division. Lashing out at his soldiers, his N.C.O.s and subsequently his junior officers, he inflicted long-lasting harm which was unnecessary and incorrect, and despite amending this misleading impression by 20 July, his initial churlish verdict was carried up the chain of command.

The fighting for the other, smaller, woods on the Somme has attracted a different reaction. The first attack on Trônes Wood was launched on 8 July, and only after eight attacks was it finally taken on 14 July by the 18th and 30th divisions. High Wood was fought over from 14 July to 15 September by elements of five British divisions. The first attack on Delville Wood was launched on 15 July and the last on 3 September by elements of several divisions, most notably the South African Brigade.

Each of these has a different reputation surrounding their eventual capture to that of Mametz Wood. Delville Wood was bought by the South African Government and is a place of pilgrimage for the families of men who fought there. High Wood has been compared to Hell itself and the action there revered, yet Mametz Wood is still wrongly associated with failure. This erroneous attitude is a slur on the men who fought so bravely to achieve the difficult task they had been set. They had captured the largest wood on the Somme but received little credit for it outside Wales, owing to the defamation voiced by one of their own commanders and their conduct being misrepresented to their Commander-in-Chief.

A contemporary illustration of the fighting for the woods on the Somme

Studying the contemporary accounts by the soldiers who were there, or who arrived in the area shortly afterwards, and the reporting of the fighting in the newspapers, it is apparent that no such stigma was held to be widespread at the time. Rather, it seems to have been fed upwards to Haig by his staff, frustrated at underestimating how long it would take to capture Mametz Wood, and at what cost. Once the fighting for the other woods in the area began, it should have been obvious to them that the 38th (Welsh) Division had, in fact, performed exceptionally well, but, fostered by the ill-informed comments of Price-Davies, the damage had been done at senior level, though the soldiers and junior officers always retained their sense of pride in what they had accomplished.

To demonstrate their admiration for the capture of Mametz Wood, the citizens and ex-servicemen of the Cardiff area subsequently raised over £7,900 to provide the 'Mametz Ward' in Cardiff Royal Infirmary in memory of the men of the 16th (Cardiff City) Battalion who had fought and died at Mametz Wood. They understood the suffering and the achievement of these men and their peers and saw fit for it to be publicly recognised.

The Mametz Ward plaque

Epilogue

HARRY FELLOWS WAS a Lance Corporal with the 12th Northumberland Fusiliers. On 15 July 1916 he was one of a number of men charged with burying the dead inside Mametz Wood. He recalled how they dug graves that were eight feet by six feet, but only two feet deep because of the tree roots. The stench of the dead bodies was unbearable and took months to clear from his nostrils. Each man's equipment had to be removed from his body before he was buried. If he was lying on his back, then the shoulder tabs were cut and the belt buckle undone to remove the equipment. If the body was lying face down, then a cut-throat razor was used to sever the belt at the back.

The body was then rolled onto a groundsheet and pulled with rope to the graveside. The dead man's wallet and pay book were removed and tied together using the string of his identity

tag. A bayonet was placed in the ground at the head of the grave and the little package tied to it. A steel helmet was then placed over it in case of rain. Six soldiers were buried in each grave, head to toe. The Germans were buried in separate graves. Where a body had been blown apart

Private Harry Fellows

by shellfire, the parts were placed in a grave using a shovel. It was reckoned that over 1,000 men were buried in this way on one day alone.

Harry Fellows never forget this terrible experience and though he survived the war, when he died in 1987 it was his wish that his ashes be buried in Mametz Wood. On his headstone are inscribed the words of reconciliation: 'Where once there was war now peace reigns supreme and birds sing again in Mametz.'

In the 1980s Tom Price, who had fought and been wounded at Mametz Wood while serving with the 13th Welsh (2nd Rhondda), visited the Somme battlefields and commented that he was disappointed that there was no memorial on the Somme to the Welshmen who had fallen there, and in particular none to his comrades who had fought at Mametz Wood.

The cause was taken up by the south Wales branch of the Western Front Association who began fundraising in 1985. A sculpted dragon created by David Petersen was created from steel and was set on Forest of Dean stone, with the three regimental crests and an inscription in Welsh. The dragon looks out across the valley at The Hammerhead and holds a strand of barbed wire in one of its claws.

It was dedicated in July 1987 but Tom Price had passed away before he could witness the realisation of his dream. Other veterans were present to witness the Welsh Dragon proudly glaring across Death Valley to Mametz Wood.

In 1930 the following newspaper report appeared:

WAS LOST AND IS FOUND
Fourteen years after he was killed in the attack on Mametz Wood, the body of Private Bryant Collins, Welsh Regiment, has been identified. Writing to his mother who lives at Arabella Street, Cardiff the Imperial War Graves Commission said identification was possible through remnants of his kit. The remains have been buried at Beaumont Hamel.'[1]

The dedication of the Mametz Wood Memorial to the 38th (Welsh Division)

John Bryant Collins had served in 'C' Company of the 15th Welsh and was reported missing on 11 July. His mother, Helen Wheadon, had remarried and he now lies buried in Serre Road Cemetery No. 2. He was 21.

In November 2012 a new name was added to the First World War memorial at Ferndale in the Rhondda Valley. Private John Murray was just 19 when he was killed on 7 July in the attack made by the Cardiff City Battalion. His body was unable to be identified and he is remembered on the Thiepval Memorial. A miner before the war, he had lied about his age and enlisted in 1914. After the war was over his parents died before the town's memorial was constructed and his brother and sisters had left the area, so there was no one to submit his name. That error was rectified 96 years after his death.

As the years pass, perhaps more men will come in from the cold as we continue to hear the voices from Mametz Wood.

Some of the Heroes of Mametz Wood

Endnotes

Chapter 1: Raising the 38th (Welsh) Division

1   *Welsh Army Corps – Report of the Executive Committee*, Cardiff, 1921. p. 3.
2   Ibid., p. 6.
3   Ibid.
4   Bowen, H.V. (ed.), *A New History of Wales*, Llandysul, 2011, p. 154.
5   Ibid. p. 12.
6   Ibid. p. 14.
7   Ibid. p. 16.

Chapter 2: Mametz Wood – The Overture

1   Brown, M., *The Imperial War Museum Book of the Somme*, Oxford, 1997, p. 127.
2   WO 95/2561/2.

Chapter 3: 7 July – The First Movement

1   Ward, D., *Regimental Records of the Royal Welch Fusiliers*, 2005, p. 204.
2   Edmonds, Brig. Gen. Sir J. E. (ed.), *History of the Great War Based on Official Documents: Military Operations. France and Belgium: Vol. II 1916*, 1995, p. 9.
3   Griffith, L. W., *Up to Mametz and Beyond*, Barnsley, 2010, p. 90.
4   Ibid. p. 100.
5   *South Wales Echo*, 11 December 1914.
6   WO 95/2561/3.
7   Ibid.
8   *Glamorgan Gazette*, 21 July 1916.
9   Ibid.
10 De Ruvigny's Roll of Honour 1914–1918.
11 Hicks, J. *Barry and the Great War*, Barry, 2007, p. 84.
12 Author's collection.
13 Hicks op. cit., p. 85.

14 *The Cardiff Times*, July 1916.
15 Ibid.
16 Ibid.
17 Courtesy of Vanessa Clee.
18 Ibid.
19 *The Porthcawl News*.
20 Author's collection.
21 De Ruvigny op. cit.
22 Gelligaer Historical Society, *Gelligaer Journal Volume 21*, 2014, p. 80.
23 *Cambria Daily Leader*, 29 July 1916.
24 De Ruvigny op. cit.
25 D.C.M. citation.
26 *The Cardiff Times*.
27 Courtesy of Ceri Stennett.
28 Ibid.
29 Ibid.
30 WO 95/2555/1.
31 Ibid.
32 Ibid.
33 Ibid.
34 Courtesy of Stephen Lyons.
35 WO 95/2549/2.
36 Ibid.
37 Griffith, L.W., op. cit., p. 99.

Chapter 4: 8 and 9 July – The Interlude

1 Papers of Lord Horne of Stirkoke, Imperial War Museum 62/54/1 to 17.
2 Ibid.
3 David Morley's Service Record.

Chapter 5: 10 July – The Second Movement

1 *The Cardiff Times*, 10 July 1916.
2 Marden, Maj-Gen. Sir T.O., *The History of the Welch Regiment 1914–1918*, The Naval and Military Press, undated, p. 386.
3 WO 95/2552.
4 Ward, D., op. cit., p. 205.
5 WO 95/2552.
6 Ibid.
7 Ibid.

8 *The Breconian*, July 1916.
9 *Brecon and Radnor Express*, 3 August 1916.
10 *Brecon & Radnor Express, Carmarthen and Swansea Valley Gazette* and *Brynmawr District Advertiser*, 3 August 1916.
11 Pearson, R., *The Boys Of Shakespeare's School,* The History Press, 2010, p 51.
12 Ibid. p. 52.
13 Hicks, op. cit., p. 89.
14 George Briggs' Service Record.
15 De Ruvigny, op. cit, pp. 171–2.
16 WO 95/2555/2.
17 Ward, op. cit. p. 206.
18 Ibid., pp. 206–7.
19 Ibid., p. 207.
20 WO 95/2555/2.
21 Ward, op. cit., p. 208.
22 Ibid., p. 209.
23 Ibid., p. 210.
24 Ibid.
25 Ibid. p. 388.
26 *North Wales Chronicle*, 21 July 1916.
27 Oliver, N. *Not Forgotten*, London, 2005, p. 227. (Oliver has the wrong date of death.)
28 Courtesy of Karen Smith.
29 Marden, op. cit., p. 387.
30 WO 95/2559/1.
31 Courtesy of General Accident Fire and Life Assurance Corporation Ltd.
32 WO 95/2559/1.
33 De Ruvigny, op. cit.
34 *The Lawrence House School Magazine.*
35 *The Western Mail,* 19 July 1916.
36 Hicks, op. cit., p. 89.
37 Author's collection.
38 WO 95/2559/3.
39 *Herald of Wales,* 22 July 1916.
40 Ibid.
41 Ibid.
42 Munby, Lt-Col. J.E. (ed.), *A History of the 38th (Welsh) Division,* Hugh Rees Ltd., 1920, p18.
43 M.C. citation.

44   *Cambria Daily Leader*, 12 October 1917.
45   Hicks, op. cit., p. 89.
46   *South Wales Daily Post*, 19 August 1916.
47   Courtesy of Mike Johnson.
48   Ibid.
49   Ibid.
50   Ibid.
51   Ibid.
52   *Llais Llafur* [South Wales Labour Voice], 5 August 1916.
53   Ibid., 21 October 1916.
54   Ibid., 28 October 1916.
55   WO 9559/4.
56   *Glamorgan Gazette*, 15 September 1916.
57   WO 95/2561/2.
58   WO 95/2561/2.
59   *The Vigornian*, No. 87, Vol. VIII (November 1916).
60   *Yr Adlais* [The Echo], 24 October 1917.
61   Records of the Royal Welsh Regimental Museum, Brecon.
62   *Penarth Times*, 20 July 1916.
63   WO 95/2548/2
64   *Monmouth Guardian,* 28 July 1916.
65   De Ruvigny, op. cit.
66   WO 95/2550/1.
67   Courtesy of Phil Colley.
68   Ibid.
69   Ibid.

Chapter 6: 11 July – The Third Movement

1   WO 95/2555/1.
2   WO 95/2555/2.
3   De Ruvigny, op. cit.
4   *North Wales Chronicle*, 21 July 1916.
5   Ibid.
6   ruthinandthegreatwar.blogspot.co.uk
7   WO 95/2557/3.
8   Ibid.
9   Courtesy of Dr Anita Jordan.
10   *Rhondda Leader*, 19 August 1916.
11   Courtesy of Vanessa Clee.
12   *Rhondda Leader*, 19 August 1916.
13   Author's collection.

14 Rugby School, *Memorials of Rugbeians Who Fell in the Great War*, London, 1918.
15 *The Western Mail*, 1916.
16 Ibid.
17 De Ruvigny, op. cit.

Chapter 7: 12 July – Coda

1   National Library of Wales, Manuscripts 3882853/190.
2   Ibid.
3   Ibid.
4   Ibid.
5   Ibid.
6   Ibid.
7   Ibid.
8   De Ruvigny, op. cit.
9   Ibid.
10 *The Parish Magazine of Cheriton and Llanmadoc.*
11 M.C. citation.
12 *Cambria Daily Leader*, 26 May 1917.
13 Ibid.

Chapter 8: The Aftermath

1   Marden, op. cit., p. 390.
2   Dunn, Cpt. J.C., *The War the Infantry Knew*, London, 1994, p. 226.
3   Dunn, op. cit., pp. 516–17.
4   Dugmore, Cpt. A.R., *Blood in the Trenches – A Memoir of the Battle of the Somme*, p.147.
5   Feilding, R., *War Letters to a Wife*, London, 1929, p. 54.
6   Author's collection.
7   Ap Glyn, I., *Lleisiau'r Rhyfel Mawr*, Llanrwst, 2008, p. 92.
8   Richards, F., *Old Soldiers Never Die*, Uckfield, 2001, p. 181.
9   Clayton, C.P., *The Hungry One*, Llandysul, 1978, p. 140.
10 Gathorne-Hardy, J., *Gerald Brenan: the interior castle –a biography*, London, 1992, p. 113.
11 Jenkins, G., *Cymru'r Rhyfel Byd Cyntaf*, Talybont, 2014, p. 147.
12 Doyle, A.C., *The British Campaign in France and Flanders Vo. III:1916*, London, 1918, pp. 73–4.
13 Marden, op. cit., p. 389.
14 Marden, op. cit. p. 390.
15 Atkinson, C.T., *The History of the South Wales Borderers 1914–1918*, The Naval and Military Press, 2014, pp. 246–7.

16 Munby, op. cit., p. 18.
17 WO 95/2552.
18 Ibid.
19 Ibid.
20 Ibid.
21 Ibid.
22 Ibid.
23 Ibid.
24 Ibid.
25 Nicholson, I. and Williams, L, *Wales: Its Part in the War*, London, 1919, pp. 66–7.

Chapter 9: The Survivors' Accounts

1   *The Western Mail*, 20 July 1916.
2   Ibid.
3   Ibid.
4   Ibid.
5   Ibid.
6   *Cambrian News*, 28 July 1916.
7   *The Western Mail*, 1 August 1916.
8   Ibid.
9   *South Wales Evening Post*, 1 August 1916.
10 *Cambria Daily Leader*, 31 August 1916.
11 Ibid.
12 *Cambrian News*, 1 September 1916.
13 Records of the Royal Welsh Regimental Museum, Brecon.
14 *Bargoed Journal*, 8 September 1916.
15 Jenkins, op. cit., p. 153.
16 Ap Glyn, op. cit., p. 90.
17 Ibid.
18 Ap Glyn, op. cit., p. 92.
19 *The Aberdare Leader*, 29 July 1916.
20 Courtesy of David Penman.
21 *Cambria Daily Leader*, 21 October 1916.
22 *Cambria Daily Leader*, 18 October 1916.
23 *The Aberdare Leader*, 28 October 1916.
24 Author's collection.
25 *Y Clorianydd* [The Judge], 24 January 1917.
26 Ambrose, F., *With the Welsh*, Cardiff, 1917, pp. 22–30.
27 *Brecon and Radnor Express*, 23 August 1917.
28 Author's collection.

29 *The Welsh Outlook*, April 1918.
30 Robinson, P. (ed.), *The Letters of Major-General Price-Davie*, Spellmount, 2013, pp. 108–9.
31 Ibid., p. 109.
32 Ibid., pp. 109–10.
33 Liddle Collection, Leeds University Library, WW1/GS/0668.
34 The Colin Hughes Archive at Cardiff University, 461/2/7.
35 Ibid., 461/1/7.
36 Ibid., 461/1/11.
37 Ibid., 461/2/18.
38 Phillips, T., *With the 38th Division in France*, privately published.
39 Ibid., 461/2/10.
40 Ibid., 461/2/11.
41 Ibid., 461/2/5.
42 Davies, E.B., *Ar Orwel Pell*, Llandysul, 1965, p. 76.
43 Ibid., p. 78.
44 *The Rhondda Pals*, Glenn Baber, undated, p. 11.
45 Author's collection.
46 Hughes Collection op. cit.461/1/1.
47 Hughes Collection op. cit. 461/1/2.
48 Ibid.
49 *The Western Mail*, 18 July 1916.
50 *South Wales Evening Post*, 7 September 1916.
51 Archives of Wrexham Museum, 3684.
52 Davies, E., *Taffy Went to War*, Knutsford Secretarial Bureau, 1975, p. 30.
53 Ibid., p. 31.
54 Ibid.
55 Ibid.
56 Ibid.
57 Ibid., p. 32.
58 Ibid.
59 Ibid., p. 33.
60 Ibid., p. 34.
61 Ibid.
62 Ibid., p. 35.
63 Ibid.
64 Ibid., p. 36.
65 Hughes Collection, op. cit., 461/2/6.
66 Graves, R., *Goodbye to All That*, London, 1929, p. 220.
67 Sassoon, S., *Memoirs of an Infantry Officer*, London, 1930, p. 61.

68 Ibid., p. 67.
69 Ibid.
70 Ibid., p. 69.
71 Jones, D., *In Parenthesis*, London, 1937, p. 174.
72 Royal Welch Fusiliers Regimental Museum, 3694.
73 Ibid.
74 Ibid.
75 Griffith, op. cit., pp. 100–1.
76 Ibid., p. 104.
77 Ibid.
78 Ibid., p. 110.
79 Records of the Royal Welsh Regimental Museum, Brecon.
80 Hughes Collection, op. cit., 461/1/4.
81 Brown, M., *The Imperial War Museum Book of the Somme*, Oxford, 1997, pp. 126–7.
82 Hughes Collection, op. cit., 461/1/3.
83 Hughes Collection, op. cit., 461/1/10.
84 *The Western Mail*, 26 July 1916.
85 Hicks, op. cit., pp. 86–7.
86 Hughes Collection, op. cit., 461/1/15.
87 Ibid., 461/1/17.
88 Ibid., 461/1/6.
89 Records of the Royal Welsh Regimental Museum, Brecon.
90 *South Wales Echo*, 25 January 1986.
91 *Cardiff City Battalion*, Bryn Owen, privately published, undated.
92 *Whitbread News*, April 1987.
93 Hughes Collection, op. cit., 461/1/20.
94 *The Western Mail*, 15 July 1916.
95 Hughes Collection, op. cit., 461/1/23.
96 Courtesy of Adrian Jickells.
97 Courtesy of family of George Groves, and David Penman.
98 Courtesy of David Penman.
99 Author's collection.
100 Charles Watkins' Service Record.
101 *Amman Valley Chronicle*, 2 January 1919.
102 Sheffield, G. and Bourne, J. (eds.), *Douglas Haig – War Diaries and Letters 1914–1918*, Weidenfeld and Nicholson, 2005, p. 199.
103 Ibid., p. 200.
104 Ibid., p. 201.
105 Ibid.
106 Ibid., p. 202.

[107] *Cambria Daily Leader*, 11 October 1918.

Chapter 10: The German Perspective
[1] Pfeffer, G., *Geschichte des Infanterie-Regiments 186*, Oldenburg, 1926, pp. 67–8.
[2] Stosch, A. von, *Somme-Nord I.Teil: Die Brennpunkte der Schlacht im Juli 1916*, Berlin, 1928, p. 176.
[3] Ibid., p. 197.
[4] Ibid., p. 199.
[5] Ibid., p. 204.
[6] Ibid., p. 216.
[7] Sporn, B., *Geschichte des Lehr-Infanterie-Regiments und seiner Stammformationen*, Zeulenroda, 1935, pp. 280–2.
[8] Ibid., pp. 316–19.
[9] Ibid., pp. 311–16.
[10] Phillips, R., *Wales and the World: The Battle of Mametz Wood*, 1916, Talybont, 2003, p. 57.
[11] Kitter, S., *Geschichte des Schleswig-Holsteinschen Infanterie-Regiments Nr. 163*, Hamburg, pp. 144–5.
[12] Miles, op. cit., p. 53
[13] Belsersche Derlagsbuchhdlg, *Das Wurttembergische Reserve-Infanterie-Regiment Nr. 122*, Stuttgart, 1922, pp. 23–9.
[14] *Cambria Daily Leader*, 28 July 1916.
[15] Wynne, Cpt. G.C., *Landrecies to Cambrai*, Helion and Company, 2011, p. 99.
[16] Ibid., p. 104.

Chapter 11: How the Press Reported the Battle
[1] Gibbs, P., *The Battles of the Somme*, Toronto, 1917, p. 89.
[2] Ibid., p. 94.
[3] Ibid., pp. 100–1.
[4] Ibid., p. 98.
[5] Various newspapers, July 1916.
[6] Ibid.
[7] Ibid.
[8] *The Aberdare Leader*, 23 September 1916.
[9] *Cambria Daily Leader*, 8 July 1918.
[10] Author's collection.
[11] Ibid.
[12] Wilson, H.W. and Hammerton, J.A. (eds.), *The Great War – The Standard History of the All-Europe Conflict*, London, 1917, pp. 87–8.

13   Ibid., pp. 88–9.
14   *Sir Douglas Haig's Great Push*, London, 1917, p. 102.
15   Ibid., p. 105.

Chapter 12: The Medal Winners

1   D.C.M. citation.
2   D.C.M. citation.
3   *South Wales Evening Post*, 7 October 1916.
4   Ibid.
5   D.C.M. citation.
6   M.C. citation.
7   *South Wales Evening Post*, 4 November 1916.
8   M.M. citation.
9   *Llanelli Star*, 19 July 1919.
10   *Glamorgan Gazette*, 29 September 1916.
11   Ibid.
12   *Glamorgan Gazette*, 27 October 1916.
13   Author's collection.
14   Parry, C.J., *The Story of the Order of St. John in the Principality of Wales*, Volume One, Newport, 1996, p. 102.
15   Author's collection.

Chapter 13: Conclusion

1   Simkins, P., *From The Somme to Victory*, Barnsley, 2014, p. 64.
2   WO95/5 GHQ War Diary. General Staff entry for 9 July 1916. National Archives.
3   Hart, P., *The Somme*, London, 2005, p. 237.

Epilogue

1   *Western Daily Press*, 3 May 1930.

Bibliography

Ambrose, F., *With the Welsh*, Cardiff, 1917.

Ap Glyn, I., *Lleisiau'r Rhyfel Mawr*, Llanrwst, 2008.

Atkinson, C.T., *The History of the South Wales Borderers 1914–1918*, The Naval and Military Press, 2014.

Baber, G., *The Rhondda Pals*, Undated.

Barlow, R., *Wales and World War One*, Llandysul, 2014.

Belsersche Derlagsbuchhdlg, *Das Württembergische Reserve-Infanterie-Regiment Nr. 122*, Stuttgart, 1922.

Bowen, H.V. (ed.), *A New History of Wales*, Llandysul, 2011.

Brown, M., *The Imperial War Museum Book of the Somme*, Oxford, 1997.

Clayton, C.P., *The Hungry One*, Llandysul, 1978.

Davies, E.B., *Ar Orwel Pell*, Llandysul, 1965.

Davies, E., *Taffy Went to War*, Knutsford Secretarial Bureau, 1975.

Doyle, A.C., *The British Campaign in France and Flanders Vol. III:1916*, London, 1918.

Duffy, C., *Through German Eyes*, Phoenix, 2007.

Dugmore, Cpt. A.R., *Blood in the Trenches – A Memoir of the Battle of the Somme*, Barnsley, 2014.

Dunn, Cpt. J.C., *The War the Infantry Knew*, London, 1994.

Edmonds, Brig. Gen. Sir J.E. (ed.), *History of the Great War Based on Official Documents: Military Operations. France and Belgium: Vol. II: 1916*, London, 1995.

Feilding, R., *War Letters to a Wife*, London, 1929.

Gathorne-Hardy, J., *Gerald Brenan: the interior castle – a biography*, London, 1992.

Gelligaer Historical Society, *Gelligaer Journal Volume 21*, 2014.

Gibbs, P., *The Battles of the Somme*, Toronto, 1917.

Graves, R., *Goodbye to All That*, London, 1929.

Griffith, L.W., *Up to Mametz and Beyond*, Barnsley, 2010.

Hart, P., *The Somme*, London, 2005.

Hicks, J., *Barry and the Great War*, Barry, 2007.

Hughes, C., *Mametz – Lloyd George's Welsh Army at the Battle of the Somme*, Gerrards Cross, 1982.

Jenkins, G., *Cymru'r Rhyfel Byd Cyntaf*, Talybont, 2014.

John, S., *Carmarthen in the Great War*, Barnsley, 2014.

John, S., *Carmarthen Pals*, Barnsley, 2009.

Jones, D., *In Parenthesis*, London, 1937.

Jones, G., *Mametz Wood – Three Stories: Tales of Wales*, Bretwalda Books, 2014.

Kitter, S., *Geschichte des Schleswig-Holsteinschen Infanterie-Regiments Nr. 163*,

Hamburg, 1926.

Lewis, B., *Swansea Pals*, Barnsley, 2004.

Lewis, B., *Swansea in the Great War*, Barnsley, 2014.

Macdonald, L., *1914–1918 Voices and Images of the Great War*, London, 1991.

Marden, Maj-Gen. Sir T.O., *The History of the Welch Regiment 1914–1918*, Uckfield, Undated.

Miles, Cpt. W., *Official History of the Great War, Military Operations, France and Belgium 1916 Volume 2*, London, 1938.

Mulmann and Mohs, *Geschichte de Lehr-Infanterie-Regiments und seiner Stammformationen*, Thuringen, 1935.

Munby, Lt-Col. J.E. (ed.), *A History of the 38th (Welsh) Division*, Hugh Rees Ltd., 1920.

Nicholson, I. and Williams, L., *Wales: Its Part in the War*, London, 1919.

Oliver, N. *Not Forgotten*, London, 2005.

Owen, B., *Cardiff City Battalion*, Undated.

Parry, C.J., *The Story of the Order of St. John in the Principality of Wales, Volume One*, Newport, 1996.

Pearson, R., *The Boys Of Shakespeare's School*, The History Press, 2010.

Pfeffer, G., *Geschichte des Infanterie-Regiments 186*, Oldenburg, 1926.

Phillips, G., *Dai Bach y Soldiwr* in *Llafur* Vol. 6, No. 2, 1993.

Phillips, R., *Wales and the World: The Battle of Mametz Wood, 1916*, Talybont, 2003.

Phillips, T., *With the 38th Division in France*, privately published.

Renshaw, M., *Mametz Wood*, Barnsley, 1999.

Richards, F., *Old Soldiers Never Die*, Uckfield, 2001.

Robinson, P., (ed.), *The Letters of Major-General Price-Davies*, Stroud, 2013.

Rugby School, *Memorials of Rugbeians Who Fell in the Great War*, London, 1918.

Sassoon, S., *Memoirs of an Infantry Officer*, London, 1930.

Sheffield, G. and Bourne, J. (eds.), *Douglas Haig – War Diaries and Letters 1914–1918*, London, 2005.

Simkins, P., *From the Somme to Victory*, Barnsley, 2014.

Sir Douglas Haig's Great Push, London, 1917.

Sporn, B., *Geschichte des Lehr-Infanterie-Regiments und seiner Stammformationen*, Zeulenroda, 1935.

Stosch, A. von, *Somme-Nord I. Teil: Die Brennpunkte der Schlacht im Juli 1916*, Berlin, 1928.

The Welsh Outlook, April 1918.

Ward, D., *Regimental Records of the Royal Welch Fusiliers*, Uckfield, 2005.

Welsh Army Corps – Report of the Executive Committee, Cardiff, 1921.

Wilson, H.W. and Hammerton, J.A. (eds.), *The Great War – The Standard History of the All-Europe Conflict*, London, 1917.

Wynne, Cpt. G.C., *Landrecies to Cambrai*, Solihull, 2011.

Other sources

The archives of the Regimental Museum of the Royal Welsh, Brecon.

The archives of the Royal Welsh Fusiliers Regimental Museum, Caernarvon.

Papers of Lord Horne of Stirkoke, Imperial War Museum 62/54/1 to 17.

The Colin Hughes Archive at Cardiff University.

David Jones letters in the collection of Wrexham Museum.

National Library of Wales Manuscripts 3882853/190.

War Diaries – held in the National Archives, Kew
113th Brigade – WO 95/2552
13th Royal Welsh Fusiliers – WO 95/2555/1
14th Royal Welsh Fusiliers – WO 95/2555/2
15th Royal Welsh Fusiliers – WO 95/2556/1
16th Royal Welsh Fusiliers – WO 95/2556/2
114th Brigade – WO95/2557/3
10th Welsh Regiment – WO 95/2559/1
13th Welsh Regiment – WO 95/2559/2
14th Welsh Regiment – WO 95/2559/3
15th Welsh Regiment – WO 95/2559/4
115th Brigade – WO 95/2560/1
17thRoyal Welsh Fusiliers – WO 95/2561/2
10th South Wales Borderers – WO 95/2562/1
11th South Wales Borderers – WO 95/2562/2
16th Welsh Regiment – WO 95/2561/3
19th Welsh (Pioneers) – WO 95/2548/2
119th Brigade Royal Field Artillery – WO 95/2546/1
120th Brigade Royal Field Artillery – WO 95/2546/2

121st Brigade Royal Field Artillery – WO 95/2546/3
129th Brigade Royal Field Artillery – WO 95/2549/1
129th Field Ambulance – WO 95/
130th St John Field Ambulance – WO 95/2549/2
131st Field Ambulance – WO 95/2550/1
123rd Field Company Royal Engineers – WO 95/2547/1
124th Field Company Royal Engineers – WO 95/2547/2
151st Field Company Royal Engineers – WO 95/2547/3
38th Division Signal Company – WO 95/2548/1

Acknowledgements

Damian Farrow for his translation of E. Beynon Davies' work, David Jones' and Meredydd Ffoulkes' letters, the reports and poems in *Llais Llafur* and Arthur George's poem.

Lieutenant-Colonel Ian Gumm for drawing the map of the Mametz Wood area.

Alison Harvey of Cardiff University for granting me access to the Colin Hughes Collection.

George Heron for the recollections of Harry Fellows.

Bernard Lewis for his generosity in supplying original material.

Dr Gethin Matthews for giving me access to original material.

Robin Mellor for the death card of Franz Schachtner, the photograph of the 38th Divisional Ammunition Column football team and the photograph of John Noyes' medals.

Lieutenant-General Jonathon Riley for supplying original material.

Jack Sheldon for his support in providing the German accounts.

Anke Yee for her translation of the German accounts.

Photograph of Joseph Bailey courtesy of Tony Tullett.

Photograph of Charles Edward Bond courtesy of David Bond.

Photograph of Gwilym Charles courtesy of Gareth Madge and Swansea Museum.

Photograph of Henry Benedict Cowie courtesy of General Accident Fire and Life Assurance Corporation Ltd.

Photograph of Emlyn Davies courtesy of his daughter, Dilys Thomas.

Photograph of John Thomas Davies courtesy of Alun Davies.

Photograph of Sergeant Edward Evans courtesy of Jeremi Cockram.

Photograph of Thomas Fergusson courtesy of Marilyn Tipples.

Photograph of Ted Gill courtesy of Peter Strong, Gwent WFA.

Photograph of Thomas Pryce Hamer and information courtesy of Ceri Stennett.

Photograph of Henry and Tom Hardwidge courtesy of Garron Evans.

Photograph of Tom Hardwidge and information courtesy of Vanessa Clee.

Photograph of Emrys Elwyn Hughes and information courtesy of Diana Lambert and Margaret Colwell Kenwood.

Photograph of John Hughes D.C.M. and information courtesy of Alun Salisbury.

Photograph of W.S. Jeffreys courtesy of Sherborne School.

Photograph of Charles Henry Johnson and information courtesy of Mike Johnson.

Photograph of Gwilym Jones and information courtesy of Gareth Jones.

Photograph of John Jones courtesy of Karen Smith.

Photograph of Raymond Jones courtesy of Phil Colley.

Photograph of William Anthony Jones provided by Jennifer Browne.

Photographs of the Lehr Regiment courtesy of Bernard Lewis.

Photograph of Oliver Loosemore and information courtesy of Dr Anita Jordan.

Photograph of the McConnell brothers courtesy of Mary Daubney.

Photograph of William Henry Peters and information courtesy of Terry Peters.

Photograph of Christian Gibson Phillips courtesy of the King's Own Royal Regiment Museum, Lancaster.

Photograph of Edward Price courtesy of Phillip Price.

Photograph of Frederick Rowlands courtesy of Louvain Rees.

Photograph of Arthur Thomas by kind permission of Glamorgan Archives.

Photograph of David Thomas 14th Welsh courtesy of Mrs D. Court.

Information on David Thomas R.A.M.C. courtesy of Rob Thomas.

Photograph of George Tucker by kind permission of Glamorgan Archives.

Wartime diary of G.H. Jickells by kind permission of the 130th St John Field Ambulance website.

Diary of Ieuan Phillips, letter from Captain Ffoulkes and letter from Timothy Richards courtesy of David Penman.

Photographs of the Mametz Memorial Dragon courtesy of Gary Williams and Jean-Paul Payen.

All other photographs are part of the author's collection.

My thanks go also to my friends and Western Front Association colleagues who have assisted me in my research: Paul Kemp, Trevor Tasker, Daniel Richards, Simon Lee, David Warren, David Hughes, Philip Davies and John Dixon.

Also by the author:

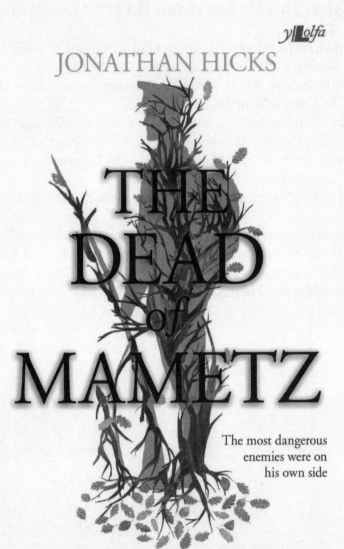

y Lolfa

JONATHAN HICKS

THE
DEAD
of
MAMETZ

The most dangerous
enemies were on
his own side

THE FIRST THOMAS OSCENDALE NOVEL

£8.95